A History of England

A History of England

E. L. WOODWARD

LONDON

First published in 1947
Reprinted twice
Second edition, revised and reset, 1962

First published as a University Paperback in 1965
Reprinted nine times
Reprinted 1987

Reprinted 1991, 1992 by
Routledge
11 New Fetter Lane, London EC4P 4EE

ISBN 0 415 07842 3

© 1962 E. L. Woodward

Printed in Great Britain by
T J Press (Padstow) Ltd
Padstow, Cornwall

Preface

AN ATTEMPT TO write the history of England in 65,000 words is like trying to pack the crown jewels into a hat-box. You can do it only by leaving out the settings. Therefore it would be idle for me to pretend that my small book is more than an introduction to some of the people who have lived and to some of the events which have happened in Great Britain since Julius Caesar landed on our coasts two thousand years past. These people and events have become so familiar to me that in writing about them I have the illusion that I am writing my own recollections. I can well understand why George IV thought in later life that he had taken part in the battle of Waterloo. I do not need much more day-dreaming to convince myself that I was present at the battle of Hastings.

Thus every page of the book has given me pleasure; a pleasure which is open to anyone to share if he will but turn his thoughts to the sequence of the past and to this procession down the long alleys of memory. My own enjoyment has been greater because in writing as though I were thinking aloud I have been able to give myself the liberty proper to conversation. Thus I have interrupted the argument here and there with 'asides' in the form of footnotes. These 'asides' can be ignored by readers wanting to keep to the main theme, but, if I may advise, less hurried travellers will take them as signposts pointing to quiet and most desirable English by-ways.

Oxford, 1947

Preface to Paperback Edition

I HAVE TRIED in this revised edition to bring my book up to date in the light of the most recent research. This revision has meant a number of small changes in the text. Otherwise the book is as I wrote it fourteen years ago.

Princeton, N.J., 1961

Preface to Third Edition

I HAVE ADDED to this book three chapters on English history since 1918. The scale of these chapters dealing with recent events is unavoidably rather different from that of the earlier chapters. I should not want to give the impression that the earlier history of England is being pushed into the background merely to serve as an introduction to an account of recent events.

I ended my original text with the words: 'History itself touches only a small part of a nation's life. Most of the activities and sufferings of the people of Great Britain . . . have been and will remain without written record.' I quoted familiar words from the book *Ecclesiasticus*: 'Some there be which have no memorial; who are perished as though they had never been, and are become as though they had never been born.'

The historian writing of the few who are remembered must always keep in mind these many who have no memorial, whether they were peasants or craftsmen a thousand years ago, living in harsh conditions and subject to the violence of strangers, or whether they are the anonymous millions of a 'welfare state' in danger of being crushed by the machinery and institutions devised for their happiness.

Oxford, 1965

Contents

I   BRITAIN UNDER THE ROMANS   *page*   1

II   THE ANGLO-SAXONS   7

III ALFRED: THE DANISH INVASIONS: THE NOR-
     MAN CONQUEST   15

IV   THE ANGEVINS AND THE GREAT CHARTER   25

V   EDWARD I AND 'PARLIAMENTS'   36

VI   THE HUNDRED YEARS WAR: LANCASTRIANS
     AND YORKISTS   46

VII THE END OF THE 'MIDDLE AGES'   55

VIII THE TUDOR MONARCHY AND THE CHURCH   69

IX   THE ELIZABETHAN AGE   83

X   THE BREAKDOWN OF THE ROYAL GOVERN-
     MENT   93

XI   THE CIVIL WAR: OLIVER CROMWELL AND
     PURITAN ENGLAND   103

XII THE REIGN OF CHARLES II: THE REVOLU-
     TION OF 1688: THE WAR AGAINST LOUIS
     XIV   115

XIII ENGLAND IN THE EIGHTEENTH CENTURY   125

XIV WALPOLE: CHATHAM: THE LOSS OF
     AMERICA: THE DEFEAT OF NAPOLEON   137

XV   ENGLAND IN THE NINETEENTH CENTURY   147

XVI FREE TRADE: SIR ROBERT PEEL AND LORD
     PALMERSTON   156

CONTENTS

XVII   MR GLADSTONE AND IRELAND: IMPERIAL-
        ISM: THE SOUTH AFRICAN WAR   166

XVIII   THE EARLY TWENTIETH CENTURY AND THE
        FIRST GERMAN WAR   175

XIX   GREAT BRITAIN BETWEEN THE TWO WARS:
        DOMESTIC   POLITICS   AND   ECONOMIC
        PROBLEMS   191

XX   BRITISH FOREIGN POLICY FROM 1919 TO
        1939   211

XXI   THE SECOND GERMAN WAR AND AFTER   221

        INDEX   235

CHAPTER I

Britain under the Romans

IT IS EASY but dangerous to generalize about the history and character of the English people and then to explain such generalizations by reference to the facts that Great Britain is an island just off the continent of Europe and therefore slightly out of the main lines of European development; or that within this island and south of the Cheviots the land falls into two divisions, the northern and western highlands, and the lowlands of the south and east. Thus the country most attractive to an invader is also nearest to the Continent and accessible because it contains a number of good harbours and easily navigable rivers. There is even less to be gained by attempting to draw conclusions from the present physical make-up of the English people. It has been said that Englishmen can afford to be impartial about the Norman Conquest because most of them must have had ancestors on either side at the battle of Hastings.[1] One might go back a thousand years earlier and remember that the men who watched the landing of Julius Caesar were also of mixed stock and that each successive wave of invaders carried with them a biological history in which the term 'race' has little meaning.

Hence it is safer to begin with a date. There is no doubt that in the year which we reckon as 54 B.C. Julius Caesar, after preliminary reconnaissances, put an army ashore near Walmer, or what is now Walmer. What did he find? About and behind this coastal area there was a population divided politically into a number of small tribes, and working the heavier soils which more primitive

[1] This is not mere guesswork. Allowing only four generations a century (a low estimate in view of the age of marriage in earlier times) the ancestors of an Englishman of today could have numbered 2^{36} in 1066; a figure large enough to allow full discount for marriages of persons of common descent. A more precise claim to an ancestor who fought at Hastings is difficult to prove since the names of only about forty of William's followers are known for certain, and it is doubtful whether any of their direct male descendants can be identified.

agriculture had left untouched. These latest invaders had not long come from northern France. They were slowly pushing their settlements northwards and eastwards at the expense of people less advanced in their way of living and therefore keeping mainly to hut villages, hill forts, and the areas of lighter soil. To the south of Caesar's line of march lay the great forest of the Weald. Away to the middle west there were other tribes, more or less backward in agriculture but with some organized government and very considerable skill in craftsmanship. Others again were established to the north of the midland forests in country which later was to form part of Yorkshire. In the north, north-west, south-west, and in Wales conditions were more primitive; few instruments of metal, for example, were in daily use.

To their highly civilized contemporaries of the Graeco-Roman world these islanders had no special significance. Even their name – Pretani – was not certain. It is likely that Caesar, whose expedition started from a region near Boulogne inhabited by people known as Britanni, thought that the Pretanic name was a mistake and corrected it to Britannia. Why then did Caesar find it necessary or at all events worth while to invade the Pretanic isles? Probably, like most conquerors, he found himself drawn on from one frontier to another; an unsubdued territory within sight of the north coast of Gaul might become a centre of revolt or at least a source of border raids.

Caesar was recalled to meet trouble in Gaul before he had conquered Britain. He went as far as Hertfordshire, and obtained, none too easily, the submission of Cassivellaunus, the king of the most important tribe among the recent settlers. Then he left Britain. For about a hundred years no other Roman army attempted a landing. Meanwhile a new wave of invaders had come, apparently from Normandy, to the Hampshire coast, and at the end of the century the more civilized tribes were ranged in some five kingdoms covering roughly the basin of the Humber and all southern, middle, and eastern England from the Fens to Somerset and Dorset. London was already a trading settlement.

The Roman conquest of Britain was undertaken at the orders of the Emperor Claudius, probably for the reason which had decided Julius Caesar to invade the country. Claudius's general, Aulus Plautius, landed at Richborough in A.D. 43. The conquest even of the lowlands took some time. The Britons had at least one good leader – Caractacus – and after his betrayal resistance broke out again in the wild revolt of Boadicea (Boudicca). The Romans never attempted to bring the whole island under their direct control. After an advance to the line of the Clyde and Firth of Forth they fixed their boundary farther south between Solway Firth and the Tyne. Here, about A.D. 122, in the reign of the Emperor Hadrian, they built the fortification known today as Hadrian's Wall. This work was more than a wall with a ditch in front of it. There were fortresses and defended camps at intervals; behind the ramparts was another ditch,[1] while a military road ran from the Cumberland coast to Wallsend. Some fifteen to twenty years later a fortified line, less elaborate and expensive, was built between the Clyde and Firth of Forth. This work did not mean the beginning of another forward move; within half a century the new wall was abandoned. Hadrian's Wall remained the boundary of the area under permanent occupation, and to the south of it the country was at peace.

A description of the machinery of civil government in Roman Britain belongs more to the history of the Roman Empire than to the history of England. This government changed, as the Empire itself changed, in the direction of centralized despotism. It suffered from the same defects as Roman government elsewhere and decayed for similar reasons. Many important details about it will never be known; there is no record of the public expenditure or revenue of Britain. Within the framework of the provinces into which the Empire was divided Roman institutions were essentially urban. The highest rank of provincial town was the *colonia*, or settlement of retired legionaries.[2] Britain had four of these colonies: York, Lincoln, Colchester, and Gloucester. Each had its own local officials or 'magistrates' and senate of ex-magistrates modelled on the august and far-off senate of Rome. Native tribal organization was adapted to this system, with a town, as a tribal centre, an 'order'

---

[1] This second ditch, which must have cost a million days' labour, is an example of the bureaucratic extravagance which did so much to ruin the Roman Empire. A ditch on the Roman side of the wall cannot have been intended as a military obstacle; it was probably built for the convenience of the customs officials who were distinct from the military organization. Within a short time the ditch was filled in – also at considerable cost.

[2] There was also a *municipium* (a lesser sort of *colonia*) at Verulamium (St Albans).

of elected magistrates, and a senate. Thus the Durotriges had as a centre Durnovaria (Dorchester), near to their earlier fortification of Maiden Castle.

If there is much uncertainty about the government of Britain, the facts about the condition of the governed are also incomplete. There are no statistics to show the numbers or distribution of the population. Probably the figure of one million would cover lowlands and highlands alike. The area of civilian occupation was south of a line drawn from Chester to York. The whole of this lowland zone seems to have been romanized to some extent; everyone used Roman pottery, though only a few were touched by the higher ranges of Roman civilization. In the early stages the army – about 55,000 to 60,000 strong – and its camp-followers brought a large number of foreigners into the country. Most of the first garrisons came from Gaul, Spain, the Danubian provinces, and the Rhineland; later, when recruits could not be found locally, drafts were taken mainly from the Rhineland. Italians, whether soldiers or civilians, were too few to leave any lasting physical trace on the population. On the other hand, Italian ideas influenced the planning of towns, each with its *forum* or market square, and an aisled and colonnaded hall or basilica. In general the public buildings were very large in proportion to the numbers who would use them; so large that the cost of their construction and upkeep may be among the financial burdens under which the Empire collapsed. The towns themselves were small. London, already a seat of government, had a population at most of 15,000. On the other hand, these small places had amenities not to be found in Birmingham or, for that matter, in Westminster, at the end of the eighteenth century. The streets were paved and drained, with sideways for foot-passengers; the houses had central heating, and nearly always a public water supply.

This Roman town life did not last. The damage to the well-to-do classes through high taxation; the ruin of trade through depreciation of the coinage and the lack of free, productive industry; the multiplication of officials; civil war, and the plunder of cities by rival armies; these were some – though not all – of the reasons why from the middle of the third century the towns began to lose their amenities. In Britain, for example, the *forum* of Wroxeter was destroyed by fire about the year 300; it was never rebuilt. At

Silchester there is evidence that towards the later period of the life of the town a less civilized class came into possession of the fine houses and did their cooking on the tessellated pavements. At Verulamium the theatre became a stone quarry.

The decay of town life did not mean at once the end of Roman culture. The economic basis of the Empire was agricultural, and the Roman *villa*, like the Roman army and bureaucracy, survived long after the Roman town had become a squalid slum. The *villa*, or country-house, large or small, was not the sole unit of this agricultural life. Most Romano-Britons lived on primitive farms and cultivated their small fields much as they had done before the Romans came to Britain. They gained from the suppression of tribal war, but against this benefit must be set the increasing power and exactions of the bureaucracy and the subjection of the poorer class to the State and the great landlords. In the last resort the population lost the power of defending themselves, since they were not trained to arms.

The village represented the poor, that is, the majority; the *villa*-owners included the few rich and the larger number of well-to-do. A *villa* was not, like the later manor, an administrative unit which normally, though not always, controlled one or more villages. On the other hand it was not just one man's home, but the centre of an economy which was self-sufficient or nearly so, after the decay of the towns and the shrinking of markets. The *villas* varied in size and comfort. Their comfort must not be exaggerated. They had Roman fittings, in a modern phrase, but their ground-plan, a line of rooms linked by a corridor with wings at either end, was more Romano-Celtic than Italian. None the less nearly all of these country-houses were more comfortable than the homes of the English kings throughout the greater part of the Middle Ages.

For their luxuries the richer *villa*-owners had to rely on imports from the Continent. Even before the decline in commerce, a Romano-British importer had not much to offer in exchange.[1] The mineral deposits of Britain, especially the lead mines, were a source of wealth, but mines and quarries were State property. Much corn was grown, yet here again taxation in kind for the benefit of the army and the bureaucracy took a great part of the surplus available for export. Hence those who wanted luxuries had

[1] Hunting dogs, bears (for the arenas), oysters, pearls, and woollen rain coats.

to develop a 'substitute existence' – or so the Romans of Italy would have thought it – in which beer took the place of wine, tallow the place of oil, and pewter was used instead of silver. Pottery of a standardized kind was made in large quantities and distributed throughout the country; a rudimentary capitalist organization of the industry existed side by side with the local 'craft' productions. Brick and tile making; a textile industry important enough to bring about some rural depopulation through the conversion of arable to sheep-pasture; a glass manufacture; these and other minor industries did not tilt the balance from agriculture to manufacture. As far as distribution was concerned, long-distance communications by road were good. In a sense they were too good. The main roads ran in straight lines from one centre to another, often without touching the smaller towns or the relatively more populous areas.

The products of Romano-British industry, with few exceptions, were artistically poor. This fact is remarkable, because in the period before the Roman occupation British workmanship was at a high level, and at the end of the Roman period there was a considerable revival of Celtic art. It is impossible to explain why this delicate non-representational art disappeared only to reappear again. We might perhaps know more about the matter if we had any information about the thoughts and ideas of the Romano-British people. Our knowledge even of their religion is purely external. Archaeological evidence shows that the 'official' Roman cults were practised; that the local Celtic deities also survived and that the Romans, once the demands of the religion of State were satisfied, were ready to assimilate Celtic gods and goddesses with those of Olympus or to regard them with the politeness which Roman imperial authority always showed to local cults of no political danger. There are signs that Christianity was introduced early into Britain and that here as elsewhere it rose in the social scale after its adoption in the fourth century by the Emperors.

CHAPTER II

The Anglo-Saxons

ALREADY IN THE last years of the third century the coastline of
Britain from the Wash to the Isle of Wight had been fortified
against pirates and was known as 'the Saxon shore'. The end of
the Roman Empire in Britain, as elsewhere, was accompanied by
catastrophe and followed by darkness, but the collapse of classical
civilization was more like the slow sinking of the soil before the
advance of the sea than sudden calamity through fire or earthquake.
The barbarians who settled in the ruins of the Empire had no wish
to destroy it. They did not think in such universal terms. They
wanted particular things; plunder and land.

The legend is that barbarians under Hengist and Horsa, introduced to defend south-east Britain against other barbarians, turned
upon their employers. Whether Hengist and Horsa did or did not
exist, the invaders came as pirates or settlers from the area between
Slesvig and the Rhine. Their own country was unfertile; pressure
of population as well as the westward move of other peoples – Huns
and Avars – probably compelled them to migrate. The term
'Anglo-Saxon' is as good as any other to denote the main tribal
composition of the migrants. The Teutons were not neatly par-
celled out in their own country. The invasion and occupation of
Britain would have required submission to an enterprising leader
and the Teutonic kings and princes were accustomed to collect
followers from more than one people. It is likely that the first of
these expeditions for settlement and not merely for plunder took
place about 450–60. The invaders established themselves in Kent
and in Sussex south of the forest of the Weald; a little later others
settled beyond the Sussex coast in Hampshire, and also in Surrey,
Essex, and Middlesex. For some time, raiders in force from these
areas of occupation plundered and destroyed over most of southern
and middle-western England. Between 490 and 516 the British

population rallied under a certain Ambrosius Aurelianus. The raiders were defeated at Mons Badonicus, a place now unknown, and driven back to their holdings. Here they stayed for about a generation, but the results of the British victory were not permanent. The British had neither sufficient resources nor permanent organization to keep out an enemy who came in, literally, with the tides. The invaders followed the rivers flowing into the Wash until they reached higher ground inland beyond the marshes. They spread north and south of the estuary of the Humber.

The history of these invasions and early settlements is obscure. It is not known, for example, whether the West Saxons came up the Thames or whether they landed on the east coast and reached the middle Thames valley by taking the Icknield Way to the neighbourhood of Wallingford. Their royal family may have come from the south and set up a kind of military rule over the different groups settled in the good lands of this middle and upper Thames valley. Whatever their origin, these early adventurers are of great interest, since they were the remote founders of the kingdom of Wessex and ultimately of the kingdom of England.

The Teutonic settlers, advancing by land or by water, entered a country more civilized than the regions from which they came. Did their coming mean a breach of historical continuity in the sense that they destroyed or let go to waste all this civilization only to recover a part of it on their conversion to Christianity? Did they drive out the Romano-British population? Did they forget none of their Teutonic customs and learn nothing from the people whose land they conquered?

It is easier to raise these questions than to answer them. The conquerors were too near in physical characteristics to the conquered to allow generalizations from skull measurements and the like. The Romano-Britons were not purely Celtic; the Anglo-Saxon invaders were not purely Teutonic. Place-names cannot always be relied on for guidance. Teutonic names, except for important natural features, took the place of Celtic names; this change may not imply that the inhabitants vanished with the names of the places in which they had lived. The evidence, such as it is, seems to show that urban life, as understood by the Romans, disappeared; in other words, the decay of the towns, which had begun long before the arrival of the Anglo-Saxons, now became complete. Canterbury was a partial exception; London faded out of history from the middle of the fifth to the early seventh century. The Roman *villa* system also broke down, but it would be going beyond the limits of ascertainable fact to say that there was no continuity between the agricultural life of the Romano-Britons and that of the Anglo-Saxons. In general the conquerors took little or no account of the Roman civilized past; there is no need to assume that they killed or drove out or even reduced to slavery all the occupants of the country in which they settled. Until the early part of the seventh century little is known of the history of the Anglo-Saxon peoples in England. Out of the short-lived confederacies necessary for the period of conquest a number of kingdoms took shape only to disappear in the course of time before larger units corresponding to the main geographical divisions of the country. There is, however, one event of outstanding importance; the return of Roman civilization with the landing, in 597, of the missionaries sent by Pope Gregory the Great for the conversion of England. This pope was a *grand seigneur* and a statesman as well as a saint; he seems to have had in mind, when he sent Augustine to England, his duty not merely to spread the Christian faith but also to recover for the authority of the Roman see a province which had once formed part of the Roman Empire.

There was a difference between the first coming of the Romans under Julius Caesar and this papal mission six and a half centuries later. The first Roman entry into the country had been made by physical force; the success of Augustine depended upon persuasion and voluntary acceptance. Hence, although the spread of Christianity was not very rapid, the ultimate effect was deeper. This effect was nothing less than the transformation of a barbarian society by Christian ideas. The process involved, as a matter of course, compromise, distortion, and at times, defeat. In a sense the paradox of the Christian religion is that it has always seemed to be fighting a losing battle against the kingdoms of this world. Nevertheless it is possible to say that, from the hour in which the small band of monks was received at the court of the Kentish king, there was a new force at work in English history. To this new force English paganism could not offer lasting resistance. Pagan usages, common to all the Germanic peoples, survived in hidden ways long after the sanctuaries of the gods were deserted. Pagan traditions survive today in place-names, in the days of the week, in the names of certain festivals. Yule and Easter, taken over into the Christian calendar, but paganism had no stubborn organization, no body of doctrine to set against the Christian hierarchy or the teaching and law of the Church. Moreover the Roman form of this law and teaching was established within seventy years of the arrival of Pope Gregory's mission. The British Church, which had lingered on in areas not reached or occupied by the English invaders, was unlikely to get much attention even if it had concerned itself with missions for the salvation of the conquerors.

Celtic Christianity in Ireland, however, was not broken by political defeat, although for the most part it had lost touch with the Roman see. In the year 634 King Oswald of Northumbria, the northernmost of the English kingdoms, invited the monks of Iona to send a mission to his people. This mission settled at Lindisfarne under the leadership of Aidan, one of the most gracious of the Celtic saints. Celtic Christianity, over a distance of centuries, appears gentler, more lyrical and imaginative than the legalism of Rome. This picture may not always correspond with the facts. In any case the English needed the harder and more logical discipline of the Roman obedience. In the year 663 a synod was held at Whitby; the immediate issue was a choice between the Celtic and Roman methods of determining the date of Easter. The decision of the Northumbrian king in favour of the Roman custom carried with it a general adoption of Roman forms of order and thus prevented a division of England north and south of the Humber between two churches.

This decision would almost certainly have been taken sooner or later. The date on which it was taken is important because in 668 Pope Vitalian consecrated as Archbishop of Canterbury a Greek named Theodore of Tarsus.[1] Theodore was sixty-six years old, with a high reputation as a scholar. He had lived in Rome and was not predisposed to regard the contemporary political division of England into a number of small principalities as part of the scheme of things. He established the authority of the see of Canterbury

---

[1] The kings of Northumbria and Kent had agreed upon the choice of a certain Wighard. Wighard went to Rome for consecration, but died of the plague after presenting his credentials to the Pope. Hence the Pope felt justified in filling the vacancy by an appointment of his own.

throughout the country, created new bishoprics, called an ecclesiastical council at Hertford (in 672) for the whole of England, and
laid down the basis of administrative order for the Church and a
moral code which the clergy were to attempt to enforce. Theodore
could not carry out all his plans of episcopal foundation. He did
little in Wessex, but the general implication of his policy was a
united kingdom.

There is something symbolic about the presence in England of
this man[1] who knew the Greek and Roman worlds even at a time
of their decline. Theodore came to England at the bidding of a
Roman official. He belonged to a class which claimed authority
and respect for reasons unconnected with birth or physical strength
or success in war. For their own protection and for the security of
their church the clergy required written laws and written evidence
of the possession of land. They alone maintained a tradition of culture. The body of knowledge regarded by Churchmen as essential
was, obviously, ecclesiastical in character, but it included, for example, sufficient grounding in elementary mathematics to calculate
the date of Easter. A general familiarity with the events of Biblical
history provided a wider view of the past than anything to be found
in the traditions of the Germanic tribes; the Christian idea of sin
was more fundamental than any barbarian code of right behaviour
which accepted the blood feud.

It is necessary to repeat that the working of these new ideas in
English society was slow. For a long time the Christianizing of a
scattered pagan population was especially difficult because there
were no parish priests and indeed no parishes. The bishop was the
pastor of a great diocese. He might be helped by monastic foundations. Such monasteries were more often houses of clergy living
together than of monks obeying the rule of an order; the anglicized
word 'minster' gives an idea of the kind of church which they
served. The parish as such could not come into existence until
landlords had endowed churches on their estates; it is typical of the
mixture of worldly and other-worldly motives that the establishment of a church might be undertaken as a good investment, since
the lay founder could stipulate for a share in the fees paid to the
priest.

Although the influence of the clergy in strengthening the

[1] An African scholar named Hadrian came with Theodore.

'systematic' elements in Anglo-Saxon society can hardly be exaggerated, the Church was not working among people without institutions or any understanding of law. The Teutonic settlers had brought with them notions of kingship and of a graded society in which the free man (or rather, the free household) was the unit. Below the free householder, or *ceorl*,[1] were the unfree; most *ceorls* owned slaves. Above the *ceorls* were the magnates of royal descent and the king's immediate followers, the military 'companions' by whom, according to ancient custom, he was surrounded. The settlement in England brought about, in the course of time, a number of social changes. These changes cannot be described neatly because – as in all societies ruled by unwritten law – there were wide local diversities; Kent had arrangements unlike those of Wessex or, for that matter, those of Essex on the other bank of the Thames. The Scandinavian invaders who later established themselves during and after the ninth century in the area north and east of Watling Street added to those regional differences.

The dominant economic factor in English life until long after the Norman conquest was the struggle with nature; the labour of peasants, owning few instruments and practising (in modern eyes) a rudimentary technique, to maintain and extend the areas of cultivation. This harsh, incessant work, in an environment of insecurity and violence, provided the surplus out of which the king and his entourage of military retainers, the magnates and their followers, and the foundations of the church were supported. The surplus was originally in kind. Kings and grandees were perpetually on the move to eat and drink these accumulated stores. The king had other revenues – increasingly as time passed – but his chief means of giving permanent rewards to his followers, above their keep when in his company, was to grant them land. Similar grants were made to communities of monks and clerks. These grants, strictly speaking, were not grants of land, but of rights over the land – the 'farm', as it was called, of a particular district, the dues and services which the king could claim for himself. Theoretically the status of the free peasantry was unaffected by these transfers. In fact the grants marked the beginning of a long development in which the *ceorl* gradually lost his freedom and became the serf of a lord.

---

[1] The social decline of this word into 'churl' reflects the course of history over several centuries.

What were the reasons for this decline in status? Again it is necessary to consider the struggle of peasant families for a living. The margin over subsistence level was small and liable to be destroyed by war. The first condition of success was security, but what security had the peasant against the devastation caused by the wars of kings or by the incessant quarrels of local magnates? The solution was for the peasant to put himself and his land under the protection of a lord. The lord's bounty might keep him and his household alive in the evil days of famine as well as of war. The Danish invasions and the measures taken to ward off these invaders or to regain the country occupied by them added to the burden of the peasants. They were unable to meet the increasing burden of taxation and the line of least resistance was to offer the lord labour instead of the rent in kind due to him. The lord would use this labour to cultivate land, the 'demesne' in a later term, which he had been acquiring for himself.

Thus the combination of the need for protection and of the change from the supply of commodities to the supply of labour brought about a position of fact dangerously near to serfdom. The free man had become the 'man' of a lord for whom he performed services of a kind done by the unfree; the difference between accepting a lord's protection and holding land in dependence on him was small. The drift towards dependency also resulted from the policy of the 'central government', if this term is not too elaborate to describe the household of an Anglo-Saxon king whose treasury might be a box in his wardrobe. It was desirable that everyone should be under some authority strong enough to enforce the peace and to suppress the common crimes – house-breaking, cattle-stealing, murder – of primitive rural communities. The king could not exercise this authority directly; the landowners could do so, and found the work profitable. Hence grants of land came to imply the bestowal of jurisdiction as well as of revenues, and the peasants came to accept the lord's house as a centre of government as well as of economic organization.

It is characteristic of the lack of material for answering the most interesting questions about early English history that there are few means of dating accurately the stages in this immense transformation. The change was spread over half a thousand years and affected a whole people. It was complete enough at the time of the Norman

Conquest for the foreign clerks of William the Conqueror, when
drawing up the great 'Domesday' survey, to describe as *villani*[1] the
average peasant landholders who supplied the lord's demesne with
labour and to use the loose term 'manor' to denote the average
centre around which the smaller holdings were grouped. The
'villein' was not yet the serf of a manor; the 'feudai'[2] pyramid' – a
king, the king's military tenants-in-chief, the military sub-tenants
of the king's tenants – was not yet built up in law with a multitude
of serfs at the base, but the conditions of feudalism existed. The
primary bond of society was the relationship of lord to man and
man to lord. This relationship was bound up with the holding of
land, and the work of society was being specialized, broadly,
among three classes; those who fought, those who prayed, and
those who worked the soil.

[1] A *villanus*, or villein, is, simply, a villager. Here again the social decline of
the word sums up a great deal of the history of the English poor. See also below,
pp. 24 and 57–9.
[2] This term is derived from the late Latin *feodum*, a 'fee', or estate held on
condition of homage and service. In order to avoid the impression that medieval
society was consciously and logically 'planned' on a 'feudal' basis, it may be
pointed out that the English adjective 'feudal' was a technical term used by
seventeenth-century lawyers and antiquarians, and that very few of Shakespeare's
contemporaries would have known what it meant.

CHAPTER III

Alfred: The Danish Invasions: The Norman Conquest

IN THIS GENERAL setting, the political history of Anglo-Saxon England becomes less of a meaningless jumble. The history can be summed up as the consolidation of three kingdoms: in the north, the kingdom of Northumbria; in the midlands, Mercia – the 'march', or boundary folk; in the west, Wessex, the land of the West Saxons. The West Saxons were on the way to establishing themselves over all rivals before the Danish invasions meant that the work had to be done over again. The recovery of the Danelaw, or country settled by the Danes, was also nearly complete when a new conquest under Canute brought about the unity of England as part of a short-lived Scandinavian Empire. In the short time between Canute's death in 1035 and the coming of the Normans in 1066 the central power of the kings was not sufficient to control that of the great territorial magnates, and on the death of Edward the Confessor the successor to the greatest of these earldoms, Harold,[1] son of Godwin, earl of Wessex, became king only to be defeated and killed within ten months.

Certain figures stand out in this turbulent history. During the second half of the eighth century, after Northumbria had fallen into anarchy and before the rise of Wessex, King Offa of Mercia established a predominance over all England. Offa was great enough in his day to correspond with Charlemagne on something like equal terms and to have the chance of marrying his daughter to one of Charlemagne's sons.[2] The Mercians had advantages in

---

[1] Harold was the second son of Earl Godwin. His elder brother Sweyn died on his way back from a pilgrimage to Jerusalem.

[2] This proposal caused a rift between the two great men. Offa would not accept the marriage unless his own son married Charlemagne's daughter. Offa's family was more ancient, but Charlemagne thought that Offa was asking too much.

their central position, but, on the whole, the balance of geography was against a middle kingdom. Mercia was open to attack on all sides by a coalition of enemies. There was no natural frontier against the Welsh. One of the most remarkable feats, measured in terms of labour, of Offa's reign was the construction of a dyke running, with lesser earthworks, from the estuary of the Dee to the Wye. Similarly, Offa's attempt to establish a Mercian archbishopric at Lichfield shows the importance of the fact that the ecclesiastical capital of England was in the hands of his enemies.

Within thirty years of Offa's death in 796 Mercia had been conquered by Wessex. Except for a short interval, this conquest was lasting. The West Saxons had a much stronger strategic position. The Britons of Cornwall or 'West Wales' were not a serious danger. The smaller kingdoms of south-east England could be absorbed without much difficulty; London, which had been for long under Mercian overlordship, Canterbury, and the coastal ports were rich prizes. Above all, the West Saxon royal house produced men of outstanding ability over a long period of time. By singular good fortune Alfred, the greatest Englishman before the Norman Conquest, was young and vigorous at the most critical time of the Scandinavian invasions.

These invasions began in 835. They might have come earlier[1] if the Swedes had not turned eastwards for their conquests and if the Norwegians, for whom expansion from a narrow territory was a necessity as well as an adventure, had not found land for colonization in the Orkneys and Shetlands, Caithness, Sutherland, the Hebrides, and the coast of Ireland. As for the Danes, Charlemagne and his son after him had taken care to keep on good relations with the Danish leaders. There was, however, no Carolingian fleet to prevent raids across the North Sea. When these raids began they were not limited to England. At first the Danes wanted plunder rather than land for settlement. Hence they came indifferently to English or to Continental harbours. Their plan was to establish themselves, in some thousands at a time, at a port or even far up a navigable river – Reading, for example – and then to seize horses and raid the surrounding country.

In 865, after thirty years of this ravaging and destruction, the

[1] There were in fact earlier raids on areas as far apart as Lindisfarne and Portland.

Danes brought a great army in order to rob more systematically. They overran most of Northumbria and East Anglia and partitioned Mercia. They might also have partitioned Wessex but for the resistance of Alfred. In the spring of 878 Alfred withdrew, after defeat, to the Isle of Athelney above the marshes of Sedgmoor. About two months later he was able to collect a force strong enough to defeat the Danes at Edington, near Chippenham, and to compel them to leave Wessex. For a time Alfred could do little outside Wessex. In 886 he recaptured London. It is of interest that this feat made a deep impression on the rest of England and secured the submission of all the English not under Danish rule. Alfred himself did not annex London to the West Saxon kingdom, but gave it to the ruler of 'English' Mercia. He was now able to treat with the Danish king Guthrum on equal terms for the division of England south of the Humber on a line running along Watling Street and through Bedford to the Lea.

Alfred had freed half of England, yet he could be sure that the Danes would attack again. He began the construction of a series of fortifications from Surrey to the Tamar, in order to secure Wessex, and built a fleet to destroy the Danish raiders at sea and prevent the concentration of their armies. If this were all, Alfred would stand out in history as the most notable military leader of the English on English soil. The measure of his greatness is that throughout these wars and preparations for war and at a time when administrative science did not exist, at all events in the lay sphere, he worked as an enlightened Christian king to raise the standards of civilization among his people. The means which he thought essential to this end were the spread of religion and knowledge.

Alfred belonged to an age when men of imagination were bound to envisage improvement in terms of the recovery of something lost from the past. He had been twice to Rome as a child and (so long and so strange is the continuity of history) had been invested by Pope Leo IV with the honorary title of a Roman consul. He took Latin culture, by which he meant the culture of the Carolingian revival, as the ideal for his own country. In order to prepare the way for a similar revival in England, he proposed in the first place to provide translations from Latin books. He also tried to arrange that all English boys of free birth who could be spared to do so should go to school and there learn to read English; all boys intended for the priesthood were to stay at school long enough to learn Latin.

Alfred made himself responsible, with the help of scholars, for the most important English translations. He took first the *Pastoral Care* of Gregory the Great, because this work laid down the instruction of the laity as one of the duties of a bishop. Alfred then turned to Orosius's *History of the World* (a now forgotten classic of the fifth century) and Bede's *Ecclesiastical History*. He may have delegated part of the translation of Bede to others, but he annotated Orosius, or rather added a running commentary suitable to English readers, with a section of his own composition on northern and central Europe. These books formed a basis of practical knowledge. After their completion Alfred could begin to deal with speculation. Again he chose the classics of his age: Boethius's *Consolation of Philosophy* and St Augustine's *Soliloquies*.

In order to realize the magnitude of Alfred's undertaking it is necessary to remember that this translation was pioneer work. English poetry, mainly of a heroic kind, went back beyond Christian times. This poetry (most of it is now lost) was not read; it was recited to an audience who knew what it was about and expected a certain kind of action or description. Such prose as existed, other than short statements of law, custom, and fact, was written in Latin, and, with the great exception of Bede, in eccentric and clumsy Latin. Bede (673–735), a monk of Jarrow, could base his scholarship and, to some extent, his style on examples which he found in the good library collected by the founder of his monastery. Alfred had no models for his translations; he carried them out not in the quiet of a monastery but as an incidental part of the overwhelming business of government and war.[1]

Owing to Alfred's many-sided genius the reconquest of the areas occupied by the Danish armies was only a matter of time and determined leadership. The Danish war-chiefs were not united among themselves. They could not easily take the initiative against the fortified frontier of Wessex; they had less reason, once the chances of easy plunder had gone, to fight for an independent

---

[1] This is not to 'write down' Bede. Bede is the only historian of the early Middle Age whose work can stand up to modern standards of criticism. The date on any letter or paper at the present time is a reminder of Bede's learning, since he introduced the dating of events from the year of the Incarnation.

existence. In the reign of Alfred's son Edward the Elder the over-lordship of Wessex was carried as far as the Humber. Edward's sister had married the king of Mercia; after her death, Mercian allegiance to Wessex continued for reasons of self-interest. When the Danish menace grew less, Edward made sure of Mercia by a *coup d'état*. Edward's son Athelstan continued the advance beyond the Humber into a country broken by Norwegian and Irish raiding and settlement as well as by the earlier inroads of the Danes. One of the most remarkable contemporary poems describes the battle of Brunanburh (937) in which an army from Wessex and Mercia defeated a coalition of Northmen from Ireland and the kings of Scotland and Strathclyde.

Athelstan thus reigned over all England. He liked, or the clerks of his court liked to give him, high-sounding titles suggesting an imperial power, but the unity of his kingdom depended upon the personality of the king. Hence, after the death of his nephew Edgar[1] in 975, disaster came when a revival of Scandinavian raids coincided with a weak king. The new attacks took the familiar form of raids followed, after some years, by an army ready to do more than loot. The attacks of this army continued from 997 to 1002. In the spring of 1002 King Ethelred 'No-Counsel', as he seems to have been nicknamed,[2] bought them off with money. A year later, possibly in revenge for a massacre of Danes at Ethelred's order, King Sweyn of Denmark came in person to attack England. After a time he too was bought off, but not for long. Finally Sweyn decided on the conquest of the whole country. He died in 1014; his son Canute (or, more accurately, Cnut) continued the war against the English. In 1016 Ethelred also died; his son Edmund Ironside, a much better man, survived his father only by seven months. Canute was therefore left without a rival.

For a short time Canute united Norway, Denmark, and England in a single kingdom. He was an administrator as well as a soldier, yet he found, like his predecessors, that he could not control a large area without delegating power and that power once delegated could not easily be regained. Canute's division of England

---

[1] There is a story (which may be true) that six kings – including Kenneth, king of Scots – gave their submission to Edgar after his coronation and that they rowed him on the Dee at Chester.

[2] The Anglo-Saxon word is 'Unraed' formerly misinterpreted as 'Unready'.

into four great earldoms was not very different from the delegation of authority by the Anglo-Saxon kings to the earldormen[1] of the shires. One of his later earls, Leofric of Mercia, was the son of an earldorman; another earl, of less high descent, was Godwin of Wessex, who accumulated lands and offices in his own hands and in those of his family to the undoing of England.

Canute's empire thus broke up after his death. After another period of confusion the kingship returned to the old royal house in the person of Edward, son of Ethelred 'No-Counsel' by his second wife Emma of Normandy. Edward had been a refugee in Normandy. Even if his importation of Norman favourites has been exaggerated he had no long-standing personal support in England. In any case this man of monkish temperament was not of the tough fibre necessary to bind to himself his own magnates, and least of all the proud family of Godwin, or to check the feuds which divided English strength. Edward had no son; the only other claimant to the throne of royal West Saxon descent died in 1057, leaving a son who in 1066 was still a child. Therefore, on the death of Edward the Confessor, in January, 1066,[2] there was every likelihood of a dispute over the succession, and the more so because Anglo-Saxon custom did not give exclusive recognition to the claims of birth. It could therefore be said – and also denied – that Harold Godwinson, who took the throne at once, had as much right to it as anyone else if he could get the assent of the great men of Church and State.

Harold could not wait on ceremony, because he knew that he would be challenged by William, duke of Normandy.[3] William also did his best to make his claim look respectable, but his conquest of England was a move to turn the fighting energy of his Norman subjects to his own advantage. The Scandinavian settlers in Normandy played a part in European history out of proportion to their numbers. Over-population was one reason why many of them emigrated to south Italy. Other countries, however, have

[1] An earldorman (the term lives on in our civic 'aldermen') was already administering more than one shire.

[2] Edward was buried in his new abbey of Westminster which had been consecrated only nine days earlier.

[3] Edward himself seems at some time to have recognized William as his heir. There also appears to be no doubt that about 1064 Harold himself had taken an oath – under compulsion – to assist William to the throne, although the circumstances which enabled William to extort this promise are uncertain.

endured over-population, and a consequent lowering of the standard of life, without this active response of men who loved adventure for its own sake. Moreover, although they showed little military inventiveness in the sense of developing new weapons, the Normans were quick to employ tactics invented by others, and, in particular, to combine offensive methods of fighting on horseback with a defensive use of fortified positions.

These tactics of fighting on horseback, together with a clever use of archers against the English shield-wall of men on foot, won the battle of Hastings for William.[1] Harold had less experience in war, but he was a good soldier. Immediately before the battle of Hastings he had defeated a strong Norwegian force under Harold Hardrada which had secured the surrender of York. The losses incurred in fighting the Norwegians probably weakened English resources. In any case Harold had been compelled to leave the south coast and to go as far north as Yorkshire at a time when William's landing was expected on the first favourable wind. Nevertheless, if for reasons of economy Edward the Confessor had not dispersed the English fleet some sixteen years earlier and contented himself with makeshift arrangements for collecting ships and crews and for provisioning them when assembled, William's venture might have been cut short by his own capture. William left the estuary of the Somme on the night of September 27–8. His ship was in the van, and, being less heavily laden than the transports, outdistanced them during the night and appeared alone at dawn off the English coast.[2] There was no English fleet to seize this great prize, because the English sailors, without provisions and tired of their long wait, had withdrawn their ships to the Thames.

Within a few weeks of his victory at Hastings, William had secured London and the submission of the English magnates. Although he had to deal later with rebellion, his position was safe by

[1] The numbers on each side were about 6,000–7,000. Harold, who did not wait in London for reinforcements from Mercia, had fewer trained and well-armed men. William's strategy of a 'feigned flight' during the battle was possible only with trained horsemen and also with trained horses. The transport of these horses added to the risks William took in his passage. There exists today, in the embroidery known as the Bayeux tapestry, a most remarkable representation of the whole story of the Conquest.

[2] In order to calm the nerves of his entourage, William ordered a large meal, with spiced wine, for himself while waiting for the other ships to appear above the horizon.

1070. He had conquered a kingdom of about one to one and a half million people, and had succeeded where for almost nine hundred years after him every attempt at foreign invasion has failed.

What, then, is the significance in English history of this Norman Conquest? Throughout Europe the second half of the eleventh century and the whole of the twelfth century were periods of progress (to use a term which medieval men would hardly have understood). The setting of life was feudal; the general tendency was towards order. Order in the simple, physical sense of freedom from the wildest forms of war and plunder by less civilized or alien invaders. At the same time there developed a more ordered condition of mind. Government and society were not concerned only with the elementary tasks of putting down crimes of violence and theft. Violence and theft remained common crimes, but there were other matters which occupied attention. The change can be seen all over western Europe in the movement for Church reform. The Church became once again a universal society; the papacy ceased to be a prize in dispute between local Italian nobles. The Christian faith, which was in danger of breaking up into local cults of saints and relics, was given philosophic study. Public opinion demanded a higher standard of clerical behaviour; a reformed papal court and episcopate could claim, in their relations with secular authority, to stand for a principle which did not rest upon brute force.

Secular life itself began to take new forms. Once the era of large-scale piracy and raiding had passed, some slight accumulation of capital was possible. Men were not beaten down, again and again, to the bare margin of existence. There was greater freedom of movement, and, since freedom of movement is a necessary condition of the prosperity of towns, the towns and cities of Europe once more gained in importance. The townsmen used the profits of trade and industry to buy privileges which ultimately proved stronger than the feudal rights of the nobles.

It is impossible to say whether the English response to the tendencies of the age would have been greater or less if Harold had won the battle of Hastings. They had already shown notable originality in art and letters. They had earlier taken the initiative in sending Christian missionaries to the Germans and later to parts of Scandinavia. They had close connexions with the European mainland through the Low Countries, and it is a mistake to talk either of their 'backwardness' or their 'isolation'. On the other hand, once the evils of a forcible change of régime were over, the English had an advantage over their Continental neighbours in the establishment of a strong monarchical government; it is doubtful whether the house of Godwin could have set up this government against their English rivals. The Normans[1] began with the whole country at their disposition. England was not too large for them to control; they were not too large a community to be absorbed in England. Furthermore, William himself, after rewarding his most important followers lavishly, was able to keep a domain which raised him in wealth far above the richest of his magnates. He also found in existence the general tax known as Danegeld – Ethelred's tribute levy – as well as the ancient customary payments to the king.

William maintained that he was Edward's legitimate successor; that he was restoring the 'good law' of Edward's time, and that he was making no change in English institutions. To a certain extent these claims were true. Nevertheless, the conquest was a military affair, and William's arrangements with his own followers were directed towards providing him with an armed force to hold the kingdom which he had won. Each of these tenants-in-chief, some 170 to 180 in all, was bound to bring to the king's service a round number of knights. The tenants-in-chief and churchmen with similar obligations found the knights either by maintaining them in their own households or by creating military tenancies of their own. The sub-tenants – their number was about 4,000 – differed in wealth and standing; a Norman knight was merely a man with a horse and armour, not even necessarily a person of much local importance.[2] It is, however, significant of the new power of the monarchy that at the end of his reign William made his tenants' tenants swear an oath of fealty directly to himself.

[1] Not all of William's followers were Normans. There were Bretons and Frenchmen from other parts of northern France.

[2] Within a century of the Conquest the practice of paying 'shield money' – a tax at a recognized rate per head – instead of providing the actual knights was common. The king then hired fighting men as he needed them. Thus many holders of land by military service ceased to be knights. On the other hand the status of the landholding knights rose; they concentrated on improving their local position to the neglect of the reason why they held their land. The expenses of the knight also rose as armour became more elaborate, and its weight required stronger war-horses.

This type of organization based primarily upon the needs of defence was something new in England. Hitherto military service had been a personal matter, although, for obvious reasons, it was associated with some basis of wealth and this wealth could be drawn only from land. Henceforward the association was formal as well as practical. The contract might be verbal; there was no doubt about the conditions. Moreover, William's detailed survey of England, known from its air of finality as Domesday Book,[1] was not a statistical inquiry undertaken out of interest, but an inventory of the resources which could be put at the king's disposition.

The contractual ties uniting the king and the host of mounted knights separated the latter still further from the peasants who tilled the land. The position of the peasants became simplified. Once again simplification meant an emphasis on dependency, and emphasis on dependency for men already on the vague borderline between freedom and unfreedom meant a 'sharp downward thrust'. Over most of England the average peasant[2] had to stay where he was, do what he was told, and work for others as well as for himself, since otherwise the feudal contract could not be fulfilled by his social superiors. The dependency was, in a real sense, mutual; if the social system were not to break down, someone, or rather, some one class, had to provide the labour from which the fighting man could be maintained. The legal development of serfdom throughout western Europe was therefore a part of the tendency towards functional order and rationalization. The Norman Conquest hastened this development in England. It is unlikely that the English peasantry would have fared otherwise if their humble place in the scheme of things had continued to be described in Anglo-Saxon words.

[1] Domesday Book (there are, in fact, two volumes, one covering Essex, Suffolk, and Norfolk, and the other the rest of England except for the northern counties) was a digest – arranged for reference – of the information obtained by commissioners who travelled from place to place, and, in the words of a somewhat scandalized contemporary, noted down every ox, cow, or swine, as well as the name of every landowner.

[2] Here also it is necessary to mention the danger, with regard to any medieval century, of dealing in averages. Furthermore, if many went down, others went up. Slavery practically disappeared in Anglo-Norman times.

CHAPTER IV

The Angevins and the Great Charter

WILLIAM THE CONQUEROR died in 1087. He left Normandy at his eldest son Robert, and England to his second son William. William Rufus (the Red)[1] reigned for thirteen years and then was killed about the age of forty by an arrow in the New Forest. The Conqueror's third son Henry I (1100–35) had more of his father's administrative ability. He began his reign by a charter of liberties; the meaning of the charter was that Henry would not abuse his rights as Rufus had done. He was equally determined to enforce these rights against unruly barons.[2] His position was not easy because his brother Robert tried to turn him out and remained a supporter of English rebels until in self-defence Henry seized the duchy of Normandy.

Henry's reign marks the beginning of the absorption of the Normans into England. His queen, a daughter of the king of Scotland, was descended on her mother's side from the royal line of Wessex. In order to please[3] the Normans, Henry changed the queen's name from the Anglo-Saxon Edith to the French Matilda, but the marriage was a sign that Henry was considering his English as well as his Norman subjects.[4] These latter were falling into two classes: those who held lands only in England, and a smaller class

---

[1] He was so nicknamed from his face, not from his hair. The fact that Rufus quarrelled with the Church was likely to secure him harsh treatment from contemporary historians, all of whom were Churchmen.

[2] 'Baron' is a term which has risen in the social scale. In classical Latin it meant a 'blockhead'. As the term (or a homonym) emerged from late Latin it came to denote a tenant by military service, and more narrowly, a tenant-in-chief of the king. It was not a personal title until the reign of Richard II.

[3] The Normans were not pleased. In contempt they spoke of the king and his queen by the common English names of Godric and Godgifu.

[4] Henry had at least 19 bastards.

with interests also in France. Unluckily, and here perhaps lies the greatest misfortune of the conquest of England by a duke of Normandy, the king himself was in the second class. Henry's decisive move to strengthen his position in France was an alliance with the powerful house of Anjou. Henry's son William was married to the daughter of the count of Anjou. William died in 1120. In 1127 his twin sister Matilda, widow of the Emperor Henry V, was betrothed[1] to Geoffrey, nicknamed Plantagenet,[2] the count's son and heir. Geoffrey and Matilda would thus in time control a block of territory stretching from the Scottish border to the Loire.

This policy was an early example of manipulating the balance of power. The Anglo-Norman barons disliked it because they did not want a king who would give lucrative offices to Angevins. The king of France feared it because it would create in France a single power stronger than his own. On Henry's death the barons refused to recognize Matilda as queen since they would also be accepting Geoffrey as king. There was a rival candidate; Stephen of Boulogne, a younger brother of the count of Blois and Champagne, the eldest male descendant of the Conqueror. The barons had no fear of Stephen's French connexions; the king of France supported him because these French relations represented a rival grouping to that of Normandy and Anjou.

Stephen was a fighting man of his time whose failure to govern has become one of the best-known facts of English history. The anarchy of his reign has been exaggerated, but the lack of governance allowed the local magnates to carry on their own feuds unchecked and gave a free hand to the powerful rogues who had been afraid of Henry I. Whatever the cause of war, the peasants were likely to suffer. In the last resort the self-interest of the great lords brought an end to the dispute over the kingdom between Stephen and Matilda (Geoffrey died in 1151). Stephen was no more able to defend his Continental lands than those in England; hence the barons who held lands in Normandy were in danger of losing them if they opposed the Angevin claims. Consequently in 1153 Matilda's

---

[1] Matilda was ten years younger than Geoffrey.

[2] 'Plantagenet' was not used as a family name until Richard of York adopted it about 1450 to assert his dynastic claims. The name may have arisen from Geoffrey's habit of planting broom (genista) on his hunting covers.

son Henry was accepted as heir. A year later, on Stephen's death, Henry became king.

Henry II[1] was a man of fierce and passionate energy, a scholar, a great builder, a great hunter, and, at the same time, the friend of a saint like Hugh of Lincoln.[2] Some of this many-sided energy went to waste in the effort of keeping together his Continental principalities; in England, the largest unit of his possessions, the king was little troubled with considerations of defence and therefore able to exert his strong will in the recovery of royal rights lost by Stephen and in building up a system of administrative control. This latter term must not be understood in a modern sense. There was still no distinction between the king's interests and those of the State; central government, as far as it existed, was no more than an extension of the king's household. The Anglo-Saxon kings had taken their treasure about with them or stored it with a reliable keeper like St Dunstan, in the strong monastic house of Glastonbury. They had no separate financial organization; no records survive, if there were any to survive, of their financial transactions. Their accounts would have been an undifferentiated medley in the sense that the same lists would have carried the king's dinners and the king's wars. In important matters the kings took advice, by tradition, from their companions. As England became more settled and the king's followers became great landowners, this advice was given in the Witanagemot, or meeting of wise men, lay and clerical. Here again it is impossible to define with legal precision the status or powers of an assembly which stretches back to the local meetings, or 'folk-moots', of tribal warriors. The kings had practical reasons for wanting to know the opinion of their great men. Whether they accepted or rejected this advice depended upon themselves.

[1] Henry II had a stocky, aggressive figure; he was reddish in complexion (like William Rufus), freckled, with a harsh voice, and grey eyes which glowed in anger.
[2] Hugh (?1140–1200) was the son of William, lord of Avalon in Burgundy. He entered the Carthusian order and was brought to England by Henry to form a small Carthusian house which the king had founded at Witham. Henry became a close friend of Hugh and in 1186 secured his election to the see of Lincoln. Hugh was admired for his charity and fearlessness in denouncing injustice as well as for his ascetic piety. He was canonized in 1220 and his cult became almost as popular in the north of England as that of St Thomas in the south.

William the Conqueror and his sons, for obvious reasons, continued these meetings, with the difference that under the Norman kings attendance at the king's court became a military duty, which the tenants-in-chief were bound to fulfil; they imposed a similar duty of 'suit of court' upon their own tenants. It was said of the Conqueror that 'thrice a year he wore his crown' and that there were then with him 'all the rich men over all England'. The routine business of the kingdom, however, had to be conducted from day to day without the presence of these magnates in the great councils. Hence there developed a smaller council over the composition of which king and barons long disputed. Furthermore some machinery had to be devised, and continually extended beyond the rudimentary arrangements of Anglo-Saxon administration, to meet the needs of government. The first stage towards modern administrative *expertise* was in the establishment of specialized branches of the court, that is to say of the king's household. The first of these departments was the Exchequer as organized by Henry I. The name was taken from the chequered tablecloth used for reckoning by counters; this method was itself an adaptation of the *abacus* or counting-board, recently introduced again into western Europe.[1] Henry I also sent 'justices' from his court to the courts of the shire and thus linked up the local and central administration. Once more it is necessary to see these justices as their contemporaries would have seen them. The king had an interest in the maintenance of order throughout his kingdom. He wanted to know what was going on and also to safeguard his rights; the execution of justice, through the confiscation of the chattels of wrong-doers, was itself a source of revenue. Justice, in the words of a contemporary of Henry II, was not merely an ideal; it was *magnum emolumentum*. In spite of the grants – long become customary – of some of the king's rights in this respect to landowners, the old courts of the shire and hundred had continued, and the king was interested in the business done in them.

Henry II continued these experiments in specialization and in more careful supervision of the king's agents. The justices went more often to the shire courts. There they used for the king's

[1] The Exchequer had two chambers; one for the receipt of money from the sheriffs, or royal representation in the shires, the other for the audit of the sheriff's accounts.

purposes the local knowledge of representatives on oath, in other words, a jury. Here again it is important not to confuse the notions of the twelfth and twentieth centuries. Law meant custom; something which everyone knew, and which was written down, if at all, as an *aide-mémoire* or in order to secure uniformity. No early medieval king promised more, new, and better laws; the appeal was rather to the 'good law' of the past. The business of a court was to declare the law, that is to say, the ancient custom. There was no examination of evidence whether an accused man had broken the law. Such an examination would have required procedure beyond the capacities of those attending the court. The court was a group of neighbours; peasants who did not move from place to place. The men of the 'neighbourhood' knew the characters of everyone within the territorial jurisdiction of the court. They also knew the 'law'. Hence they could judge on the basis of character and reputation whether the accused man was likely to have broken the law. In case of doubt the judgment was left to God; trial by ordeal of battle, or by a test such as walking on red-hot ploughshares. If the decision of God – the *judicium Dei*[1] – was in the accused man's favour, he was held to be innocent.

The judicial measures of Henry II introduced certain innovations into this system. Henry was unwilling in every case to allow accused men to clear themselves by the ordeal. Men of ill-repute, if 'presented' to his itinerant justices as suspect of law-breaking, had to leave the kingdom even though they might have satisfied the test of the ordeal. Another inroad into the custom of trial by ordeal was of the widest significance for the king's subjects. The king extended to them his own privilege of getting a right decided by the opinion of a 'jury' of sworn representatives of the neighbourhood. The advantages, for example, in the case of disputed possession or ownership of land were obvious; a dispossessed claimant no longer had to meet trial by battle.

A king of this temper of mind, extending and modernizing the area of royal power, was unlikely to avoid differences with the Church. Disputes over ecclesiastical privilege were not new. They were indeed one of the consequences of the reform of the Church

---

[1] Enlightened opinion already doubted the immediate working of Providence through the ordeal. The Lateran Council of 1215 forbade priests to countenance the ordeal.

and of the improvement of secular government. The bishops were the representatives of an international society and also great landowners. In such circumstances the quarrel over lay investiture[1] to ecclesiastical office was in the last resort a conflict over the freedom of the Church. The reformed papacy could not permit these appointments to fall under lay control; medieval kings, fighting to secure a strong central authority, could neither allow the disposition of large properties to be made outside their control nor lose the chance of rewarding their own clerical servants[2] by ecclesiastical promotion. This long-drawn dispute exhausted the two main European combatants, the Pope and the Emperor. In England the dispute was settled in Henry I's time by a compromise with Archbishop Anselm, whose learning, piety, and personal humility were impressive arguments in favour of his order.

The king, however, gained more than the Church. The bishops agreed to do homage as the king's tenants; the king promised freedom of election. The bishops were thus held to their feudal obligations, and the king could always find means to influence the elections. In any case disputes over ecclesiastical privilege continued. In Henry II's time they came to a crisis over the king's definition of his rights in relation to the Church and, in particular, over the royal claim to punish criminous clerks who had been dealt with in the Church courts according to Church law. The violence and notoriety of this dispute went beyond its intrinsic importance owing to the murder of Archbishop Becket. Becket's claim to saintliness lay mainly in the routine virtues of personal asceticism and did not prevent him from following another convention of his age in the endowment of his relations with rich ecclesiastical preferments. He had nothing of the spiritual power of Anselm; even after his murder at the altar steps had shocked Western Christendom the cause which he had upheld to the death was not altogether won. Henry II had his way on many of the definitions with which he limited the

---

[1] i.e. 'investing' a man with the insignia of office (in the case of bishops, a ring, a pastoral staff, and a white woollen band symbolical of episcopal authority). The bestowal of these insignia implied the right to appoint to the office and therefore to receive the allegiance and submission of the person appointed.

[2] In the twelfth century 'clerks in holy orders' were the only clerks in the modern sense of the term; the Church alone provided means of education, and when the higher ranges of administration began to require educated men, the kings could find them, with few exceptions, only among these Churchmen trained to 'clerical' work.

freedom of the Church. The sweep of Henry's administrative reforms affected the whole life of his kingdom. For example, the appointment of justices to sit in permanence at Westminster established London as a capital city.[1] London had long been the largest of the English towns, but its importance in Anglo-Saxon times was more economic than administrative. There could be no 'capital' of England as long as the king's government moved about with the king and the assemblies of magnates were called to any place which the king might find convenient. London, on a tidal river near to the Continent, was, however, a centre for merchants from northern France, Lorraine, the Low Countries, and the Germanic towns. Apart from London, the only towns before the Conquest with a population of about 6,500 to 8,000 were York, Norwich, and Lincoln.

The Anglo-Saxon and Anglo-Norman towns never lost their connexion with agriculture. London kept for its citizens the right of coursing in the Chilterns. Trade in the smaller places was never very great, and a number of towns had been established as part of a system of frontier defences. Most towns were fortified;[2] it is therefore more accurate to speak of trade coming to fortified places rather than of the fortification of trading centres. There were other reasons, apart from the safety of the trader and his stores, why trade was limited to towns. Trade in a town could be controlled. The buyer could be more certain that he was not being offered stolen goods; buyers and sellers alike could get witnesses to their transactions. The grant of privileges to a town was thus in most cases a deliberate act by the king; landowners, lay or clerical, began early to follow the king's example because there was profit to be gained from the dues paid by the traders. The ground-plan of many towns shows that it was impossible to get through them without passing into the market centre where the dues were collected.

After the Conquest the establishment of towns continued. The Norman castles offered good protection; the strategic sites chosen

---

[1] The chief office of the Exchequer remained at Winchester until the death of Henry II.

[2] 'Town' (tun) meant a fence or hedge and then something enclosed by a fence. The more specialized term 'borough' (burh) meant a strong place. The general term 'port' in later use applied to inland as well as to coastal towns, e.g. Langport, or any of the Newports founded many miles from the sea. A 'port' is a gate as well as a harbour.

for them were generally at a ford or bridge or meeting-place of roads and therefore convenient for the coming and going of traders. In Henry I's time there were probably about a hundred towns in all, although only about one in five had more than five hundred householders. Nevertheless, throughout the twelfth century the profits of trade were being used by these townsmen to buy privileges for themselves. They wanted the right to manage their own affairs and to deal with their own economic problems. As in every other sphere of medieval life, progress and action were through association. A merchant could do little by himself; a member of a merchant gild could at least appeal to his fellow-gildsmen.

The merchant gilds which negotiated and paid for these privileges thus tended to become the governing authority in the towns. There was no conscious usurpation of administrative functions; political and economic questions were not and could not be kept apart. Furthermore, until the later Middle Ages the members of the merchant gilds could hardly be described as oligarchies. They were merely small traders, living under the conditions of a local market in which fluctuations of demand came mainly from the calamities of nature or the devastations of war. They used their corporate influence to secure a fair sharing of trade and to enforce a fair price, since on a competitive basis there would have been no alternative ways of livelihood for the unsuccessful competitors, and attempts to raise prices by limitation of output would have been intolerable to buyers without alternative places of purchase. Competition was to the medieval mind something like getting out of one's place in a queue. Except for hawkers and pedlars in the countryside, who did not compete with the townsmen, there was also no room in this system for middlemen or foreigners, and a foreigner was a fellow-countryman from another town as well as a stranger from another country.

In the short reign of Richard I (1189–99) the townsmen found the king unusually ready to sell the privileges for which they asked. Richard needed money for a crusade. His long absences[1] from England made it impossible for him to continue the supervising

---

[1] Richard was in England for about four months in 1189. He came back early in 1194 and left in the same year. He was never in England again. He had nothing to do with the development of parliamentary government. It is therefore odd to find him singled out for commemoration by an equestrian statue in the precincts of the Houses of Parliament.

work of Henry II who was never too far away to deal with English business. The situation was more serious because Richard's brother John was likely to drive the baronage into an assertion of their rights against the increasing power of the king and the novel activities of bureaucrats. John (1199–1216) was an able, bad man, violent and lazy by turns and always treacherous. The opposition to him, which reached its highest point in the enforcement upon the king of the demands set out in *Magna Carta*, can fairly be called general. It was expressed in feudal terms because Englishmen thought in such terms. The leaders were the great men of Church and State because no other class in England had any means of opposing the king.

The terms of *Magna Carta* seem broader today than they were intended to be in 1215. Many legal words in its clauses have changed their meaning. Thus a 'free man' in the thirteenth century – set against a background of serfdom – was a privileged person whose claim to be tried by his peers had not the large political significance which it acquired several hundred years later. Similarly the limits put upon the king's powers to extract money meant to the barons and churchmen who drew up the charter that without their consent the king and his agents must not demand more than the customary payments due from a tenant to his lord. Even the name 'Great Charter' is misleading; the term was not used until after John's death.[1] It seems to have been then employed to distinguish the main charter, which was reissued in 1217, from a smaller charter containing only the clauses dealing with the abuse of the special laws applied to forests.

Nevertheless a king who was hateful to his subjects and who had hired foreign mercenaries against them was compelled to acknowledge his obligation to govern according to ancient customs of which public opinion approved. He was pledged not to turn these customs into tyranny. The baronage acted, as other classes before and since, in their own interest. They did not invent any permanent constitutional machinery for dealing with a king who went beyond the accepted limits of royal power. Their charter is a mixture of generality and precision, a catalogue of minor feudal privileges and a few claims belonging logically to a distant future. Yet it would be

---

[1] Other lords than the king could issue great charters. The earl of Chester granted one to his tenants.

a mistake to write down the importance of the assertion that the holders of power must not abuse their privileges.

The difficulty of controlling the king without recourse to the dangerous method of rebellion is the main theme of English history in the long reign of Henry III (1216–72), and intermittently for two centuries after him. The barons were not content with promises of the most solemn kind. These promises could be evaded by fecklessness as much as by deliberate policy. A more likely method of permanent control was to ensure that the king was surrounded by counsellors who could be trusted to compel him to keep his word. With such a council the appointment of royal officials – the use of the term 'ministers', though not totally incorrect, might mislead twentieth-century readers – would also be in safe hands. This plan failed because any clear or absolute distinction between royal and public business was still unrecognized in the actual machinery of administration. The king could escape control by using officers of his personal household for the government of the kingdom and by putting men of straw into the few 'differentiated' positions of State. Thus he might employ the clerks of his wardrobe (who looked after his private and most valuable possessions) as a means of evading the checks which the Exchequer and Chancery were exercising over policy and expenditure.

Henry III was an extravagant and politically foolish man[1] without the deep purpose of establishing a tyranny. His evasion of control by appointed counsellors might have been checked more easily if the barons had been united among themselves. They were rarely united for long. Simon de Montfort,[2] the most persistent leader of reform, was a man of remarkable character: a fine soldier, a friend of the noblest churchmen and scholars of his age, one of the few magnates with a sense of the rising importance of other classes than the greater feudal baronage. He was, however, too proud and masterful, too careless of vested interests and personal feelings to

---

[1] Posterity may be kinder than Henry's contemporaries were to this extravagance, since much of Henry's money was spent in works of art – including the rebuilding of the greater part of Westminster Abbey and St Stephen's Chapel. Henry's effigy in the Abbey is very far from being a likeness – the king was of middle height and stoutly built.

[2] Montfort was a castle on a hill between Paris and Chartres. Simon's only family connexion with England was through the marriage of his grandfather Simon with the daughter of Robert de Beaumont, earl of Leicester.

be a successful innovator. The king, or rather the king's son Edward, was able to win over some of the most powerful of the barons and to defeat Simon at Evesham in 1265. Simon was killed in the battle and his supporters scattered and broken. None the less the emergence of a middle rank – the 'mesne gent' – in English society was something which military defeat could not check. It was not merely a matter of chance that Simon de Montfort's opposition to Henry III coincided closely in time with the writings of Bracton. Bracton's treatise on the laws and customs of England (*De legibus et consuetudinibus Angliae*) is the first attempt to deal methodically and on a large scale with the 'common' law of the royal courts; a law to which in time all classes in England, including kings, would do service.

CHAPTER V

Edward I and 'Parliaments'

EDWARD I – the only English king to succeed to the throne while on his way from a crusade – was, like most English medieval kings, a fine figure of a man, tall, well made, and handsome.[1] He was much abler than his father and even if he had not known from experience the dangers of rebellion, his own temperament would have led him to the policy of strengthening his kingdom in every possible way. The first condition of strength was that he should be master in Great Britain, and the first step towards this mastery was the completion of the conquest of Wales.

At the time of the Norman Conquest of England, Wales had been divided into four independent principalities. After a few years these principalities were reduced to two, but the Welsh could not resist steady pressure from the great earldoms of Hereford, Shrewsbury, and Chester established by the Conqueror. In Stephen's reign the 'marcher' [2] lords were occupied with English feuds. Much of their work in Wales was then undone and the lost territory had to be regained under Henry II. Up to this time the English kings had been willing to leave the marcher lords to deal with the Welsh. The conquest of Ireland by a group of Anglo-Norman barons changed the political situation. This conquest is a story in itself. It would not have been undertaken if the Irish had not been quarrelling among themselves. One of their leaders, Dermot Mac-Murrough, invited the interference of Henry II, and, on the king's refusal, secured the help of a number of notables from Pembrokeshire. The first landing was made in 1169. In the following year Richard de Clare, known as Strongbow, came with a larger force. In 1171 the king himself felt bound to appear in order to establish his overlordship.

[1] Except for a drooping eyelid.
[2] i.e., the 'march' or boundary between England and Wales.

36

If the overlordship of Ireland was a shadowy affair from the king's point of view, it provided a good reason for securing solid support for royal authority in Wales. The Anglo-Norman land-holders in Wales had become more interested in the extension of their fortunes in Ireland. The Welsh themselves were united under Llywelyn ap Gruffydd, whose position as Prince of Wales was formally recognized in 1267 by Henry III. This unity depended upon the prestige of one man; Llywelyn himself realized that sooner or later the English advance would be resumed. He tried to keep Edward I occupied by encouraging opposition to him in England; these intrigues made it more necessary for Edward to deal with him. In 1277 Llywelyn was compelled to give up the greater part of his principality. Five years later he was rash enough to head a Welsh rebellion. He could not hold out long against the force which the king of England was able to bring against him by land and sea. Rebellion was to break out again in Wales but there could be no more chance of independence.

Scotland was a more difficult problem. The country was larger, less accessible from the centres of English power, more advanced in culture, and richer in resources. There could hardly be a question of conquest and assimilation or even of permanent military control. Edward could work only through the feudal method of subordinating the king of Scotland to his overlordship. A disputed succession gave him in 1292 the chance of awarding the crown to a nominee of his own, John Balliol. This move failed because the Scottish people forced Balliol into rebellion against his overlord. Although Edward defeated the Scots at Falkirk, one defeat was not likely to break Scottish resistance. In 1307 Edward died on his way north-wards to put down another rebellion. Seven years later an English army was defeated at Bannockburn. The battle of Falkirk had shown the military value of the long-bow;[1] Bannockburn had less military importance (the Scots won because they were better led) but greater political consequences, since it decided the course of Anglo-Scottish relations for several centuries and gave to the Scots a sense of national power which helped to preserve their independence far on into modern times. Thus, when at last England and

---

[1] The long-bow (as distinct from the short-bow or cross-bow) was used by the Welsh against Edward I. The archers at Falkirk were Welshmen. The effective range of the long-bow was about 280 yards.

Scotland formed a single kingdom, the union came about in circumstances which meant gain to each side.

Edward's policy needed money. He began his reign by a careful inquiry into his rights throughout the kingdom. He cut away most of the feudal encroachments of the disturbed period since Henry II by refusing to admit baronial claims which were not attested in writing or could not be shown to have operated since the coronation of Richard I in 1189. His administrative efficiency and, after he had begun his wars, his expenses led him to measures which had results greater than he or his contemporaries realized. In the year 1295 Edward was at war with France and likely to be at war with Scotland. He decided to summon an assembly at Westminster and to give this assembly a certain *éclat*. The appearance of his great officials was taken for granted. The king summoned his magnates, his archbishops, and bishops, that is to say, the personages who would be expected to come to any 'great council'. He instructed these prelates to secure the attendance of their archdeacons and of representatives of the cathedral chapter and clergy of each diocese. He also ordered the sheriffs to summon two knights from every shire and two citizens or burgesses from each city or borough in the kingdom. The knights, citizens, and burgesses were to be elected and to come with power to bind those by whom they had been chosen. The magnates were told in fine language, borrowed from the Emperor Justinian, that 'what touches all should be approved by all'.

The Emperor Justinian, who lived some seven centuries before Edward I, was an absolute ruler from whose laws and edicts it is impossible to extract maxims of democratic intention. The phrase – one of the slogans of the age – was used by Edward's clerks as a tactful way of asserting that 'what is approved by all, touches all'. Historians formerly described this assembly of 1295 as a 'model parliament'. Contemporaries did not see it in such a light. They were apt to use another general term 'colloquy' (*colloquium*), and anyone who called the assembly of 1295 a 'parliament' (*parliamentum*) would not have been giving the word a precise or single meaning. Chaucer applied it to a colloquy of birds. It was used for any 'parley' of an important kind; a conference of envoys or an assembly of the clergy. There was nothing, except the importance which Edward gave to it, to distinguish the assembly of 1295 from earlier assemblies. The addition of knights, citizens, and burgesses was not new. Edward himself had invited them, though not in exactly similar terms, in the spring of 1275. Later in 1275 he had called to another parliament knights but not burgesses. Simon de Montfort in 1265 had also invited knights and burgesses to an assembly directed to the coercion of the king. Still earlier, in 1213, John had summoned four 'discreet knights' from every shire 'to speak with him about the business of the kingdom'. This meeting was not held, but if it had taken place it would not have implied any surrender of authority on John's part. The king was merely continuing the practice of getting local knowledge from persons representing the opinion of the neighbourhood.[1] There was also no idea of bargaining. John wanted these knights probably because they could tell him what the 'neighbourhood' was likely to be able to pay. This would be the knights' part in the colloquy about the business of the realm. John and his officers would do the rest of the talking.

Edward I was therefore taking the simplest method of transmitting his demands to all parts of the kingdom. The growing wealth and importance of the towns meant that they too would be summoned to share in the colloquies. The summons was more of a burden than a privilege. The small fry, these knights and burgesses, knew why they were called. They were invited into a feudal assembly: the king in his council in parliament. The lay and clerical magnates attending this assembly had developed an attitude of their own towards the king, but their sense of corporate resistance was limited to their class. They were the 'kingdom'; their 'assent' implied the assent of everyone below them in status. The knights and burgesses, living chessmen in the game of high politics, could not make moves on their own initiative. They did not deliberate with the great men; the parliament continued not merely after they had withdrawn from the assembly, but after they had gone home. Finally, the king could deal with representatives other than knights or burgesses. He could consult the merchants of England as a separate body. The lower clergy, on their part, found it more convenient to leave 'parliament' and to vote the king's demands in their own convocation.

When all this has been said, the summoning of knights of the

[1] Representatives of the 'neighbourhood' already came to the king's court when a case was transferred to this court from the local courts.

shire – the men from whom Simon de Montfort had drawn his supporters – and of burgesses to take part with 'the king in council in parliament' was a matter of immense importance. Parliament had begun as a general term, but it soon acquired a special meaning for Englishmen – a meaning of a practical kind. The king himself had used the meetings for all manner of business. The reforms which Edward I carried out in large matters and small were embodied in written 'statutes' to which parliament gave assent. The 'statutes' were more in the nature of legal decisions, or amplifications, than laws as we know them today. They were regarded as 'new remedies' for 'new wrongs', but no one thought of them as items in a legislative programme. The general view of a meeting of the king in council in parliament was that of a court – the highest court – where justice was done. The fact that this court was the place where representatives of the 'neighbourhood' came for the redress of grievances for which there was no local remedy made it easier for these men of the third estate to raise their complaints when they were assenting to extraordinary grants of supply. The royal demand for supplies might itself be a subject of complaint. In effect this complaint was made as early as 1297. The indignation of all classes at the drain of taxation for a war which was thought unnecessary and the fear that extraordinary taxes would come to be regarded as ordinary taxes produced demands to which the king had to give way. The demands took the usual medieval form; the affirmation of existing charters: *Magna Carta* (which was already becoming legendary) and the Charter of the Forest. The significant point is that new clauses were added, including a statement that no new tallage or aid[1] should be levied without the consent of the lords spiritual and temporal, the knights, burgesses, and other free men. Already the phrase of Justinian about common consent was being turned against the king.

Institutions have a double interest for historians. They are interesting for what they are and for what they become. Out of these expedients of Edward I developed the parliamentary system of modern England. The development was slow and could not have been foreseen. It is dangerous to credit any thirteenth-century

[1] A 'tallage' was a tax levied upon towns and the demesne lands of the king. An 'aid' was a contribution from a vassal to a lord. Each tax was a contribution from a 'feudal' inferior to a superior.

statesman with a belief in representative assemblies and majority rule. It is equally dangerous to speak of an innate genius of the English for self-government. Other nations developed assemblies of estates, including representatives of the third estate; owing to the accidents of history these assemblies did not grow into representative bodies of a modern kind. It may well be that the English acquired the habit of self-government because they had a parliament rather than that they acquired a parliament because they had a talent for self-government. Indeed the whole matter may be and perhaps should be put in a different way. The immediate fact of the thirteenth century was not the rise of parliament but the incessant pressure upon the discreet knights of the shire to provide the information and to devise the local administrative machinery required to meet the demands of the central authority. From this angle of view, Englishmen, often against their inclination, learned the practice of self-government at home long before they set about taking control of the business at Westminster.

The reign of Edward II shows that in the fourteenth century, king, lords, and commons did not think in terms of modern constitutional theory. Edward was a second-rate man; he had the good looks of his family, but nothing of his father's *savoir-faire* and seriousness of purpose. He spent his time amusing himself; many of his amusements – swimming, working at a smithy, thatching houses – seemed undignified to his contemporaries and above all to the magnates who were even more scandalized by the king's delight in practical jokes at their expense. Edward's greatest friend, Piers of Gavaston, was a Gascon, distrusted as a foreigner (though indeed he was one of the king's French subjects) and despised as a peacock of a man.

Within a few years the magnates dealt with Gavaston. His end was typical of medieval 'chivalry'. He took refuge in Scarborough castle and surrendered after three weeks on terms that, if no agreement were reached about him between the king and the barons, he should be allowed to go back into the castle, which his enemies would then once more besiege. The terms were broken, but Gavaston's execution did not change Edward's habits.

In 1310, during these troubles over Gavaston, the barons had forced the king to promise that he would keep a series of ordinances

issued by themselves. As before, this remedy failed. The barons had
no new ideas. New ideas were unlikely to be found among a body
of men who boasted, almost in this year 1310, that they 'had no
knowledge of letters but were learned in knighthood and the rule of
arms'. The barons refused to face the fact that the king's revenues
were not enough to meet his expenses. They thought that all would
be well if the king's affairs were properly looked after and if he
took the advice of the barons and gave them the most important
offices in the realm. This attempt to control the king's administration could never succeed while the king was free to find new ways
of action through his household when any one avenue had been
blocked. The barons might stop one or other of these channels of
evasion – they were more or less successful in dealing with the
king's use of wardrobe officials; they could not provide a substitute
administration of their own. Indeed the interest of Edward II's
reign seen in distant retrospect – though, again, one must remember that contemporaries could not see it in this way – is the
slow but continuous development of an 'impersonal' administration,
outside the wrangles of king and barons. This development was
due, in the last resort, to the pressure of 'things' – the increasing
complexity of business, that is to say, the number of practical
problems which had to be solved, and, above all, to the cost of war.
The defeat of Bannockburn was in part a consequence of the king's
failure to finance his campaign even by devious means. The Hundred Years War in the next reign was to show that, ultimately, a
national administration alone could cope with a national policy.

In their opposition to Edward II the barons made matters worse
by choosing as their leader Thomas of Lancaster, the greatest
magnate of the realm. They could hardly choose anyone else, but
Thomas was an unbusinesslike, irritable man, richer though not
wiser than his peers and the more dangerous because he had managed to acquire a reputation for statesmanship in the country at
large. So matters drifted until in 1318 a middle party brought about
a reconciliation between Thomas and the king. The reconciliation
was given solemn form in a parliament at York. Representatives of
the commons were called to this parliament; they were now summoned as a matter of course, but not all those who were called
obeyed the summons, and those who came to York had little to do
with the business in hand. The great men managed the affair and

for a time the familiar remedy – baronial control – seemed to work. There was, however, no finality about the barons' plan; within a short time their own rivalries, together with the king's folly and the rise of a new family of favourites, caused more trouble. These years of dispute are of no interest to posterity. The king finally lost his throne over a sordid quarrel about the queen's behaviour. Edward was deposed in January 1327 and died, or was murdered, nine months later. There is nothing to be said for the queen; she was living in open adultery with one of the magnates.

The reigns of Henry III, Edward I, and Edward II, covering more than a century, may be considered from a standpoint very different from that of the development of institutions. During this period Gothic architecture reached its noblest development in England. Medieval architecture, like medieval scholarship, was at first more regional than national, and the patronage of the Church gave it something of a universal or, at all events, a general western-European character. The regional development of styles gradually became national; indeed the emergence of styles to which the term 'national' can properly be applied is one of the signs that the 'Middle Ages' were changing into modern times.

The English contribution to these regional developments was greater in all the arts, and in every century from the eighth to the fifteenth than is commonly believed. The churches of northern France were more magnificent; France, considered in its modern boundaries, was a richer country with more capital and labour available for the production of works of art. There are only three English cathedrals – Lincoln, Wells, and, on a smaller scale, Exeter – with a west front of figure sculpture comparable with the greatest churches of the Ile de France. The latest influence of French design may be seen in Henry III's Abbey of Westminster.

It is better to regard English buildings before the fourteenth century, as the English would then have seen them, without self-consciousness about special national characteristics. The most important technical development in the century before Henry III had been the substitution of the pointed for the round arch and the consequent freedom to build to a greater height and to secure greater freedom of construction. The significance of this new freedom can be understood in relation to the richness of colour, and with it, the place of decoration in the arts of the central and later Middle Ages.

There were obvious reasons why the major arts of sculpture and painting should turn to decoration. Medieval artists had not at their disposal the technical skill required for painting and sculpture as 'free arts'. Moreover, until the fourteenth or fifteenth centuries they worked mainly for churchmen. All buildings, from a castle to a cathedral, were functional; much of the decoration can also be called functional since it served the tasks of instruction and edification later fulfilled by the printed book. The Last Judgment carved over a church door was there for a purpose; the statues of the Virgin and Child, although providing a 'universal' subject of a humanist kind, were part of a religious cult. The larger themes of carver and painter were given to them; the scope for individual skill and expression – the chances of 'art for art's sake' – lay mainly in minor decorative detail. Gargoyles, capitals, bosses were not 'instructive' and allowed more realism than was possible in the treatment of saints or prophets or archangels, although here again there was a gradual loosening of the stiff Byzantine type of sculpture general throughout Europe before the twelfth century.

In any case the conditions of medieval life hampered the development of a free technique. Consider painting; in the early Middle Ages lack of light, which has always been a limiting feature of the arts in northern latitudes, was more serious because churches, castles, and town houses never had large windows. Improvements in construction made possible by the pointed arch allowed more light and were carried ultimately to a stage in which a cathedral became a series of great window-frames. Hence the colouring of glass and the elaboration of wall-paintings as an alternative to pictures. For similar reasons, until the general introduction of window-glass in houses and the invention of flues, the damp and smoke of an ordinary living-room made tapestry (woven by women) more suitable for decoration than paintings, even if there had been paintings available. Painting, as such, was done in books; here it was primarily decorative, an addition subservient to the written page of text, and getting a scale from the page or even from the margin of the page. In this form of art the English monasteries, where books were written and read (they were not much read in baronial castles), developed schools of their own; those of St Albans, and later of Westminster, were especially famous.

Only a few years after the death of Edward II English architecture diverged more sharply from that of France. The 'perpendicular' style, which after about 1350 took the place of the flowing lines of the 'decorated' period, had no Continental counterpart.[1] In France the builders in the 'flamboyant' style pushed the principles of Gothic to an extreme; English 'perpendicular', even with the development of fan-vaulting, is more restrained. In a sense, although it was used to great beauty in parish churches throughout the country and especially in towers such as those of Magdalen College or of Boston church, the style is more secular and business-like, less imaginative in its straight bars and squared panelling than the fashion which it superseded. In any case it is significant that a Frenchman coming to England at the close of the Hundred Years War would have noticed – for the first time in history – something more than an accumulation of local peculiarities in the difference between the newer English buildings and those of France.

[1] The change can be seen most easily in the contrast between the Lady Chapel (and Octagon) at Ely (1321–49) and the choir at Gloucester (1337–50). The new style appeared first on the grand scale at Gloucester because a business-like abbot, realizing that his abbey church could not compete in relics with other great foundations, offered a burial-place for the body of Edward II. Within a short time the king was regarded in popular view as a martyr. Pilgrims therefore came in numbers to Gloucester and on the proceeds of their gifts the monks were able to rebuild a large part of their abbey.

CHAPTER VI

The Hundred Years War:
Lancastrians and Yorkists

THE OCCASIONS OF war differ so much according to the temper of an age that our generation finds it hard to consider the Hundred Years War[1] between England and France as more than an irresponsible and tragic game of kings. The contemporaries of Edward III and the Black Prince did not hold this view. Edward III (1327–77) would have been regarded as a poor creature if he had not liked fighting. In fact, he enjoyed war, and, next after war, the mock wars of tournaments. He won victories and the prestige of these victories served him well. His parliaments gave him money; his policy was popular, partly indeed because he cared as little as his father for the work of administration and hardly minded what concessions he made as long as money was forthcoming.

On the grounds of national policy there was some excuse for his wars. He had inherited lands in France; their surrender would have affected English trade as well as the king's honour. Edward had also inherited a policy of interference in Scotland; here also he could not have left Scotland alone merely because the policy had not been successful. The war with Scotland was a contributory cause of the war with France. For obvious reasons the Scots since 1295 had been in an intermittent alliance with France, and the French kings had looked with favour on anti-English claimants to the Scottish throne. The rivalry of the English and French on French territory began after the Norman Conquest of England and had been increased by the Angevin connexion. Henry II's marriage with Eleanor of Aquitaine had added to Normandy, Maine, and Anjou large territories in the south-west of France. The French recon-

---

[1] The war began in 1337 and ended in 1453. Fighting was not continuous throughout this period; there were intervals of peace, e.g. after 1360, and from 1389 to 1403.

46

quest of Normandy in John's reign had removed the greatest danger
to the kingdom of France from a royal vassal whose power over-
shadowed that of his lord, but Gascony had remained in the feudal
possession of the kings of England after Anjou had been lost; the
great communes of Bordeaux and Bayonne valued their trade with
England and also thought that the king of France would be a
stronger master than a king of England across the sea.

The tactics of the kings of France were to try to edge out the
English. The reply of the English was to consolidate their power in
the south-west and if occasion offered, to take the offensive.
Edward III took the offensive on a grand scale by claiming or
rather reviving a claim to the French throne. Owing to the tangled
uncertainties of feudal succession this claim was not absurd in law.
The three sons of Philip the Fair, king of France, had died without
male heirs. If the crown could be transmitted through the female
line, Edward had a right to it, since his mother was a daughter of
Philip. Otherwise the nearest claimant was Philip VI, nephew of
Philip the Fair. There was no formal rule by which the matter
could be settled. For obvious reasons the French chose Philip's
nephew. Edward accepted the decision for a time, but refused to
recognize Philip VI's claim to certain territories in Gascony. Philip
then declared the confiscation of Gascony to France, and Edward
replied by reviving his own claim to the French throne. The
chances of agreement were less, because Philip VI, like Edward III,
was a man of his time, more interested in chivalry than in the
routine of government and readier to go to war than to try less
direct means of consolidating his power.

There were other causes of dispute. In return for Philip's reception of David Bruce,[1] the son of the victor of Bannockburn,
Edward gave shelter to a brother-in-law of the French king, who
had maintained and lost a claim to the county of Artois. Finally,
French interference in a rebellion of the townsmen of Flanders
against their Count put under French control Bruges, Ypres, and
other places in West Flanders. The merchants of these manufacturing towns were the best customers for English wool and their needs
could not be met at once from French markets. In order to force

---

[1] David Bruce, as a child of five, had succeeded his father in 1329. He had
been driven from Scotland by discontented magnates who obtained English
help.

the position Edward cut off the wool supply in 1337. The burghers gave way, made a treaty with England[1] and compelled the count of Flanders to fly for his life to the French court.

The first phases of this long war were typical of the slowness and inefficiency of military operations in a feudal age. War broke out in 1337. No engagement of importance was fought until 1340, when the English won the battle of Sluys and secured control of the Channel. Sluys was in name a sea-battle; in fact it was more a land-fight on ships and was won by archers. There was no decisive battle until the English victory at Crecy in 1346. The only strategic consequence of this victory was the capture of Calais after nearly a year's siege.[2] Nevertheless, Crecy was decisive in the sense that it showed the effectiveness of the long-bow and of men-at-arms fighting on foot against the French feudal cavalry. The implications of these tactics are important for the understanding of English social history. Distinctions of class in England went deep, but even in the fourteenth century there was not so sharp a cleavage between nobles and peasants as in France. French peasants were trampled underfoot by their own mounted countrymen; English peasants were trained to the use of the terrible new weapon and English men-at-arms did not disdain to fight side by side with the bowmen.

The French failed to learn the lesson of their defeat at Crecy. They were beaten again ten years later at Poitiers. This time victory was decisive in a military sense. In 1360 Edward was able to secure the surrender of a large area of land, including Poitou and the Limousin, as well as the retention of Calais by the English. These territorial gains were of little value. Throughout the war the English never realized the difference between military conquest and permanent occupation. They had no means of assimilating their conquests. They had raised a national feeling against them in France; their resources were not great enough for them to hold what they had won. Within ten years the French began to recover their losses; in 1375 of all the lands conquered since 1337 little was left except Calais and the coastal area south of Bordeaux.

The revival of the war under Henry V was therefore at best an

[1] Edward's definite assumption of the title of king of France in 1340 gave the Flemings a legal justification for supporting him.

[2] Shortly before Crecy Edward claimed to have found at Caen a plan for a second Norman conquest of England. He sent the document home to be read in all the churches of England.

act of misjudgment. Civil dissensions among the French gave Henry V a chance of taking the side of the duke of Burgundy, the greatest leader of faction, against the French king, but there was no reason for going to war except Henry's stubborn desire – which he interpreted as a duty – to recover his rights. Henry V landed in France in August 1415. After five weeks he took Harfleur and began a march to Calais. On his way, with a force at most 13,000 strong, he was met at Agincourt by a French army of 50,000. The English archers and men-at-arms, fighting in late October on fields too muddy for bringing up cannon – newest weapon of all – utterly defeated the French. The rest of the work, though slow, was easy. In 1417 Henry began the reconquest of Normandy. He had occupied the whole of it, except Mont St Michel, by the end of 1419. In 1420 he made peace on overwhelming terms. He married Catherine the daughter of the king of France, and was recognized as the king's heir (although Catherine's brother was living). He also kept Normandy even during the king's lifetime.

Henry V impressed contemporaries so greatly because he was a medieval not a modern king. Otherwise he might have seen the impossibility of maintaining these terms. Feudal rights could no longer determine the policy of nations; the claim to the French throne came to nothing, and by 1453 the English had been driven out of every place in France except Calais. The French learned to counter English tactics; at the battle of Patay in 1429 they attacked suddenly and thus gave the English archers no time to get ready. The war died out in a series of sieges, where the French showed greater skill in the use of cannon. In the last resort the expulsion of the English was due to the revival or rather to the emergence of national patriotism in France. This flame of liberation will be associated for ever with the history of Joan of Arc. For the shameful treatment of Joan, Frenchmen must take as much blame as the English. The English put her to death; she was betrayed to them by her own countrymen and condemned by a court presided over by a French bishop. The record of her life and death becomes incredible only if an attempt is made to rationalize it or to take it out of a medieval context in which, as in the minds and acts of children, good and evil, innocence and devilry could exist side by side.

The history of the Hundred Years War can be written in terms of its effect on English institutions. The king was out of England for long campaigns and always in need of money. Hence the king's subjects in parliament found it easier to make conditions when they granted extraordinary taxes. They asked for pledges about the spending of their money; they claimed the right to audit the king's accounts and to inquire whether his pledges had been kept. They postponed money grants until the end of a session and thus secured the redress of grievances before the vote of supplies. Parliament itself was taking a distinct form. It was no longer an enlarged meeting of the king's council; the statutes which had become the legal expression of parliamentary decisions began to be regarded as more important than the ordinances of the council. The two 'houses of parliament' were also assuming something of their modern form. The title 'house of lords' dates only from the sixteenth century, but in the early part of the fourteenth century certain families, or rather the holders of certain estates, were receiving writs of summons as a matter of course. By 1400 this summons by special writ was coming to be regarded as a hereditary right. Before the death of Edward III the knights and burgesses were putting their case to the king and lords through a Speaker; the fact that they met to discuss their answers outside the parliament house and in the chapter-house or refectory of the Abbey of Westminster added to their consciousness of themselves as a body separate from the lords spiritual and temporal. It is also significant that, although statutes and petitions were still written in Latin or, more often, in a debased Anglo-French jargon,[1] parliament was opened in 1362 for the first time with an English speech.[2] In his old age Edward III allowed the affairs of the kingdom to be mismanaged by a corrupt clique of household officials, with the connivance of his mistress Alice Perrers and the support of John of Gaunt. A parliament of 1376, known as the 'Good Parliament', took matters in hand by enforcing upon the king a council of advisers. This action – it succeeded for only a short time – was taken not, as fifty years earlier, by a baronial party acting on its own responsibility, but by a joint committee of lords and commons.

It is, however, necessary once again to look at developments of this kind as they would have appeared to contemporaries. The knights of the shire and the burgesses of the fourteenth and fifteenth

[1] The royal assent to bills is still given in the French terms: 'le roy le veult'.
[2] See also below, p. 65.

centuries would have regarded the king and the magnates as the deciding force in the country. They did not consider themselves as competent to settle high policy and anyhow wished to avoid financial responsibility for it. In 1348 the king consulted the commons about the French war. They begged to be excused; they said that they were too ignorant and simple to give advice. ('Nous sumes si mesconissantz et simples qe nous ne poons en conseiller.') The king should do what he thought best on the advice of the great and wise men of his council; the commons would agree, though their agreement did not in fact keep them from sharp criticism of the royal policy when it came to paying for it.

Furthermore, owing to their great local power, the nobles were able to influence the composition of parliament and to secure the return of men under their control. The Speaker of the commons in the Good Parliament was the steward of the earl of March; in the following year the Speaker was a steward of March's rival John of Gaunt. John of Gaunt himself was an example of a new feature which had come into the relationship of the king with the magnates. Edward III's policy of endowing his large family, of whom John of Gaunt was one, by marriage with the heiresses of vast estates offered in the second generation the danger of powerful candidates for the throne.[1] This danger of faction was more serious because the greater nobles were getting a large share of the increasing wealth brought to the country by the wool and cloth trades and were consolidating their hold over wide areas of the country. Furthermore, the French wars which impoverished the Crown added to the power of the nobility. For these men military service was no longer a personal and tenurial duty, but a matter of business. The king hired the retainers of the magnates, and the latter found it profitable to increase the numbers available for hire. In order to keep such bands of men at their disposition, their lords had to employ 'tammany' tactics and to use their local influence to overawe the king's administrative officers. Hence the breakdown of government which is the theme of so many complaints in the fifteenth century; hence also the Wars of the Roses.

The remedy would have been a strong council. Here again a small group of powerful families dominated the council and divided

---

[1] Edward III and Richard II created (sparingly) new grades of duke and marquis in the peerage.

it by their feuds. This dominance was inevitable during the first years of Richard II's reign (1377–99). The king was only ten years old when he succeeded his grandfather, Edward III. Richard was temperamental, artistic, capable of acts of great generosity, yet unable to sustain the harsh and patient effort necessary for re-establishing the royal authority. He failed in his first efforts to free himself from the tutelage of his uncles. He reasserted himself soon afterwards, and for eight years there was little open trouble. His old enemies, however, were working against him. He turned against them suddenly in 1397. Nevertheless he was not strong enough to keep the position which he had gained by something like a *coup d'état*. His vague theories of high prerogative could be used against him; the real trouble, however, was that he offended too many powerful interests. On John of Gaunt's death[1] Richard seized the Lancastrian inheritance. He had already exiled Henry of Lancaster,[2] John of Gaunt's son; the confiscation of his estates forced Henry into rebellion. Henry landed at Ravenspur in July 1399. Richard, who had taken hardly any precautions to deal with rebellion, was tricked into surrender. Henry compelled him to abdicate and took his place as king on the ample grounds of descent, conquest, and election. In 1400 he ordered Richard's murder.

In this manner the house of Lancaster came to a throne which they lost much as they had won it. Henry IV (1399–1413) was a fine figure, well educated for a king, and with a sense of what was popular, but the need to keep his followers and his popularity made it difficult for him to act in the only way likely to affirm his position. All he could do was to husband his resources, to show firmness about the rights of the crown, and, as far as possible, to employ men outside the influence of the great lords.

Henry V (1413–22) was less willing to count the cost or to consider the remoter consequences of his actions. At the same time he was ambitious on the heroic scale. He reopened the French war as the first stage in a plan to end the papal schism and lead a crusade of all Christendom. Henry died in 1422 at the age of 35; his successor

[1] 'Old Gaunt indeed, and gaunt in being old.' 'Time-honoured Lancaster' was under fifty-nine at his death.

[2] In 1390 Henry had joined the Teutonic Knights in a 'crusade' against the Lithuanians (who were nevertheless Christians). During this crusade Henry's English archers did well at the siege of Vilna. In 1393 Henry went on a pilgrimage to the Holy Sepulchre.

was an infant of nine months. Hence for years to come the quarrels between the great men on the king's council were likely to continue and indeed to grow more acute as the English lost their hold in France. The faction fights went on after the king's boyhood. Henry VI was pious, quiet, gentle by nature, weak of body and impaired of mind. He was unable to deal with a situation which drifted into civil war. Richard, duke of York and great-grandson of Edward III, and father of Edward IV, now took the part which Henry of Lancaster had played half a century earlier.

The Wars of the Roses[1] were less important than the contemporaries of Shakespeare believed. Although they lasted for a generation, fighting was intermittent; there were nearly twelve years of peace after 1471. The armies were small; only about 4,000–5,000 fought on each side in the battles. Casualties were also on a small scale, even if in the later stages there was an increase in cruelty. No large towns were besieged because each party needed the support of the towns, especially London, and therefore treated them with caution. The details of the war are hardly worth pursuing. The fighting seemed to have come to an end with a final victory of Edward IV in 1471, ten years after his accession. Edward was only nineteen when he came to the throne. He had a large inheritance, and increased it by confiscations, but he did not live long enough to establish his family against all rivals. He died in April 1483. Once again the heir to the throne was a child. Within three months Edward's brother Richard, duke of Gloucester, usurped the kingdom and, soon afterwards, appears to have procured the murder of Edward's sons in the Tower of London. Richard III was not much worse than other contemporary princes, nevertheless his acts shocked opinion enough to lose him general support. There was no Lancastrian in direct male descent[2] to challenge him, but Henry Tudor,[3] earl of Richmond, was a great-grandson of one of John of

---

[1] The name was not used until Tudor times. The Yorkist badge was the heraldic white rose; the Lancastrian red rose was less common. Many other badges of great lords were worn (e.g. the white hart and the crowned swan). The issue at the battle of Barnet was affected by the confusion between two similar private badges: a star and a *rose-en-soleil*.

[2] Richard's only son had died in 1484.

[3] Henry was born at Pembroke Castle in 1457. His grandfather, Sir Owen Tudor, claimed to be of ancient descent from the British kings. Henry's mother, Lady Margaret Beaufort (who was under fourteen at the time of his birth), came later in life under the influence of Bishop Fisher of Rochester. Fisher,

Gaunt's children by his mistress and third wife Catherine Swynford. Henry had been taken for safety to France in 1471. In August 1485 he landed at Milford Haven. He had made known his intention of marrying the Princess Elizabeth, daughter of Edward IV; his succession might therefore put an end to the disputes of faction. He met Richard at Bosworth in Leicestershire. Richard went into battle with the crown on his head, and died fighting.

although he died as a martyr for catholic orthodoxy, persuaded her to use her large fortune not, as she had intended, for the endowment of religious houses, but for the development of learning at the universities, and particularly at Fisher's own university of Cambridge.

CHAPTER VII

The End of the 'Middle Ages'

IT IS A commonplace of historians to point out that behind these fights of selfish and over-powerful nobles there were new forces at work in English society undermining the foundations of the feudal kingdom of the Middle Ages. Such a description is fair enough if it is not taken to imply that a way of life which reached its noblest external form in the thirteenth century had anything static about it and that the two following centuries were periods of decadence in which a 'medieval culture' was 'breaking up'.

The term 'middle age' is a convenient way of referring to some five hundred years of modern history during which, as always, there was continuous change. In many respects England in the fifteenth century would have seemed as unfamiliar and bizarre to Henry II as it appears to us. The England of Henry II would have seemed no less strange to Alfred and even stranger to Bede. Nearly every detail of medieval life had altered between the wars against the Danes and the battle of Bosworth. Moreover, in the early period these details have to be seen against a background of pagan and barbarian custom yielding slowly to the Christian civilization centred in Italy where, in Hobbes's words, the papacy was 'the ghost of the Roman Empire sitting crowned upon the grave thereof'. At the end of the 'middle age' this description had not lost all validity, but it would be more accurate to speak of an increasing sophistication brought by wealth; the beginnings of religious indifference, disguised under formal submission to religious authority; the emancipation of the peasantry; the rise of a middle class and spread of capitalism from small beginnings in medieval industry and in the exploitation of the land.

Nevertheless there were certain structural arrangements common to the medieval period. Throughout these centuries the average man was a peasant. The townsman was exceptional, and peasants and burgesses alike lived less by individual enterprise than by ancient custom, regulated by self-governing associations. The physical setting of the peasant's life changed very little between the twelfth and the fifteenth centuries. Over the greater part of the midlands, as far north as York, and in the nearer western counties the small two- or three-roomed cottages of the peasants were clustered in villages.[1] These huts of wattle, mud, clay, and thatch had no chimneys; even in the fifteenth century window-glass was rare. Livestock was separated, if at all, only by a passage-way from the house. Most villages would have had a manor-house,[2] possibly a bailiff's house, and a church. There would be orchards of apple, pear, or cherry, a duckpond and a fishpond. Around the village would be some meadow land and two, or three, open fields, one of them in fallow. In summer these fields were roughly enclosed to keep out the cattle; beyond them, according to the nature of the country, extended the uncleared, and uncultivated 'waste'. 'Waste land', in a peasant economy, was not useless land. Pigs were kept on it, and firewood gathered from it. Cattle were pastured in forest glades. The open fields were divided into strips, and ploughed mainly by oxen. Oxen were stronger though slower than horses and their keep cost less. In any case horses could not have been used for the plough until the tenth century because a suitable collar was not devised before this time.

These divisions into strips were confused and uneconomical; the holdings of lords and their tenants, free and unfree, were inter-mixed and there was little symmetry about anyone's possessions. Such confusion provided a motive for consolidating the strips, but for men who knew every foot of land upon which they and their fathers had worked, the divisions would be less haphazard and troublesome than they appear to us. The lordships were as mixed as the holdings. There might be several lordships, each regarded

[1] Conditions in the north and west and in East Anglia were different. Even in the more uniform central area the king's forest enclosures were under their own special (and severe) laws. These forests covered a great deal of country. Except for a relatively short distance in Oxfordshire, it was possible to walk through royal forests north-eastwards from the Solent to the Wash. The forest areas were not kept for deer alone: cattle and dairy farming might be practised in them.

[2] A manor was originally just a house of someone of local importance. As with so many medieval terms, lawyers' definitions and the process of economic change between Domesday Book and the fifteenth century had given it a technical meaning.

as a manor, in one village; the villagers of one manor might hold land elsewhere; a villein might 'belong' to more than one lord.

The lord's strips were cultivated by labour services performed mainly by the villeins who also owed other services of various kinds. Here again it is difficult to draw a firm distinction between free and unfree, in spite of the lawyers' elaboration of the status of serfdom. By the thirteenth century lords could exercise in theory almost unlimited rights against 'their' villeins. The villein could not leave his land; at least until after 1300 the average peasant in a medieval village was unlikely to want to leave it. The amount of his services probably meant more to a villein than any question of status. Moreover, a villein was unfree only in relation to his own lord.[1] He was not a slave; he shared the burdens incumbent upon freemen, although this privilege could not have brought him much satisfaction. As early as the thirteenth century the distinction between free and unfree began to apply more to the status of land than to that of persons; once again, the matter came down to one of service rather than to any sense of a class of beings unfitted for citizenship.

The change in the position of the peasantry resulted from the gradual 'commutation' of these labour and other services for money payments. This process, which was not uniform, took place for many reasons. The medieval landlord, like most of his kind before and after, was always short of money. As the standard of living rose, the lord's demand for commodities increased; so also did his shortage of funds. Labour services were never economical; most lords found that it paid them to take money in their place and to hire labour or even to give up farming their own demesnes. The peasants were able to raise small sums because there were always markets in towns; with the increase in these markets, it became easier to dispose of surplus products. Once the change from service in labour or kind to money rents had taken place the lord had more interest in securing the payment of his rents than in keeping villein tenants

[1] One mark of unfree status regarded as degrading was the payment of a fine on the marriage of a daughter. Other incidents of unfreedom can be explained in relation to the manorial economy. Thus a villein could not sell an ox or a horse (at all events until the fourteenth century) because the sale would lessen the stock on the estate. He could not set up millstones in his house because he would be competing with the lord's mill. He could not send his son to school or apprentice him to a handicraft without the lord's consent because he would be taking labour from the estate.

on the land. As the value of money declined, the peasants who paid a fixed rent instead of services gained at the lord's expense.

It has been estimated that in 1300 about one-half of the peasantry was free. In the middle of the fourteenth century this slow movement away from serfdom was affected by the terrible accident of plague. Accident is hardly an accurate description of the recurrent visitations of the Black Death, since this catastrophe was the direct result of medieval conditions; dirt and vermin, and ignorance of the consequences of dirt and vermin. The immediate cause of the plague which reached England in 1348 was the spread of the black rat over Europe; this rat seems to have come from the East two centuries earlier in the ships of the Crusaders. The rats moved westwards along the waterways and crossed the narrow seas in ships and barges. The Black Death ravaged all western Europe. It was more fatal to the young and the middle-aged than to the old; although the incidence of the plague varied locally, about one-third of the population died.

The social effects of this plague are hard to estimate. To some extent they can be described as disintegrating, without an immediate return wave of creative activity. They account, or seem to account, for some of the more feverish and tortured symptoms of late medieval culture. Possibly the general effect was less demoralizing than that of the spread of syphilis early in the sixteenth century. One of the economic consequences of the sudden decrease in the numbers of the population was a rise in the importance of labour. Hired labour became almost twice as expensive, while customary rents in money remained unchanged. Hence the king's Council, representing the interests of landlords, tried to fix scales of wages and prices. These scales were enforced, but medieval administration was never able to secure uniformity. The lords competed with one another for the service of free labourers; the villeins had more incentive to run away from their holdings and to work elsewhere for higher wages. In the confused years following the plague it was easier to run away; many estates, for example, were in the hands of minors. The lords also increased the leasing of land for money and the area put to sheep.[1] The increase in sheep-farming must not be exagger-

---

[1] This does not mean that sheep-farming in the fifteenth century was becoming more profitable. On the contrary, with the fall in population, there was for a time a slump in prices and profits, but arable-farming was more affected than

ated; for years past, and almost for centuries, wool-growing had been one of the main sources of wealth. Even before the Norman Conquest the Abbey of Ely owned over 13,000 sheep, and from the thirteenth century the great landlords ran something like sheep-ranches in wide pastoral areas such as the Cotswolds, the Welsh borderlands, and parts of Lincolnshire.

The reaction of the peasants to a state of things in which their services had suddenly become of greater value to the lords was, naturally enough, a desire to get rid of these services altogether and to secure the benefit of higher wages. For the first time in England, and not in England alone, there was a movement of a real revolutionary kind; a desire for something better and not merely for a return to the 'good customs' of the past. In addition to this unrest the burden of taxation was another cause of discontent; the cost of the French war had to be met by a smaller number of taxpayers. Hence after the imposition of a badly graded poll-tax there were peasant insurrections all over England. These revolts were especially violent in the south-east, where commutation had made least progress. The suppression of the revolts was not difficult, but the rate of change accelerated by the Black Death continued throughout the next hundred years. The change meant the end of the old manorial system and the disappearance of unfreedom.[1]

The popular agitation of a levelling kind included an attack upon class distinctions as contrary to Christian teaching. Although this attack was not directed against Christian doctrine it may be taken as a sign of the times that the established order in the Church as well as in the State was not accepted without question. The lower clergy, near to the peasants in origin, sympathized with their grievances and were themselves jealous of the wealth and encroachments of the religious orders. The friars, who had given up in fact their practice of apostolic poverty, were especially obnoxious, since they were outside the jurisdiction of diocesan bishops and could interpose between the parish priest and the souls – and offerings – of his congregation. Moreover, doubts about certain aspects of the

sheep-farming. The export of wool declined, but that of cloth increased. The rise of capitalism in the wool and clothing industries is worth study as a corrective to a good many loose generalizations on the economy of the Middle Ages.

[1] Serfdom continued on a small scale throughout the sixteenth century. As late as 1586 the Privy Council intervened on behalf of a mayor of Bristol whom Lord Stafford 'challenged' to be his bondsman.

ecclesiastical order were general among laymen. The sources of discontent were mainly the financial exactions of the Roman court and
the use by the pope of English benefices for the enrichment of his
nominees. The scandal of these provisions to benefices was exaggerated; in any case the king was as great an offender as the pope.
Statutes were passed to prevent papal abuses, but the repetition of
such laws shows the unwillingness of all parties to observe them. The
papal captivity at Avignon added greatly to English indignation,
since it was thought, again not altogether fairly, that English money
was being sent overseas to serve the cause of the king's enemies in
France. The papal schism and the failure of the great Church
councils of the fifteenth century to reform abuses were a deeper
shock to the consciences of serious men.

Thus, for different reasons, there was a slow but real growth of
anti-clerical feeling. Even the massive stronghold of scholastic
doctrine was not entirely unshaken. The career of Wiclif shows the
transition from an attack on Church organization to doubts about
the dogmas of faith. John Wiclif (c. 1330–84) was a Yorkshireman[1]
who went to Oxford and was for a time Master of Balliol. His
career was not on the lines of that of Chaucer's parish priest. Wiclif
held three livings in turn and for long periods did not reside in them.
In 1362 he added a prebend[2] in a collegiate church. He obtained
this preferment by papal provision and kept it until his death. He
would have taken another prebend, but the pope gave it to the
illegitimate son of an English soldier whom he wanted to maintain
in his service.

Although Wiclif was not consistent in his attitude towards papal
abuses, his attack was popular. He did not begin to question Church
doctrine and to express heretical views about the Sacrament of the
Altar until after the papal schism. These views lost him the support
of John of Gaunt, who had been ready enough to back plans for
the partial disendowment of the Church. Wiclif's opinions were
also too strong for the University of Oxford. He was forbidden to
perform any academic act, yet he kept the living of Lutterworth

[1] It is a curious fact that the Yorkshire family of Wiclif remained Roman
Catholic after the Reformation.
[2] A 'prebend' (from a Latin term meaning 'something provided') was an
endowment in land or money for the maintenance of a priest at a collegiate or
cathedral church, i.e. a church in which a governing body of canons was presided over by a dean.

THE END OF THE 'MIDDLE AGES'

until his death. Forty-four years later his bones were taken out of consecrated ground and thrown into the river Swift.

Wiclif was neither a saint nor a humanist. It would be difficult to call him a clear thinker. He was a scholar according to the over-elaborate learning of his time. He undermined rather than attacked the dogmatic content of this learning. The translation of the Bible carried out under his encouragement (probably not by himself) had an equally disintegrating effect. Wiclif did not say that Church doctrine was not to be found in the Bible; he invited Christians to look for it there. Similarly he did not say that papal authority was invalid; he claimed that only a good Christian could exercise dominion. Who was then to decide whether this or that pope was a good Christian, or to judge between different interpretations of Biblical texts?

Wiclif's teaching, popularized and distorted by earnest and often ill-instructed preachers, was mainly responsible for the only important English medieval heresy. 'Lollardy' [1] also continued the criticism of the existing social order current at the time of the Peasants' Revolt. Hence the Government was as much afraid of it as the Church. The Lancastrian kings were orthodox and even bigoted; they were willing to suppress Lollardy on grounds of faith and policy alike. As in the case of the peasants' rebellion, suppression of open heresy was not difficult, but there is danger to a Church which has recourse to the secular arm for the suppression of opinion. The Lollard tradition survived, in a somewhat vague but radical form, especially among the poorer classes in the towns. Anti-clerical feeling thus persisted, although the general hold of Church observance was as strong as ever and the new rich in town or country still spent large sums in rebuilding, enlarging, or decorating their parish churches. The Yorkist kings were too much concerned with the task of establishing a strong administration to attack the Church even if they had wished to do so, yet it was by no means certain that the monarchy would always be on the side of Church authority or of catholic orthodoxy.

According to European, or at all events according to Italian,

---

[1] Lollen: to sing softly, or to mumble. The word was first used in the Netherlands and the 'Poor Preachers' who spread Wiclif's doctrine were also an importation from abroad where they had come into existence as a result of schism in the Franciscan Order.

standards, Wiclif's learning and the late scholasticism of Oxford were already a little out of date. There had been a change in the attitude of scholars as well as of artists towards traditional modes of expression and canons of thought. The terms 'renaissance' and 'revival of learning' have been used to describe this change of view. These terms are a little misleading. The so-called revival of learning was largely an abandonment of out-moded types of learning. It was not altogether a discarding of lumber; much of it was only a change from rhetorical and argumentative pedantry to a pedantry of an etymological and stylistic kind.

Nevertheless a change of attitude towards received knowledge must mean an intellectual effort in the selection of different facts and the employment of a new emphasis. There was also one real revival; the study of Greek literature in the original Greek.[1] These new interests were slow in reaching England. The monasteries had ceased to be active centres of scholarship; the new learning did not begin in the universities because the scholastic mandarins rejected anything which lowered the prestige or the economic value of their repertoire.

Thus the introduction of the new learning and of the new art was due much more to a few rich men, dilettanti rather than scholars, and cosmopolitan in outlook. Humphrey, duke of Gloucester (1391–1447), and John Tiptoft, earl of Worcester (?1427–70), were very different from the later humanists. The duke was a Machiavellian prince; Tiptoft was one of the cruellest men in England. Although duke Humphrey left a collection of books to Oxford and Cambridge, neither he nor any other of these great patrons can be regarded as educational reformers, still less as moral enthusiasts. On the other hand, the greatest figure of the Italian renaissance, Leonardo da Vinci, was a scientist as well as an artist and the interest of Englishmen in Italian learning was not confined to literature. Linacre (?1460–1524), for example, went to Italy mainly to study medicine.

The study of Greek was of little general importance in England during the fifteenth century. Erasmus in 1505 found only five or six men in London whose scholarship was good both in Greek and Latin;

---

[1] Although Aristotle was one of the main sources of medieval learning, his work was studied in Latin translations, some of them from Arabic texts which were translations of Syriac versions.

eleven years later, when Richard Fox, bishop of Winchester, founded Corpus Christi College, Oxford, there was some opposition within the university to his endowment of a lectureship in Greek. No Greek book was printed in England until nearly half a century after duke Humphrey's death. Even the later humanists did not think of themselves as revolutionaries. They were removing abuses or recovering a learning which had been forgotten. None the less their work was revolutionary; the grammarians struggling with 'the enclitic δὲ,' were opening a new world.

For a long time this world remained closed to the mass of people. There is a sense in which the increasing culture of the richer merchant classes[1] and a section of the nobility widened the gulf between them and the peasantry or the proletariat of the towns. The sign of the separation was the appearance of the educated layman. In the early Middle Ages learning had been left to the clergy and had become their prerogative. It would be a mistake, however, to suppose that most of the clergy were educated and all the laity illiterate. Only a small élite of either class regarded education as an end in itself; a change of attitude in this matter was perhaps the greatest innovation of the humanists. Book-learning in the Middle Ages was a means of acquiring the technique for performing certain duties. A lawyer must know the law; a priest must be able to recite his office. There were economic advantages attached to learning but no social prestige. The only education with social prestige attached to it had not much to do with books. Training in chivalry separated the sons of gentlemen – the greater and lesser magnates of the kingdom – from the education given at universities or schools. Such training in chivalry was concerned with the profession of arms, and with the rigmarole of etiquette and deportment.

This 'licking of young cubs' was not mere snobbery. It included singing, rhyming, the speaking of French and of a little Latin. In an age of rough manners it had a certain civilizing value and was not without some influence for good on the status of women. It has been described in this respect as a counterpart to the commercialism of medieval marriages. Anyhow it was more elaborate and painstaking

[1] The increasing complications of his own business made it necessary for a rich merchant to have some general education, e.g. in the sixteenth century English merchants adopted the Italian practice of double-entry book-keeping. They also borrowed the Italian symbols £ s. d. (librae, solidi, denarii).

than the average education in the schools provided by the Church. The Church did not altogether neglect elementary teaching and deserves credit for doing something which for a long time no other body thought of doing. Almost every English cathedral church had – as some still have – both a grammar school and a 'song school'. The song school, as its name implies, was intended for the training of a choir in music and in the rudiments of religious knowledge. The song-master could take other children; the English reputation in the Middle Ages for music and singing may owe a good deal to this simple discipline.

The grammar school was on a higher grade. Medieval learning was ranged in seven arts; the grammar schools taught (in Latin) the three minor arts of rhetoric, dialectic (i.e. argument according to logical rule), and grammar. The best schools also taught the rudiments of the four major arts of arithmetic, geometry, astrology,[1] and music. The standards were low; arithmetic, for example, was not much more than calculation by Roman numerals with the help of a counting-board. The main purpose of the grammar school was to teach the language of business. For a long time this language was Latin. Latin was thus spoken rather than read. Indeed boys at grammar schools did little reading because they had no books of their own. The only textbooks – and these were works in general circulation throughout northern Europe – were the property of the teacher whose business was to dictate from them lessons to be got by heart.

From the fourteenth century the number of schools increased. Many priests serving chantries[2] added to their small incomes by teaching children. Laymen began to found schools. There was also some direct connexion between the schools and the universities.[3] William of Wykeham's colleges at Winchester and Oxford, and the royal foundations of Eton and King's College, Cambridge, are out-

---

[1] The respect paid to astrology is less odd if it is remembered that from the point of view of medieval learning, the earth was the centre of the universe but inferior in 'essence' to the stars. The influence of the higher elements on the lower was a natural deduction from the observed connexion between the sun, moon, and stars and the seasons, changes of the tide, etc.

[2] A chantry was a chapel or altar where Masses were endowed for the repose of the founder's soul.

[3] The term implies an association or *universitas* of persons, not a place where any subject could be studied. The medieval term applying to subjects was *studium generale*.

standing examples. Eton and Winchester were not intended for the very poor but for the middle orders of society – the sons of small landowners or merchants. The universities were predominantly for the clergy. This did not mean an overwhelming predominance of theology; canon law was in many ways more attractive as a study because it opened the way more easily to preferment. The undergraduates were very young; only a minority of them stayed to take degrees. The organization of a university was indeed similar to that of any other craft. Seven years of residence, corresponding to an apprenticeship, were necessary before the grant of a master's degree gave the right and privilege of teaching; another seven years were required for a doctorate. As in the schools most of the teaching was oral. There were practically no examinations; fee-paying and keeping terms were more important. The length of the 'long' vacation was not to allow time for study at home; the times chosen covered the hay and wheat harvests. There could be no study at home without books.

The invention of printing and the increasing use of English as the language of learning and business changed the outlook of the ordinary educated man as well as of the professed student. The history of the English language is a tale by itself. 'Literary' English, such as it was, almost disappeared (except for popular homiletics) after the Conquest when the language was left mainly to peasants and other unlettered people. In any case the language in its various dialects changed with use; English translations of the homilies of Aelfric, written about A.D. 1000, were 'modernized' twice in the twelfth century in order that they might be better understood. On the other hand English might have reasserted itself sooner in high places if there had not been a reinforcement of French-speaking officials with the coming of the Angevin kings. In spite of this second wave of invasion, two centuries after the death of Henry II French, even 'the French of Stratford-atte-Bowe', was not well known in England. In 1362–3 English took the place of French, though not of Latin, in the courts of law.

This English was not the West Saxon dialect spoken and written by Alfred, but the dialect of the midlands. 'Middle English' came into general use partly because it was an intermediate dialect and therefore more or less intelligible to north and south, and mainly because it was the dialect of London and therefore of the court.

Even so Caxton found it difficult to choose words understood by all his readers. In this respect the printed book, which made the eye rather than the ear the judge of language, tended towards uniformity of vocabulary.[1]

The printing press, set up by Caxton[2] at Westminster in 1477, cheapened the multiplication of books and made study possible outside a few libraries; the books would have been of less use if there had been nowhere in a private house to read them. Leisure and opportunities for reading were thus part of a rising standard of life. This rising standard again enabled readers to recover for themselves more easily the world of high individual culture in which the Greek and Latin classics had been written. In this respect the improvement in the housing conditions at least of the wealthier classes may be taken as an index of the degree of escape from the material and spiritual conditions of the Dark Ages. From the sixth to the fourteenth centuries there were no houses in England comparable in largeness of comfort and civilized purpose with the Roman *villas*.

After about 1350 it could be said that this civilized purpose had returned to architecture. A rich man's house was no longer built for defence. The number of rooms had increased; these rooms were well lit,[3] with glazed windows and chimneys. There was a certain comfort in the furniture. The introduction of table forks in the fifteenth century brought an improvement in table manners. Medieval food remained heavy and monotonous; hence the use of spices as a luxury. Honey was an inadequate substitute for sugar;[4] tea, coffee, and potatoes were unknown. Beasts were killed off in the

[1] Caxton, in 1490, told a story of an English merchant whose ship was held by contrary winds in the Thames, asking at a house, apparently in a northern dialect, for meat and eggs. The lady of the house said that 'she did not speak French.' The merchant replied that he was not speaking French, but was asking in English for eggs. A bystander explained that he meant 'eyren'.

[2] Caxton (the name was pronounced as Cauxton or Causton), was born at Tenterden in Kent. He learned printing at Cologne in order to multiply copies of his translation of the popular romance 'Le Recueil des Histoires de Troye'. In fourteen years, he and his few assistants printed more than 18,000 pages, nearly all of folio size, and about eighty separate books. Caxton also did a great deal of translation.

[3] The improvement was of special importance owing to the rudimentary character of glasses for correcting defective sight. Medieval dentistry was even more rudimentary.

[4] The sugar-cane was introduced by the Arabs into Sicily and Andalusia as well as into Morocco. The first reference to a cargo of sugar brought into England dates from 1319. Sugar was, however, a costly luxury and was long

late autumn owing to the shortage of winter keep; sea fish (and fish was an incidental requirement of religious observance) had to be salted for transport inland. Oranges and lemons were rare, and other fruits depended wholly on the English season. As seaborne trade increased, the luxuries of the few came within reach of larger numbers and higher standards of comfort spread slowly through society. In spite of the filth and stench of a medieval town[1] the merchants who entertained Edward IV lived in circumstances which would have astonished the Anglo-Norman kings.

This increase in wealth arising from a greater variety of demand had its bad side. Medieval ideas of right and wrong in economic relationships had developed against a background of sparseness. Traditional views about a 'just price' or about equality among 'brethren' in the sharing of trade disintegrated under the temptations of wealth. The gild system broke down in the conflict between richer and poorer and ceased to be a binding force in town life. Specialized craft gilds had done as much for the organization of a common life as the earlier gild merchant had done to secure civic liberty. The minute regulations of the crafts protected consumers as well as producers; their fraternities were the medieval counterpart of modern friendly societies. The richer gilds maintained schools; every gild of importance held an annual pageant, and these pageants, with their traditional 'mysteries',[2] prepared the way for the English drama of the sixteenth century. Nevertheless, in an age of expanding business, merchant and craft gilds tended to oligarchy and restriction of trade with the result that trade itself began to leave many of the older towns for places where there were no such limitations on freedom. The separation of the merchant from the craftsman meant too often the depression of the latter into a manual labourer and the end of a system of small groups of producers controlling the production and marketing of their work.

This fading out of customary rules and restraints allowed the

used mainly as an ingredient of medicines. (As late as 1700, the annual import of sugar into England was only 10,000 tons.)

[1] It is fair to remember that this filth and stench were hardly less noisome in the age of Dr Johnson than in the age of Chaucer.

[2] 'Mistery' as a trade comes through the French *métier* from the Latin *ministerium*. A 'mystery' play was a play about the 'mysteries' of religion, i.e. scenes from the Old or New Testament or, in the case of 'miracle' plays, representations of the miracles or martyrdoms of the saints. The 'mistery' performed the 'mystery' play, but the two words have a different origin.

emergence of new types of business-men without scruple and without pity. It would be absurd to suppose that medieval economic life was an idyllic companionship of fellow-workers on equal terms – town records are full of regulations against every kind of cheating and dishonesty – but the development of plenty did not mean plenty for all and the new freedom did not necessarily carry with it happier conditions of work. Although the medieval belief that usury[1] – lending money without risk – was a deadly sin rested on an imperfect analysis of economic services, it implied social and moral obligations in the employment of wealth and therefore set limits to the acquisitiveness of individuals. The *nouveaux riches* who dominated England in the century after the Wars of the Roses may astonish us by their energy; the uses to which this energy was put included the expansion of the African slave trade, a wild search for gold, and the beginning of a 'robber' exploitation of the world's treasures in life and material.

Nevertheless, if the new individualism is considered under every aspect, good and bad, the balance tends towards liberty of choice and the emancipation of human life from the lowest servitudes to nature. Without this emancipation the deepest culture of the mind would have been impossible except in the occasional and limiting conditions of a monastic order, a college, or a hermit's cell. In the last analysis there is some truth in Renan's verdict upon the Middle Ages as 'a thousand years' tyranny of priests and crowds', even though a fairer judgment would remember that these 'priests and crowds' built monuments of timeless beauty, such as Chartres Cathedral, reclaimed thousands of square miles of uncultivated land, and worked out theories of law and right which remain the basis of free societies.

[1] Medieval theory sanctioned the lending of money at interest when the borrower shared in the risk. There were few speculations in the Middle Ages which did not involve large risk; the sin of usury thus consisted in lending money at interest without risk to borrowers who would bear the whole risk of an enterprise. Medieval rates of 'lawful interest'—e.g. payment of damages or compensation if a loan was not returned at the agreed time—were very high: 20 per cent was not unusual. Up to 1290, when Edward I turned them out of the country, after he had largely ruined them by his extortions, the Jews were the chief lenders; they advanced money, among other purposes, for the building or enlargement of cathedrals and monasteries. Italian moneylenders who succeeded them also lost large sums to Edward III.

CHAPTER VIII

The Tudor Monarchy and the Church

AGAINST THE RISING standards and increasing diversity of occupation and interest in England, the Wars of the Roses were an anachronism. All classes of society felt the need of political and administrative order. The lack of order at the highest point – the central administrative system – was less tolerable because ordinary life was becoming more systematized and complicated. The development of the machinery of the State had lagged behind the development of society; such a time-lag is familiar to us in the international sphere, and as most of our present remedies imply the creation of some strong international authority, so at the end of the fifteenth century the remedy for disorder was the concentration of power in the hands of a strong monarchy. The medieval remedy of conciliar government had failed both in Church and State. The break-up of the old order, therefore, far from implying confusion, led to greater security and better justice.

The establishment of a strong monarchy meant the rise of nation states. Medieval conditions, in which action tended to take place through associations, were unlikely to produce 'positive' national feeling, although it would be unwise to assume that 'patriotism' did not exist before the fourteenth century or to think of medieval 'regionalism' as entirely different from later nationalism. A feudal order of society is no more incompatible with nationalism than a communist order; the conquered English in the eleventh century who were compelled to pay a special fine if a Frenchman were found murdered, must have thought in terms of nationalism without knowing it. The distinction between French and English or between English and Germans was strong enough in the reign of Edward III, but until the fifteenth century nationalism tended to be little more than a negative dislike of foreigners.

National patriotism of a modern kind is associated with England under the Tudor monarchy, but it began certainly as early as the time of Henry V. It could not take a modern form until the feudal allegiances, which were jumbled much as the ownership of strips in a medieval field, had given place to a clearly defined and consolidated sovereignty of a king without feudal rivals. Nationalism was bound to develop once this sovereignty had emerged. The king of England was not a modern sovereign while rival English armies wore the badges of great nobles. As soon as the English and French monarchies were masters without dispute in their own territories, the countries of England and France became rival units in a world of independent sovereign states.

The view of the coronation of Henry VII as a landmark in the history of England is therefore justified if it is also remembered that there was no break at this time in the continuity of English development. Tudor England must be seen against the background of Lancastrian and Yorkist England. Such a perspective gets rid of a good many adjectives loosely applied to the fifteenth and sixteenth centuries. There is less 'decadence' in the later Middle Ages and less originality in the sixteenth century than is commonly believed. The Tudor monarchy represented 'the greatest effective concentration of power' in England since the Norman Conquest, but the monarchs, fortunately for England, were not absolute in the sense that they controlled a large army and bureaucracy, disposed of immense revenues, and ruled over subjects whose habit of obedience knew no limits. The Tudors never had a large army and could never have afforded to hire mercenaries for war on the scale practised by the sovereigns of France or Spain.[1] They were much wealthier than their predecessors because they gained from the impoverishment of the great families in war and from the confiscations which Lancastrians and Yorkists had alike enforced. Henry VII and Elizabeth were parsimonious by temperament. Henry VIII had the windfall of church property, although much of it went to his subjects. The rise in the cost of living offset a good deal of the increases in revenue and, in the end, finance (above all, the cost of governing Ireland) wrecked the monarchy. Finally,

---

[1] On a rough estimate the population of England and Wales at the accession of Henry VII was 2½–3 million. The population of Spain was more than twice as large, and of France more than five times as large.

so far from obtaining constant obedience from their subjects, the Tudors were never free from the danger of conspiracy or even from rival claimants to the throne.[1] With the exception of Mary, the Tudor sovereigns were more acute than the Stuarts in judging public opinion; the growth in the importance and self-esteem of parliament shows that public opinion had to be considered.

The Tudors made a success of government because – again with the exception of Mary – they had the personal qualities necessary for the work. They were well above the average in intelligence; they could be cruel and heartless, but they knew how to watch their subjects. Bacon's description of Henry VII illustrates the faculties required in a king who had to make his way with caution. Henry was 'full of thoughts and secret observations, and full of notes and memorials of his own hand, especially touching persons; as whom to employ, whom to reward, whom to inquire of, whom to beware of, what were the dependencies, what were the factions, and the like'. It is characteristic of Henry that more is known of his diplomacy than of his private life. His 'secret observations' were a guard against rebellion. He suppressed the custom by which the great nobles kept bands of armed retainers; this suppression was easier because the nobles found more profitable ways of employing and multiplying their capital. Henry used men of lower standing than the great families. As his medieval predecessors had long realized, the employment of Churchmen was cheap, since they could be rewarded out of Church preferments. Henry also avoided creating rivals at home to his own family and increased his standing abroad by marrying his children to foreign royalty. His eldest son Arthur, who died young, married the daughter of the king of Spain; his second son Henry married Arthur's widow. His eldest daughter Margaret married the king of Scotland. Each of these marriages was of diplomatic importance. A close dynastic connexion, and ultimately a personal union[2] of the two crowns, was the best

---

[1] Henry VII's title to the throne was established by a statute which eluded any difficulty about hereditary right by referring to 'Our now sovereign lord, King Henry'.

[2] At the time of this marriage, a personal union of the two crowns must have seemed unlikely, since Henry's two sons were alive. The marriage itself was celebrated with a romantic magnificence. At their second meeting Margaret Tudor, as evidence of her accomplishments, danced a bass dance with Lady Surrey, and James, as proof of his courtliness, accompanied her on the lute.

solution of the problem of Anglo-Scottish relations; an alliance with Spain was necessary to counterbalance the dangerous increase of French power through the absorption of Brittany into the kingdom of France.

Henry VIII (1509–47) gained by his father's diplomacy and steady accumulation of wealth. Time had given him a more secure title; he was the first king since Henry V who did not have to fight a battle to win or keep his throne. He was handsome, a good musician, and a good scholar. As a young man he could tire eight or ten horses in a day's hunting. He was a fine archer and a tennis player. Although in later years his thick frame became heavy with fat and his legs bloated, there was always a certain magnificence about him. Henry was a prince after the fashion of his age. He was neither deep nor prophetic, but in all things politic, selfish, and intensely national. He was unable to pursue aims as far-reaching as those of his fellow-sovereigns in Europe, since England had not the resources of France, still less those of Spain after Charles V in 1519 had united in his person the Imperial and Spanish crowns. Charles had the wealth of Spain, the Netherlands, part of Italy, and the Spanish conquests of the New World. Henry VIII was not even king of a united Great Britain and did not dispose of an ounce of the gold or silver mined in America. Hence, apart from spending money on ships of the royal navy, Henry could only use England as a make-weight in the balance of power in Europe. The rivalry between Francis I of France and Charles V allowed full value to be taken from this policy, but Wolsey,[1] partly out of self-interest – he wanted Charles's support of his candidature for the papacy – and partly from miscalculation, came down on the Spanish side in 1521. Four years later the army of Charles V completely defeated Francis I at the battle of Pavia. When the two rivals made peace in 1529, England was not even consulted.

This failure would have been enough to cause Wolsey's fall even if Henry had never wanted the divorce of his Spanish wife Cather-

[1] Wolsey came of a humble, though not poor family. He obtained the degree of B.A. at Oxford at the age of fifteen. He was dismissed from the bursarship of Magdalen because he applied money without authorization for the completion of the tower. He entered the road to political fortune through the help of the marquis of Dorset to whose sons he was tutor. Wolsey was uncanonically married, and left a son and a daughter. The daughter became a nun; the son was given valuable ecclesiastical preferments.

ine of Aragon. Henry's wish – one might use the term passion – to be rid of Catherine was the occasion rather than the cause of the English Reformation. Neither too much nor too little must be made of this divorce. There were reasons of State for it.[1] Henry had no male heir. No precedent, other than the doubtful case of the Empress Matilda, existed for the rule of a woman in England; king and nation alike might fear the dangers of a disputed succession. If the king were to be divorced, not even Wolsey's cleverness could extort the consent of the pope, since the papacy was now under the control of Charles V who was Catherine's nephew. If the pope would not grant a divorce, Henry was likely to take matters into his own hands.

Nevertheless the king could not have gone so far in repudiating papal authority if he had not been sure, for better or worse, of popular support. It is difficult to judge Henry's religious policy as it appeared to the king himself and to his contemporaries. Few Englishmen guessed how far the 'reformation' of the Church would go. Educated laymen and many of the clergy believed reform to be necessary. Reform meant the removal of administrative abuses, the raising of clerical standards of conduct and knowledge, the abolition of observances which had degenerated into popular superstition. A 'reformation' of this kind involved the whole question of papal finance; it did not imply fundamental change in Church doctrine or government. Church authority and ceremonial, Church teaching or law touched secular life at almost every point. The separation of Church and State was inconceivable; the tradition of Western catholicism was so strong, so ancient, and so deeply rooted that its continuance was taken for granted.

Nevertheless for this very reason there were chances of conflict and disaster. If the Church had influenced for centuries every aspect of the life of Western society, ecclesiastical institutions had themselves taken a medieval shape. At a time of very rapid change in the temporal sphere, these institutions became out of harmony with their environment. In particular they were out of harmony with the development of independent national sovereignties. Church

[1] On ecclesiastical grounds Henry's argument was that his marriage to Catherine – the widow of his brother Arthur – had been possible only owing to a papal dispensation. If this dispensation could be pronounced illegal, the marriage would be annulled.

doctrine had also been expressed in medieval form and expounded in scholastic terminology. The intellectual changes of the age required an extremely large adjustment. The differentiation of the individual, the loosening of the habit of action through associations and communities led to an assertion of the right of private judgment, both personal and national, and to the rejection of authority from outside, whether external to the national state or to men's private consciences.

The conflict between Church and State, or between Church and society, had begun in Germany before the first phase opened in England. The dispute over ecclesiastical jurisdiction was intolerably sordid. The dispute over Church property was not less sordid; greed or need or both against vested interests. Once the breach with Rome had been made, doctrinal changes were bound to follow. They were accepted by the English people, not easily but with less opposition than might have been anticipated. Such acceptance does not show either cynicism or religious indifference. It would be impossible to explain the intensity of religious feeling in the seventeenth century if religion in the latter half of the sixteenth century had been something irksome or unwanted in English life.[1] The acquiescence of the nation in successive doctrinal changes imposed from above was due partly to the length of time over which the changes were spread and partly to the ingenuity of the government in devising ambiguous formulae and in providing a form of worship which was a compromise between old and new. It is possible also to think that the doctrinal differences[2] meant less to the average man than the religious attitude of mind and presuppositions common to all parties. Although the protagonists would not or could not admit the fact, or even understand it, no other explanation covers the partial success in Europe alike of the protestant reformation and of the catholic counter-reformation. Neither movement required a fundamental and revolutionary change of outlook towards human life and destiny.

It is thus not a paradox that the reform of the Church should have been associated with persecution. There is little to choose here

---

[1] A less likely explanation would be that the English people became more religious after the middle of the sixteenth century.

[2] Visible changes – surplices and whitewashed walls – probably meant more to the ordinary man than variations in doctrine.

between catholics and protestants. Religious persecution in England, though not in Ireland, was on a smaller scale and less ferocious than in continental Europe; English civil wars were also less ferocious. The reason lies outside matters of doctrinal difference between catholics and protestants. Some persecution was inevitable, and the form of it – torture and death – belonged to the grimness of the age. The idea of toleration, which was the true corollary of the differentiation of the individual, would have been far more revolutionary than any new theory about sacramental grace and could not have been entertained by men so close in time and thought and habit to the group-life of the Middle Ages. Moreover, the practice of toleration would have been far from easy in a society where Church and State were so closely bound together, and uniformity was necessary because there were no governmental means of dealing with dissent. No administrative machinery in the sixteenth century or for many years after it was flexible enough to cope with great diversities of opinion.

The first step in the English Reformation, which was carried through by parliament, was, characteristically, an attack on the fees of Church courts for the probate of wills. Henry himself began his assertion of the royal supremacy in matters ecclesiastical by a piece of chicanery. He had already confiscated Wolsey's property on the plea that the exercise of authority as papal legate was a breach of a statute of 1393 forbidding any transactions with the court of Rome which were against the interests of the king or realm of England.[1] The use of this statute against Wolsey was unfair because the king had authorized him to exercise legatine powers, and Wolsey had employed them in the king's interest. Henry now accused the clergy as a body of a breach of the statute of 1393 because they had obeyed Wolsey. He allowed the Convocation of Canterbury to buy a pardon by a payment of £100,000[2] and an acknowledgment that he was 'Supreme Head of the Church and clergy of England' as far as the law of Christ allowed.

In other circumstances there would not have been much novelty about this declaration. The king of England had always

[1] This statute of *Praemunire* (*praemunire facias*, i.e. 'see that you warn': an order to a sheriff to warn someone to attend in answer to a charge) was part of the legislation of the fourteenth century against clerical abuses.
[2] The Convocation of York paid only £19,000 – a sign of the relative poverty of the north.

acted as Governor of the Church in matters temporal within his realm; the pope had made little objection as long as his own overriding superiority had been recognized. The trouble was in Henry's intention not to recognize such superiority but to decide for himself what the law of Christ did or did not allow. Meanwhile the clergy were in difficulties. They could not avoid dealings with the centre of Church government. Were all these dealings with Rome treasonable? In 1532 parliament, probably at the king's dictation, presented a general complaint against the exercise of ecclesiastical authority. Most of this document repeated familiar grievances, such as the delays of Church courts, or nepotism in the conferment of benefices. There was something new in the charge that the clergy were too much inclined to 'catch out' heretics on minor points.

The clergy gave way before the storm. They promised not to legislate (on ecclesiastical matters) in convocation without the king's authority and approval. Hence they debarred themselves from action against the king in the affair of the divorce. At the same time the king put financial pressure on the papacy. Here again he was able to beat up popular and parliamentary support by raising the old complaints about the 'great and inestimable sums of money' sent out of the kingdom. In 1533 the king married Anne Boleyn in spite of the papal refusal to grant his divorce from Catherine. He was therefore bound to prevent appeals to Rome from the ecclesiastical courts in England. An act of parliament of 1533 declared England an 'empire'; within this Empire[1] all causes, civil and ecclesiastical, were to be determined. The king forced convocation to admit that the pope could not give a dispensation permitting marriage with a brother's widow. Archbishop Cranmer then declared that Henry's marriage with Catherine was void.

There could now be no reconciliation with the papacy. The next step was to proclaim the royal supremacy by act of parliament (1534) annexing to the king's 'imperial' crown the title 'Only Supreme Head in earth of the Church of England'. There was no mention of any qualifying term. Two years later another act of parliament 'extinguished' papal authority in England. The terms of this statute were deliberately offensive to the papacy. Only nine years earlier Henry had referred to the pope as 'our most holy

[1] It is of interest that this word had nothing of its modern significance. It denoted a 'closed' national state.

Lord, the true and only Vicar of Jesus Christ on earth'. In July 1535, the noblest man in the kingdom – Sir Thomas More – gave his life rather than accept a repudiation of accepted religious authority. As for the country at large, Henry had taken care in 1532 to safeguard his subjects from the spiritual terrors of excommunication by requiring the clergy in all circumstances to continue the administration of the sacraments.

The Church in England was now at the king's mercy. Control of Church government implied control of Church endowments. Hence the attack on the monasteries was a logical consequence of the royal supremacy, especially for a king in need of money. Here again Henry had the support at least of the propertied classes. There is also little doubt that public opinion, except in parts of the north, was not on the side of the monks. In the absence of complete evidence of a reliable kind, it is uncertain how far the prejudice against them was justified. They were losing their voluntary offerings and had ceased to receive endowments. Long before Henry VIII's time a chancellor of the university of Oxford, and no friend of Lollardy, had denounced them. The universities had taken the place of the monasteries as centres of learning.[1] The general evidence about monastic conditions shows some grave scandals, some evidence of real piety and much more of worldliness and slack enjoyment of revenues. This worldliness was common among all ranks of the clergy, but the monasteries, with their large estates and visible signs of great collective wealth, were more open to attack.[2] The wealth was not spent on the purposes for which it had been given; in any case such purposes of prayer and contemplation were out of harmony with the ideas of the age. Even as landlords the monks were not examples of beneficence or of progress.

The dissolution of the monasteries, after visitations intended to produce unfavourable results, took place between 1536 and 1539.[3] The transfer of property was on a large scale; about £1,400,000 in

[1] Although the Benedictine Order had been of immense service in preserving the texts as well as the traditions of learning, monasticism as such was not intended to promote the advancement of knowledge and must not be judged by its failure to do so in the years of its decline in England. The friars had concerned themselves more than the monks with the universities.

[2] Not all of them were rich. Some of the smaller houses had remained chronically bankrupt since the financial shocks of the Black Death.

[3] The king's chief instrument in this work was Thomas Cromwell, a self-made 'go-getter', who had served Wolsey and for whose ultimate fate – execution

movables (plate, vestments, jewels, etc.) and some £130,000 a year in revenues from land, mines, quarries, mills, fisheries, timber, and other sources. If the capital and income thus diverted from the Church had been used in the endowment of education or charity or in the foundation of new bishoprics, there might have been a better case for the king's action. In fact, little of it was spent in these ways. The crown itself did not get more than a permanent increase in revenue of some £66,000 a year[1] (about one-half of the existing royal income). Some of the remainder was spent by the king as income. Much of it went in grants to officials, courtiers, and others pertinacious enough to secure a share.

From this point Henry began indirectly to approach the question of changes in doctrine. Once more he was likely to get the support of many of his subjects in discouraging the cult of saints and relics, or in exhorting the clergy to teach the elements of religion in English and the laity to read the Bible for themselves. Nevertheless the consequences of this Bible-reading soon alarmed the king. In 1543 he laid down that only the nobility and gentry and merchant householders could read so dangerous a text. Although he was afraid of the political consequences of too much private judgment and therefore enforced penalties against heresy, Henry may have intended a good deal more doctrinal innovation. He chose as tutors for his son Edward[2] men who would have supported these changes, and thus widened the gulf between the Church in England and the papacy. Henry's death meant a regency. The young king's uncle, Edward Seymour, earl of Hertford, became Protector and took the title of duke of Somerset. Somerset held 'advanced' views on theological questions, and used his position to make doctrinal changes. He was supported by Cranmer, but archbishop and Protector had to act carefully because the opponents of innovation could bring forward the royal supremacy as an argument against change before the king came of age.

after his political and ecclesiastical policy had served its purpose – it is difficult to feel pity.

[1] An increase of roughly the same amount was received from other confiscated ecclesiastical property.

[2] Edward VI (1547–53) was born to Henry in 1537 by his third wife, Jane Seymour. He learned to write a Latin letter at the age of eight. Edward's health was good until he had a simultaneous attack of measles and smallpox in 1552. Later in this year he seems to have developed tuberculosis; his death in 1553 was hastened by the mistakes of his doctors.

Somerset took stronger measures against popular religion. He forbade the use of images and dissolved all chantries; most of the confiscated endowments, in spite of a great deal of talk about education, were distributed among the court. In 1549 Somerset issued a prayer-book in English; the tone of the book inclined towards Lutheranism, but it still contained the Mass, and, in order to encourage learning, Latin, Greek, or Hebrew could be used for all the prayers (except the Mass) in the college chapels of Oxford and Cambridge.

Somerset fell in 1549, mainly through the intrigues of his less scrupulous rival and successor, John Dudley, earl of Warwick and later duke of Northumberland. Once again, with Cranmer's assent, the rate of change was quickened. In 1550 Ridley was appointed bishop of London. Ridley's views were definitely protestant; he spoke of the 'superstitious opinions of the popish Mass'. In 1552 parliament authorized a second prayer-book. This book, which appears to have been largely the work of Cranmer, did not contain prayers for the dead or provision for the reservation of the sacrament for the sick.

Edward VI was succeeded by his half-sister Mary (1553–8), daughter of Catherine of Aragon. Mary was on the losing side in English history and has been harshly treated in popular reputation. She was not unattractive in person, although she was never beautiful and became prematurely aged by illness. She was a good horsewoman, musical, and, like Elizabeth, fond of jewels and pageantry. Mary would have been cold-hearted beyond the measure of the Tudors if she had accepted the religious settlement associated with her mother's disgrace and death and the declaration of her own illegitimacy. Even so she had to begin by using the royal supremacy. The supporters of the new ideas, or as the queen called them, 'corrupt and naughty opinions', were in possession. Mary repealed the statutes of Edward VI and revived the ancient ceremonies. She also revived the laws punishing heresy and enforced them against Cranmer, Ridley, and others. She ordained a solemn reconciliation with Rome, but was unable to restore the monastic lands. Indeed she had to declare that all persons in possession of these lands could enjoy them 'without scruple of conscience' and 'clear from all dangers of the censures of the Church'.

Except towards heretics, Mary was more merciful than her father. The persecutions[1] of her reign were on a small scale in comparison with the horrors of religious war or the suppression of heresy in continental Europe. Nevertheless they shocked Englishmen. It is fair to say that the shock was due less to the cruelty of persecution than to the fact that this half-Spanish queen seemed to be supporting a minority against the majority of Englishmen and that her devotion to her Spanish husband Philip was contrary to the political as well as to the religious interests of the country.

The persecutions were a failure. Protestantism in England now had its martyrs. Long after Mary's death the violent measures of the catholic reaction did harm to the cause of the 'old religion'. In the reign of Edward VI foreign refugees from persecution abroad had little influence on the course of change in England. The English divines driven abroad by Mary came back in her sister's reign strongly affected by Calvinism, and began an attack on the religious settlement which ended by making England more protestant than Elizabeth ever contemplated.

The Elizabethan settlement was an attempt at the greatest possible measure of compromise. Elizabeth used the term 'governor' in order to avoid controversy whether a woman could be Supreme Head of the Church but she asserted her supremacy in all 'things or causes' spiritual as well as temporal, and laid down that 'no foreign prince, prelate, state, or potentate' had spiritual or temporal authority within the realm of England. Although the pope was not mentioned by name, the form of affirmation showed the nation-state in its full independency.

Elizabeth was bound to secure at least outward conformity in religious observance. She reissued the second prayer-book of Edward VI with certain modifications. The book was deliberately ambiguous over the controversial question of the Sacrament of the Altar, yet on the whole it represented a certain continuity with the ancient Church. The 'Injunctions' which followed the issue of a prayer-book were also a curious mixture of conservatism and radical change. The queen discouraged the marriage of priests and compelled them, if they wished to marry, to submit the wife of

---

[1] Some 300 in nine years. In Elizabeth's reign about 200 catholics were put to death over a period of more than forty years.

their choice to the judgment of the bishop and two justices of the peace.[1]

The queen's settlement was favourably received by most of her subjects. After all that had happened during the previous thirty years the English people were more bewildered than fanatical about Church doctrine and discipline and inclined to accept without enthusiasm any reasonable arrangement. Reception could not be merely passive because attendance at church on Sundays and Holy Days was compulsory under payment of a fine. The survivors[2] among the Marian bishops, with one exception, rejected the prayer-book and refused to take the oath acknowledging the royal supremacy. Most of the lower clergy submitted; the laity followed their example. Hostility was greater in the backward and poorer north and west than in the richer parts of the country.

The Elizabethan settlement owed its success in the first instance to the political skill with which it was devised. It is right to add that the leaders of the Anglican clergy were men of great learning and piety and that their influence secured something more than external conformity to orders from public authority. On the political side the settlement was both hampered and assisted by the attack on England on the part of catholic Spain. The violence of this attack, which had the support of the papacy, drove Elizabeth into persecution and was the ultimate reason for the execution of Mary Queen of Scots.[3] After her expulsion from Scotland in 1568, Mary was the centre of catholic intrigue. She lent herself with impetuous and tragic folly to plans which would have caused civil war in England and, as the price of success, put the country under the domination of a foreign Power. The wonder is, not that Mary was

[1] In the sixteenth century marriage was in any case mainly a matter of family arrangement.

[2] Elizabeth's work was easier because at her accession five of the twenty-seven English bishoprics were vacant by death. Five more sees – including Canterbury – were vacant for a similar reason within a year.

[3] Mary Stuart (1542–87), as the grand-daughter of Henry VIII's sister Margaret, was next in succession to Elizabeth. Her father, James V of Scotland, died a week after her birth. Mary was taken to France in 1548 on the ratification of a treaty for her marriage to the Dauphin. The marriage took place in 1558. The Dauphin succeeded to the throne of France in 1559 and died in 1560. Mary – not yet nineteen – went back to Scotland in August 1561. She reached Leith in a dense fog, foreshadowing, as John Knox wrote later, the 'sorrow, colour, darkness and all impietie' which resulted from her coming. Her subjects serenaded her with protestant psalm-singing.

executed in 1587, but that in such an age her life should have been spared so long. On the other hand the attack on Elizabeth's government, the plots against her person, and the recklessness of the catholic extremists did much to transform a state-made compromise into a national Church.

CHAPTER IX

The Elizabethan Age

THE QUEEN WHO enjoined a religious settlement upheld by grave and dignified scholars like Hooker had come to the throne as a young woman of twenty-five. Although all her portraits idealize her, she must have been handsome, and in youth even beautiful. She was of good height, auburn-haired, hazel-eyed, olive-skinned, and of fine regular features;[1] her intelligence was far above the average and her judgment sound and clear. From childhood she was used to danger. Her own father had been responsible for the execution of her mother Anne Boleyn;[2] Elizabeth herself had been at some risk of execution by her half-sister. Nothing frightened or tired her. Her interests were practical. She could speak Latin and French well and knew some Italian and German and a little Greek. She had learned these languages for speech and not for reading; she cared little for scholarship and had little artistic taste. She made no distinction between the plays of Shakespeare and those of any ephemeral hack whose works were performed for her pleasure. She was as little accustomed to pity as most other successful men or women in a cruel age. She had neither brother nor any near male relative from whom she could take advice. Her choice of counsellors, on the whole, shows her wisdom and justifies the loyalty with which she was served.

If by temperament Elizabeth did not incline towards innovation, she held firmly to her rights. It has been said that during her reign the conflict between monarchy and parliament was in suspense. This judgment is true. Although the elements of conflict were present, the main cause of possible dispute — the lack of a clear

---

[1] She nearly died of smallpox in 1562.

[2] One of Elizabeth's maternal great-great-grandfathers was a merchant and sometime Lord Mayor of London. He bought the manor of Blickling from Sir John Fastolf.

delimitation of the rights of the crown – worked in the queen's favour. The Tudors collaborated with parliament, partly because they always cared for legality even when they were using the law to commit injustice. They had no reason, however, to be afraid of parliament. The house of commons was no longer a sounding-board for the magnates. In an age when legislation was nearer to the judicial interpretation of existing law than to the creation of new rules parliament was in fact as in name a high court. The redress of grievances was not expected to require new laws. Sessions were therefore generally short; the so-called reformation parliament of Henry VIII lasted for seven years, but held only eight sessions. Henry VIII did not call a parliament between the end of 1515 and the spring of 1523. Mary held five parliaments; the longest of them sat for less than two months. Throughout Elizabeth's reign parliament was in session only for thirty-five months. Thus there could be no continuous criticism of the executive by an organized opposition. There was no organized 'ministerial' party. Privy Councillors with seats in parliament would defend the executive; no other defence was needed, because in all questions of trade, diplomacy, or war the monarch was by tradition supreme. Executive work at the centre was in the hands of the Council; local administration of all kinds – the licensing of ale-houses, as well as the repair of bridges and the fixing of wages – was done by the justices of the peace.[1]

Elizabeth maintained this system. She was indeed bound to do so, since questions of war, diplomacy, and trade were closely connected and the general position was more complicated and dangerous than in Henry VIII's time. In the haze of distance Elizabethan foreign policy, like many other features of the age, appears romantic. There was no romance about it. Elizabeth was not an idealist; still less did she care for adventures. She was always ready to sacrifice good faith to expediency, and in her view expediency meant any means of preserving the peace. The queen wanted peace because she could not afford war, but she would not be bullied or frightened into accepting peace on terms which did not suit English needs.

The drift of events led England into war with Spain. Matters of

---

[1] In the Anglican litany (which may have been the work of Cranmer), supplication is made for the lords of the council, the nobility, and the magistrates. There is no mention of parliament. A prayer for parliament (probably written by Laud in 1625) was not included in the Book of Common Prayer until 1661.

religion, trade, the succession to the English throne, and the balance of power in Europe, combined to bring about this war. Philip of Spain gave England no alternative except the loss of independence. From conviction as well as for reasons of policy Philip wanted the defeat of England. The defeat of the greatest protestant Power was necessary if Philip were to get the better of his own protestant subjects in the Netherlands.[1] As long as English help could be given to the Dutch and English ships dominated the sea-route to Antwerp, Dutch resistance might be maintained. On her side Elizabeth desired neither a complete Spanish victory in the Netherlands which would have made Spain too strong, nor a complete Spanish defeat which would have increased the danger from France. She would have accepted a restoration of Spanish sovereignty with the grant of special liberties to the protestants. For Philip a compromise of this kind was politically dangerous as well as an offence to his conscience. For the Dutch the only safety lay in full independence.

The question of trade was linked with matters of religion and the balance of power in Europe owing to the Spanish monopoly of commerce with the New World. During the first half of the sixteenth century the English had not tried to rival Spain in the Indies or in South America. They had shown little interest in voyages of exploration after the Cabots in Henry VII's reign had failed to discover the coast of Asia. For a long time there was no incentive to make forlorn ventures; the cloth trade was profitable enough in markets nearer home. Once the Spaniards had established themselves in the New World, there could be no question of an attempt to drive them out. Hence English enterprise turned to regions outside Spanish control. Trade with Turkey was one of these developments. Trade was also opened with Russia almost accidentally as the result of an attempt to find a north-east passage to Asia and, in particular, to the Spice Islands. This attempt and similar voyages in search of the north-west passage failed, but they started a new policy. The Spaniards had not occupied the Atlantic coast of North America. The sea passage to this coast from England was safe from enemies and pirates; the country itself appeared to offer unlimited possibilities for the cloth trade. Raleigh's settlement of colonists in

---

[1] Open rebellion had broken out after Philip had begun to enforce the decrees of the Council of Trent. The instrument used to suppress protestantism was the hated Inquisition.

Virginia[1] was the first of these projects for a trading settlement on the mainland, but the plan ended in disaster. The Elizabethans did not know how to open up a new country; they underrated every difficulty, including the strength of native opposition.

Hence there seemed no alternative to an attack on the Spanish monopoly. Although this attack began before the Virginian failure, the English were not the first to break into the vast treasure-house of Spanish wealth. Huguenot sailors from the western ports of France had been attacking Spanish catholics long before English sailors came in for a share. The first English voyages, made by John Hawkins, were not strongly opposed because Hawkins brought cargoes of slaves which the Spaniards were willing to receive.[2] Philip, however, could not allow the Spanish monopoly to be broken and in 1568 the Viceroy of Mexico attacked Hawkins at San Juan de Ulloa. Henceforward there could be only a state of war in the New World; private war, with plunder on the English side and harsh countermeasures by Spain against English prisoners falling into their hands.

Hawkins took no part in the raiding of the next ten years because he was employed at home in the reorganization of the navy, but Drake was one of the leading supporters of a policy of attack. Drake was not just a freebooter. He realized that Spanish wealth was being used to threaten English independence and that the way to meet this danger was to cut off the wealth at its source. The first move was to try to seize the bullion from Peru stored at Nombre de Dios – 'the mouth of the Treasure of the World' – for transport to Spain. Drake only just failed to carry off the richest part of this store in 1572; in 1573 he intercepted a treasure convoy crossing overland from Panama.[3] John Oxenham, in 1575, found the convoys

---

[1] Raleigh himself never went to Virginia, but he organized the expeditions which sailed between 1585 and 1587. One reason for the choice of Virginia was that it might serve as a base from which to reach a supposed continent south of the Strait of Magellan. Humphrey Gilbert's expedition to Newfoundland in 1583 might have been more successful – it brought England its first colony – if Gilbert had stayed there, and not turned southwards into unknown dangers and ultimately lost his life on the homeward voyage.

[2] There is irony in the names of some of the ships – *Jesus, Solomon, Gratia Dei*, and *Angel*, which sailed with these cargoes. The Spaniards were already exporting slaves from the Portuguese possessions in West Africa.

[3] When midway on the Isthmus of Panama, which runs east–west, Drake was taken by his guide to a tree on the highest ridge whence he could see the 'North

strongly escorted. Oxenham therefore built a ship in the Pacific in order to cut off the unprotected treasure ships before they reached Panama. He succeeded, but was caught in his turn while crossing the isthmus with his booty. It thus appeared that the safest method would be to sail directly into the Pacific, since the English were not yet strong enough to attack the treasure fleet between the Caribbean and Spain. Drake's voyage round the world in 1577–80 was undertaken partly to intercept these treasure ships in the Pacific, although he also had instructions to look for the western end of the northwest passage and to explore the possibility of an English settlement in California.

About 1585 Philip II seems to have decided to make a great attack on England. Unlike Elizabeth, he possessed an army large enough to conquer a country. Even so he had to build or rather to increase his fleet; the Mediterranean galleys which won the battle of Lepanto against the Turks were of little use in the stormy waters of the Channel or the wide Atlantic. Philip's plan, as finally settled, was to land the Spanish army of the Netherlands in England under cover of a protecting fleet which would also carry a large force from Spain. He expected, in view of reports from catholic exiles, that the English catholics would welcome him. In fact, most catholics would have fought against him as stoutly on land as they fought at sea, but it is doubtful whether a united English resistance would have been strong enough to meet the best-trained army in Europe under the duke of Parma, the first soldier of the age.

Fortunately for England, the test was not applied. In April 1587 Drake sailed into Cadiz harbour to destroy many thousand tons of shipping and stores. Until the end of June, Drake's ships harassed all traffic along the coasts of the peninsula. Hence the Armada was not ready before the winter. The last preparations were not completed until May 1588, and the Spanish ships were not sighted off the Lizard until July 19.[1] The Armada was an imposing sight, but

Sea' from which he had come and the 'South Sea' towards which he was going. The term 'South Sea', which became of common use in English, was first employed by the Spaniards who had made this north–south crossing of the Isthmus. The name 'Pacific' came from a Portuguese approach by sea and not by land.

[1] 'Old Style', i.e. before the reform of the calendar. In the sixteenth century nine days must be added to get the modern equivalent. The promontory from which they were sighted was the Old Lizard Point and not the present headland of that name.

half of it was made up of heavily laden transports and supply ships. In fighting ships of war the English were almost as strong. In fighting strength they were superior because their ships were faster, more easily handled, and built primarily as gun-carriers, whereas the Spanish ships, though heavily armed, still had the high superstructures designed for the old type of boarding warfare. The English divided their forces: a western fleet – the larger of the two – was to prevent a direct landing, while an eastern fleet kept Parma from sending out his transports. The western fleet followed the Armada up the Channel, 'plucking their feathers', yet failing to break their unity. The weakest point of Philip's plan, however, was the junction between the great fleet and Parma's transports. The transports could not come out unless they were protected from English attack; the nearest port deep enough to take the Armada was Flushing, and Flushing was in English and Dutch hands.

In the afternoon of July 27 the Armada anchored off Calais. About midnight on July 28–9 the English, now joined by the eastern fleet, sent eight fireships[1] against the Spaniards and drove them out in confusion. Next day, in a running fight along the coast towards Dunkirk, the range and weight of the English guns decided the issue. The Spanish Admiral could not turn back through the Channel; he was compelled to take the long course home round the British Isles. He had no pilots for these northern and western waters; the winds, which had favoured the Spanish plans in July, now completed their ruin. Late in September the remnants of the Spanish fleet entered Santander. Sixty-three Spanish ships – very nearly half of the Armada – had been lost. On the English side not one ship was sunk or captured.

The defeat of the Armada saved England from Parma's army, but it was not and could not be followed by a successful counter-attack to break the power of Spain. Within a decade the Spaniards were as strong at sea as they had ever been.[2] In the last years of Elizabeth's reign there was renewed fear of invasion. An expedition of Drake and Hawkins to the West Indies in 1595 was a failure in which both admirals lost their lives. Although in 1596

[1] Actually they were light fleet auxiliaries, used for the purpose. It is characteristic of the age that the fireships ordered from Dover by the English commander had not arrived in time.

[2] Their strategy was better. They convoyed their treasure ships with such efficiency that between 1593 and 1602 no consignment of bullion was captured.

Essex repeated, with immense destruction, Drake's earlier exploit against Cadiz,[1] another Armada set sail from Spain in 1597, but was driven back by a storm. Harvests in England were bad and trade disturbed. In 1592 and again in 1602–3 outbreaks of plague added to the distress. War expenditure was heavy in the Netherlands, in France (where an English alliance was necessary to meet a Spanish threat to Brittany), and in Ireland. Parliament became restive at the burden of subsidies three times as great as those of the earlier years of the reign.

These facts must be set against the picture of an England rising ever higher in self-confidence after the defeat of Spain. Throughout the Elizabethan age there was agrarian unrest and a large floating population of vagrants and unsettled or unemployed men. Some of the social troubles have been exaggerated. Enclosure of land for grazing – already an old complaint – was on a smaller scale than contemporaries believed it to be. The Elizabethan government was the first to recognize that society as a whole, and not certain specialized religious institutions, should provide for those whose indigence was due to age, sickness, or to circumstances outside their control.

The troubles of the times included, over the greater part of the sixteenth century (and during the reigns of James I and Charles I), a rise in prices and in the cost of living owing to the influx of silver and gold[2] into Europe from the New World. The disturbing consequences of such a change were, as always, a social *malaise* and much feverish spending. The tone of society was set by the men who had made money, and made it as they could, without regard to the general welfare. Throughout the countryside these men were not more insistent upon their rights than the old landlords; they were harsh in a new way. The typical rich man of the Elizabethan period was not a sea-captain who had taken a fortune from the hold of a Spanish ship, but a manufacturer who had bought land after doing

[1] Essex failed to prevent the Spaniards from burning a merchant fleet which he would otherwise have captured. None the less the expedition, which also included a Dutch fleet, was a good example of a successful 'combined operation'. Drake had led a great naval raid. Essex carried 6,000–7,000 men and, if he had been allowed to do so by Elizabeth, could have held Cadiz against land attack.

[2] Silver and gold rather than gold and silver, especially after the discovery in 1545 of the silver mountain of Potosi in Bolivia.

D

well in the cloth trade, in the supply of armaments or naval stores or in one of the new industries, such as silk-weaving, introduced by refugees.

Nevertheless, although some of the noblest of Elizabeth's contemporaries – Edmund Spenser, for example – disliked their own age, the intense and splendid vitality of Elizabethan England will continue to astonish posterity. The liberation of the individual was not yet clouded by self-consciousness or doubt. The hyberbole of language used about the queen may be regarded as an expression of this individuality and vigour. Elizabeth, even more than Henry VIII, was a symbol of a country favoured by fortune and able to defend itself by its exertions. The national pride was not unjustified. England had saved herself; there were visible signs of well-being. Against the vulgarity of the rich and the hardships of the very poor must be set a general and permanent rise in standards of living and a consequent improvement of manners throughout society.[1] The conceits and tiresome word-play of the lesser Elizabethan writers were little more than the exuberant features of a language which was growing in flexibility and offered almost unlimited modes of expression to active minds.

The magnificence of Elizabethan English is one of the reasons why the age has not lost its fame and lustre. It is therefore fair to remember that the reign of James I, which no one would call politically inspiring, has left even finer achievements of language – the authorized version of the Bible and the greatest of Shakespeare's plays. Elizabethan work in literature and the arts was curiously uneven. There was no school of English painting worth the name. Architecture was a mixture of styles; the only large public building of the age was, significantly, the Royal Exchange in London. The most remarkable innovations were in music and, above all, in the drama. Elizabethan song-writing was near to the grave religious music of earlier centuries and yet secular and personal in intention and effect. The English drama was given form and life by the Elizabethans out of the confusion of miracle and morality plays, 'interludes' and adaptations of Seneca and Plautus performed in the

[1] Feather beds, comfortable chairs, pewter instead of wooden spoons, table-linen, plaster ceilings, tomatoes, potatoes, and tobacco were among the novelties of the period. Tobacco was regarded as a valuable medicine, e.g. as an antiseptic as well as an anaesthetic.

halls of great men's houses, or – for larger audiences – on temporary scaffolds or in the courtyards of inns.[1] The novelty – once again a sign of the differentiation of the individual – was the portrayal of human beings and not of types. This task required literary ability and practice far beyond the scope of earlier stage productions. Marlowe's first play was produced early in 1590. Shakespeare, an actor who wrote plays, was at first regarded with some jealousy by literary men.

It is perhaps not too fanciful to regard Elizabethan interest in the drama as a sign of the vivid practical outlook of the time. This practical bent can be seen in the interest taken in geography, navigation, and the improvement of scientific instruments. There was little contribution to speculative thought, scientific or philosophical. Even in theology Hooker's *Ecclesiastical Polity* was a wise justification of the Church settlement of the realm rather than an excursion into the region of metaphysics. Bacon's philosophical writings belong to the seventeenth century, and their influence was not widespread until about the middle years of the century. Translations of foreign works on scientific subjects had a certain vogue which, in the case of medicine and surgery, went beyond dilettantism, but the first medical book of importance written by an Englishman was Harvey's *De Motu Cordis* of the year 1628. Although the Copernican theory was known to educated Englishmen, the theory itself was not universally accepted (Bacon was always opposed to it) and the significance of the discovery had not reached the public at large or weakened popular belief in astrology. There was little reason why scientific knowledge of a systematic kind and not of immediate practical bearing should reach a wide public. General education both at the universities and in the schools did not change much in the latter half of the sixteenth century. The school curriculum was concerned almost entirely with the grammar and syntax of the classical tongues. History was little more than dry-as-dust antiquarianism, and the modern political sciences hardly existed. Nearly all English political philosophy has been the result of political conflict or of doubts about the established order of society. The Elizabethans discussed ecclesiastical causes and theological doctrine; they might venture

---

[1] The first public theatre in England dates only from 1576. It is typical of the age that special buildings (with their dog-kennels) for bear- and bull-baiting already existed.

on 'new-fangled' opinions about the extent of the prerogative or grumble at the queen's demands for money. They were not compelled by events to look for a theoretical justification of their system of civil government.[1]

[1] One feature (significant for the future) of Elizabeth's reign was that, owing to an increasing shortage of timber, coal began to be used as a substitute fuel for wood in industry. Already in the first half of the seventeenth century England was the largest coal-producing country in Europe.

CHAPTER X

The Breakdown of the Royal Government

THERE IS NO abrupt transition from the Elizabethan to the Stuart period of English history. The accession of James VI of Scotland – son of Mary Queen of Scots and of Lord Darnley, a great-grandson of Henry VII – settled the question of the succession but did not settle anything else. The personal union of the kingdoms of England and Scotland under one sovereign did not prevent Scottish armies from fighting English armies in the civil war. In their English kingdom James I (1603–25) and his son Charles I (1625–49) had the misfortune to inherit questions in dispute which were not of their own making.

It would be more accurate to speak of questions in suspense. Consider, for example, the relations between crown and parliament. The Tudors were neither absolute nor constitutional monarchs. They did not work on a theory of monarchy other than that of the King's Most Excellent Majesty. None the less a time would come when a theory would be necessary because both king and parliament would try to increase their powers and each would accuse the other of encroachment. In an age which barely understood compromise and did not understand toleration any definition of right tended to extremes. Thus parliament, forgetting the great change in the status of the commons since the death of Richard III, could assert that 'the prerogatives of princes may easily and daily grow; the privileges of the subject are for the most part at an everlasting stand'.

On the other side the king could produce a theory of 'prerogative' rights of the monarchy in which the ordinary view that the government of the kingdom was a royal business was stated as though matters outside the functions of parliament were also above parliament. The next step would be to assert the doctrine of non-resistance to any royal act and to add, as a top-dressing, a rigmarole about the divine right of kings drawn from the Biblical history of the patriarchs. Hence, if parliament insisted overmuch on the rights of subjects, the king's answer would ultimately be that of Charles I: 'Remember that parliaments are altogether in my power for their calling, sitting, and dissolution. Therefore, as I find the fruit good or evil they are to continue or not to be.'

This dispute about the limits of royal power became linked with disputes about ecclesiastical government because the Church was bound to support the principle of authority and the king was bound to support the Church. James's phrase, 'No bishop, no king', was a sound deduction from the facts as he had observed them in Scotland. The facts were dangerous because Church government was a matter upon which different opinions were held with the utmost passion. Here again the Elizabethan settlement could not long remain without attack. Elizabeth herself had to deal with 'puritans'[1] who wanted a reform of doctrine and ritual in the protestant direction. Calvin's systematic theory of religion and of the relations between Church and State offered a clear-cut and easy answer to the systematic theory of catholicism associated with the counter-reformation. Such an answer would appeal to fanatical minds more readily than the 'historical' theories by which scholars like Hooker and Andrewes justified the Elizabethan settlement.

Once more differences of opinion would be stated in unyielding terms. There is little to choose in rigidity and formalism between the calvinist attack and Archbishop Laud's defence of the order and ceremonial of the Church of England. In one respect the puritans had the advantage. Each side appealed to the Bible; the anglican appeal emphasized the need of interpretation and, therefore, of an interpreting authority; the puritan appeal was more literal and was made directly to the judgment of the individual. Hence the puritans went out to make converts by preaching; the conforming clergy looked to the royal supremacy to maintain their position. The royal supremacy in religion was, however, the most majestic and, to the age, the most important feature of the prerogative. Thus, if the

[1] The word was first used about 1564. It may have come from France. The sense was derogatory – i.e. it implied an analogy between the reformers and the Novatian heretics of the early church known as Cathari (pure). The terms 'puritan' and 'catharan' are often found together.

commons in parliament began to agitate for changes in religion, they could not avoid attacking the position of the sovereign.

The risk of encroachment upon royal rights was greater because king and parliament in secular affairs had long accepted the view that extraordinary expenses of the kingdom could be met only by grants from the commons. Towards the end of Elizabeth's reign the monarchy could not meet expenses. Elizabeth did not waste money and had no family to support but, especially in the latter part of her reign, she was living partly on capital obtained from the sale of crown lands. James I was extravagant and thriftless; even if he had been more careful he could not have avoided what he called 'this eating canker of want'. The country was richer. Prices were still rising; the customs receipts gained from an increase in trade, yet the assessments for the payment of subsidies remained unchanged while the cost of administration continually increased. Even in peacetime the expense of governing Ireland was five times the Irish revenue.

James I and to a greater extent Charles I tried all manner of expedients to add to their revenues. Some of their methods affected trade and the cost of living and irritated parliament without providing sufficient money. Hence, if this money were to be obtained, parliament had to be summoned more often than in Elizabeth's reign. More frequent parliaments gave opportunity for organized criticism in matters other than finance. These opportunities must not be exaggerated. Parliament was in session only for four and a half years between 1603 and 1640, but the commons made the most of their sessions. Moreover it was certain that the attack would turn against the royal prerogative. Freedom of speech, which parliament claimed in Elizabeth's reign, meant freedom to discuss all questions. There were, however, affairs touching foreign policy and religion which fell within the sphere of government and were therefore, in Elizabeth's opinion, unsuited for inclusion within the sphere of freedom of speech. James I agreed with Elizabeth.

Nevertheless, if the commons were asked for subsidies to pay for the king's foreign policy, they would claim the right to discuss and criticize this policy. They made their claim with greater heat because James's policy was muddled in idea and ignominious in execution. Neither king nor parliament fully understood the significance of the religious and territorial war in Germany. James wanted to secure the recovery of his son-in-law's dominions in the Palatinate;[1] he hoped at first to do so by getting Spanish support for a negotiated peace. Parliament still thought in terms of a protestant alliance and a profitable war against Spain in the Indies. War, as always, might be profitable to some of the king's subjects. It brought no profit to the crown.

In the end war was declared on Spain, but the French would do nothing to restore Frederick and James wasted English lives and money in expeditions which were disgracefully mismanaged. Mismanagement and defeat continued under Charles I after a change of policy had resulted in war with France. Finally, to the disgust of the nation, the king had to abandon the protestant cause in Europe. The country gentlemen who had now established themselves in the house of commons might be out of their depth in foreign affairs; they could judge military incompetence when they saw it on a large scale. They also found it easy to ignore their own share of responsibility in failing to give adequate subsidies. The maladministration which lost so many lives in the military expeditions under James I and Charles I was due in part to the duke of Buckingham, a favourite of James to whom Charles continued to give his confidence. Neither king was a good judge of men or skilful in handling public opinion. James was a scholar at a time when scholarship was three-quarters learned pedantry. He never knew when to leave well alone or to make concessions with grace or dignity. Charles, as his portraits show, looked more like a king and had all the virtues of a private gentleman[2] except that of keeping his word, but his stiffness of mind was the more dangerous in dealing with men as obstinate as himself. He was twenty-four years old when he became king; seventeen years of experience before the outbreak of the civil war hardly taught him anything.

The failure of Charles's foreign policy brought him at least one advantage. After 1630 he was not fighting a war and therefore not

---

[1] The Thirty Years War (1618–48) developed out of a protestant rebellion in Bohemia. James's daughter Elizabeth had married Frederick, Elector Palatine. Frederick (against his father-in-law's advice) accepted the election to the crown of Bohemia by the protestant rebels in 1619, and was defeated by the catholics in 1620. As a result of his defeat Frederick lost Bohemia and also the Palatinate.

[2] Charles was a very delicate child, but grew up to be a good horseman and tennis-player. He was a fair critic of music and painting.

dependent upon parliamentary subsidies. He did not call parliament again until 1640. During this interval he might have built up a powerful position for himself if he had treated public opinion with tact and reasonableness. A considerable number of men of weight in the country disliked both the incompetence of the king's favourites and the nagging of the group of lawyers who opposed every exercise of the prerogative. The 'moderates', of whom Sir Thomas Wentworth, later earl of Strafford, was the most remarkable, wanted strong government and believed that the initiative in policy should remain with the king.[1] Wentworth might have been able to re-establish the prestige, if not the popularity, of the king, but Charles's support of Laud's ecclesiastical policy added greatly to the opposition. Archbishop Laud[2] was not a tyrant. The trouble about him was that he tried to enforce the law without distinguishing between essentials and non-essentials. Laud nearly always missed the point. He never asked himself why bishops who kept great state were unpopular or whether the poverty in which most of the lower clergy lived might not be the real reason why their sermons were unimpressive. He never considered that time might be on his side, and that Englishmen, if left alone, might tire of fanatical controversies over Church government. Laud's insistence upon uniformity in religious observances drove many sincere men into exile, irritated thousands of others, and once more brought the royal prerogative into disrepute.

The need for tact and forbearance in matters ecclesiastical was greater because the king was straining the law in his efforts to do without an appeal to parliament for money. The formal legality of the king's acts made them more unbearable, since there seemed no way of opposing them. Charles's lack of fair-mindedness offended all classes. The peers and country gentry disliked the revival of old laws inflicting heavy fines for trespass – even if three centuries old – on

[1] Wentworth's views may be summarized in his own words which also express the opinions of many men who joined the king's side: 'the authority of the king is the keystone which closeth up the arch of order and government, which contains each part in due relation to the whole, and which, once shaken, infirm'd, all the frame falls together into a confused heap of foundation and battlement of strength and beauty'.

[2] William Laud was the son of a Reading clothier. In spite of his meticulous enforcement of external observances, he was not narrow in his theological views. He seems to have had little or no sense of humour (he carried on a long feud with Archie Armstrong, the king's jester).

the royal forests.[1] Merchants and consumers alike objected that the prerogative right of regulating trade was used to confer 'monopolies' in return for large payments. The levy of ship-money was the most notorious but not the least defensible of the king's methods. Ship-money as such was neither new nor inequitable; it was required from seaports in time of urgency and as a substitute for the provision of ships. Charles extended the levy to inland towns and enforced it when there was no obvious emergency compelling him to act without parliament. Ship-money was actually used to build ships which were of use under the Commonwealth in fighting the Dutch. For the most part indeed the revenue was honestly spent; the taxes in themselves were not very heavy, but opinion fastened upon the methods by which they were obtained and upon the fact that, if the king could support himself indefinitely without parliament, parliament would be unnecessary and the liberties of subjects would certainly be 'at an everlasting stand'. Finally there was a deeper and, one might say, a more modern cause of antagonism between parliament and the royal government. At its best the 'system' of Strafford and Laud represented the old paternalism whereby the monarch regulated the lives of his subjects to the general good of the realm. The parliamentary opposition was upheld by men whose economic interests were of an individualist kind and opposed to the conservative methods of an earlier age. From this point of view Strafford and Laud in their attempt to enforce legislation against enclosures were dealing with a parliament of landlords and industrial magnates who would have disliked interference even if the king's government had not twisted the law in order to extort money or fussed about religious observances repugnant to 'tender' consciences.

There were, however, many Englishmen who agreed with Strafford's views. The 'system' might have lasted much longer if England alone had been concerned. The collapse came through Laud's attempt to extend his rules of uniformity to Scotland. In 1638 Scottish resistance took the form of a National Covenant to oppose religious innovation. The king, as usual, offered too few concessions, and offered them too late. The Scots brought together an army twice

---

[1] These measures were not less offensive because some great landowners, whose impoverishment was due to the same economic troubles which affected the crown, were also trying to save themselves by an insistence upon ancient and outmoded claims.

the size of the force which the king was able to produce from the reluctant English. In any case Charles's system of raising money could not suffice for a war. He could not afford to pay a force of trained soldiers and had to rely on the militia of the northern counties. Therefore he had to accept a compromise with the Scots. This compromise could not last because the Scots were determined to abolish episcopacy and the king was determined to maintain it.

Charles's next move was to summon the English parliament. Strafford advised this step in the belief that the king could reckon upon English dislike of the Scots and in the knowledge that he could produce evidence of Scottish intrigues with France. The commons, however, considered the king a greater danger to English liberties than the Scots and intended at last to settle with him. The king's reply was to dissolve parliament. Strafford then suggested that the army in Ireland should be used against the Scots, but Charles's military plans collapsed. The Scottish army invaded England and compelled the king to negotiate with them on the condition that they should be paid £850 a day during the negotiations, and should occupy Northumberland and Durham as securities.[1]

Charles now had to call parliament again, although it was clear that the commons would now destroy the machinery through which the prerogative had been exercised and take vengeance on Laud and Strafford. Strafford was executed (in May 1641) and Laud imprisoned.[2] Parliament abolished the courts of conciliar jurisdiction through which the policy of Laud and Strafford had been enforced. The common lawyers' jealousy of these courts, particularly of the court of star chamber, did not lessen the zeal of their attack. In order to safeguard these victories, parliament passed acts preventing a dissolution without its consent and requiring that a parliament should be summoned at least once in three years.

If Scottish affairs were the immediate cause of the calling of the 'Long Parliament', the question of Ireland indirectly precipitated the English civil war. The Tudors had not solved the Irish question of their time. The problem was beyond their resources. They had found a country in which, apart from the English settlements in the

---

[1] It may be taken as a sign of a new age that the Scots felt sure of their money because the possession of Newcastle gave them control of the important coal trade with London.

[2] Laud was beheaded in January 1645.

small 'Pale'[1] on the south and south-east coast, there were a few chartered towns, half-English, half-Irish in character, an Anglo-Norman nobility which from an English point of view had 'gone Irish', and a turbulent Celtic population following their own customs and obeying, if anyone, their own chiefs. Henry VIII had thought of trying to get the collaboration of these chiefs in a land settlement on an English model. In Edward VI's reign there was a return to the hopeless policy of conquest and extermination; in Mary's reign more expropriation of Irish land. Irish religion was as wild as other features of Irish life; Mary's catholic bishops indeed had a task no easier than that of the protestant bishops of Edward VI, but a change came with the success of the catholic missionaries of the counter-reformation. The religious significance of this success belongs to Irish history; the political consequences added another tragic element to Anglo-Irish relations. The attempt to conquer Ireland would now be more difficult, yet to the English it appeared more necessary, since there was greater danger that a catholic Power might use an Irish base for an attack on England.

Elizabeth attempted the method of plantation by private enterprise. This plan also failed. In 1598 Hugh O'Neill, earl of Tyrone, led a rebellion with the large purpose of driving out the English and making himself king of all Ireland. He had been promised Spanish help; in 1596 and again in 1597 and in 1599 Spanish fleets bringing this help had been wrecked or driven back by storm. No further assistance was sent until 1601; by this time the rebellion was being stamped out. In the spring of 1603 the English could regard the danger as over. The cost in money alone was over a million pounds and Ireland still had to be held down by force. In this ferocious record the English, although Irish memory is almost bound to hold otherwise, did not behave with cruelty or venom beyond their time. The catholic armies of France and Spain were certainly not less terrible to the population of occupied countries. The age knew nothing of the science of administration; there were no traditions of generosity towards defeated rebels, no understanding even that a generous policy might bring its own reward. None the less the English could not expect and did not deserve anything but hatred in Ireland.

James I and Charles I were unlikely to show imagination in the

---

[1] i.e. a boundary, cf. 'beyond the pale'

treatment of Irish problems. James went on with the planting of colonists – Scottish presbyterians as well as Englishmen – in Ulster. Strafford tried to restore order and efficiency[1] in the English administration. He succeeded only at the price of making himself and his policy of 'Thorough' everywhere hated. After he left Ireland in 1640, there was no one to continue even his methods of suppression. For the Irish the temptation – or rather provocation – to turn against the English in a desperate effort to gain independence was increased owing to the preoccupation of their enemies with civil disputes at home. Moreover, the possibility of puritan supremacy in the English parliament was a more serious threat to Irish religion than Strafford's policy of plantation. Hence an Irish rebellion broke out in 1641. The rebellion was accompanied, almost inevitably, by widespread massacre of English and Scottish settlers in Ulster. From Ulster the attack spread to Wicklow. The answer of parliament was to vote that popery should not be tolerated in the king's dominions and that the cost of restoring order in Ireland should be met by further confiscation of Irish land.

These measures turned the rebellion into a war. The English could reconquer the country only by sending a large army there. The king could not maintain an army without money from parliament. Parliament would not give the money for an army under the king's control, since the king might use it to restore his position at home. Hence the extreme party in the commons tried in a 'Grand Remonstrance' to get popular support by a statement of grievances and a demand for the control of the king's counsellors and for a synod of divines to effect the 'intended reformation of the Church'. This plan of reform, which affected the Church as well as the State, was too much for the moderates and anglicans who did not want the 'intended reformation' and were trying to prevent the misuse and not the traditional exercise of royal rights.

Once more if Charles had known how to wait, he might have regained support. He threw away his chances by a constitutional outrage. He sent armed men to remove from the house of commons the five members most hostile to him. The members were not there and the king gained nothing from his action. Or rather he lost

[1] The need of order may be seen from the facts that, owing to pirates at large in the Irish Sea, the Lord Deputy from England could not cross in 1630 for six months and that a pirate ship (from Dover) captured £500-worth of his linen

everything, since he had left the ground of formal legality upon which it was difficult to attack him. Parliament set out a programme of control over the council, the Church, and the militia. They knew that the king would not accept this programme. Each side now prepared for civil war.[1]

[1] The king set up his standard at Nottingham in August 1642. A high wind blew it down the same night.

CHAPTER XI

The Civil War: Oliver Cromwell and Puritan England

AT THE OUTBREAK of the civil war no man living could have seen fighting by rival armies on English soil except for the small engagement of 1640 against the Scots. Englishmen had fought abroad in the king's service and, especially in Elizabeth's reign and in the Netherlands, had gained a good reputation; a foreign commander once described them as 'always willing to go on'. There was, however, little understanding of land warfare among the nation at large;[1] most people thought that one battle would decide the issue. The division of parties was roughly geographical. The richer south and east supported parliament; the poorer north and west supported the king. The king's party included most of the nobility and gentry, and the parliamentary party most of the merchants and yeoman farmers. These lines of demarcation were never 'tidy'. There were royalist minorities in the south and east who would have come out on the king's side if they had dared to do so. There was also a good deal of regional and county rivalry. The parliamentary leaders, especially the army commanders, were of good family and, as the event showed, by no means favourable to social or even to political equality. The alignment of parties according to religion, or rather according to ideas on Church government, was clearer, but the supporters of parliament were agreed only in their opposition to the high anglicanism which Laud had tried to enforce. If Charles before the outbreak of war had been willing to allow a combination of episcopal and presbyterian authority, he might have won over most of the moderates. Cromwell himself once said that religion 'was not

---

[1] One may compare the general hurly-burly of a Shakespearian battle with the ordered manœuvres of the hosts of God and Satan in *Paradise Lost* – written by Milton after the Civil War.

the thing at first contested for, but God brought it to that issue at last'.

The control of the east and south-east gave parliament great superiority in resources. The larger part of the customs revenue was collected in London. Control of the fleet enabled the parliamentarians to supply the strongholds of Hull and Plymouth and to prevent the king from getting arms from abroad. With the fleet in his possession the king could have blockaded London by sea instead of trying to capture the city by direct attack or to cut it off from the sea by securing a hold on the north and south banks of the Thames. The failure of an attempt at the latter plan in 1643 showed the usual unwillingness of countrymen to fight at a distance from their own neighbourhood in the execution of a strategic plan. The Yorkshire contingents would not move on London until Hull had been taken; the Welsh and Cornish wanted Gloucester and Plymouth to be in their hands.

Nevertheless towards the end of 1643 the royalists were gaining ground. Parliament then agreed with the Scots to establish presbyterianism in England (and Ireland) in return for the help of a Scottish army. This agreement made reconciliation with the king's party more difficult, but the Scottish army turned the scale in the north and at the end of 1644 a parliamentary victory seemed probable. During the winter of 1644–5 parliament under the influence of Oliver Cromwell took in hand the reorganization of their army. A 'New Model' was ready for the campaign of 1645 with Fairfax as commander. The 'New Model' was given greater strength in cavalry and a train of artillery for the siege of royalist castles.[1] Within two months of taking the field the 'New Model' won the battle of Naseby. The royalist infantry were killed or captured; five hundred officers and quantities of stores and artillery were taken. The king's position was now hopeless. The war dragged on, mainly in sieges, until in May 1646 Charles put himself in the hands of the Scots. The Scottish interest in the war was centred on the establishment of presbyterianism, but Charles still refused to give up epis-

---

[1] Hitherto the royalist superiority in cavalry had been their greatest military asset. Cavalry were of special value in the open downlands of the south and in the unenclosed fields of the Midlands. Infantry were not yet armed with bayonets on their muskets, and their rate of firing was not rapid enough to keep off a cavalry charge. For this purpose they depended on pikemen.

copacy. Hence the Scottish army handed him over to the English early in 1647 and went home.[1]

The average Englishman at this time would probably have been content with a restoration of the king on terms blocking a return to arbitrary government. Parliament – the 'Long Parliament' which had met in 1640, and was now without its royalist and anglican members – might have accepted this solution, but the army and not the house of commons had defeated the king. The army had become the home of a militant religious individualism as much opposed to the uniformity of presbyterianism as to that of the anglican bishops. 'Independency' in religion, that is to say, the autonomy of separate congregations, implied independency in politics. Why should men whose consciences forbade them to submit to a presbytery give way to members of parliament? They were even less ready to submit after parliament had tried to disband them without making up their arrears of pay.

Every age has its jargon. In attempting to interpret the vivid language of seventeenth-century 'agitators' [2] (who could describe Oliver Cromwell as 'led by the nose by two covetous earthworms') it is difficult to distinguish between politics and religion or to know how far during the incessant prayer-meetings and preachings of the 'New Model' the application of religious phrases to secular matters was a mere fashion of speech. There is some truth in the saying that in the civil war the scribes and pharisees were on one side and the publicans and sinners on the other. Nevertheless, especially among the humbler ranks of society, the religious setting of life had not faded out in the hundred years between the death of Henry VIII and the captivity of Charles I. The habit of obedience to external religious authority had gone; the Christian background remained and it was natural enough for men to fit their discontent into the religious scheme of things. There might be a good deal of self-will and self-interest as well as confusion of thought in this probing and quoting of Biblical texts. At the same time, when Cromwell or

[1] Charles thought that he could gain time by playing off the Scots against the English, but the parliamentarians were business-like enough to pay the first instalment of the money due to the Scottish army for their services.

[2] The term 'agitator' meant an 'agent', i.e. someone who acted for others. The 'agitators' were the 'agents' first elected by certain cavalry regiments and then by all the army in 1647 to lay before the generals, and ultimately before parliament, their grievances in the matter of pay.

anyone else spoke in terms of 'crowning mercies', they were not speaking as hypocrites.

If the army represented the extreme views of a minority, this minority was far from unanimous. There were differences of view on political matters. Some officers and men were republicans of an aristocratic type; others, who became known as 'Levellers', supported universal manhood suffrage. A small number aimed at a social and agrarian revolution.[1] It is hardly possible for a historian to know the unspoken thoughts of poor men centuries ago and thereby to estimate how much support lay behind this revolt against the long servitude of the English peasant to rights of property. An agrarian revolution had no chance of success. For this reason alone, while there may have been many in England ready to dream of a social order determined according to the law of Christ and not according to the law of property, few were ready to risk their lives in an attempt to realize the dream.

In this setting of economic and political issues expressed in religious terms and of religious issues bound up with politics, the events of the next few years could be deduced almost by process of logic. The decision would rest ultimately on force. This force would be in the hands of an organized body – the army – and at the disposition of the strongest man in the kingdom, but one man even with an army behind him would be unable to change the traditions of the English people. After his death, the old habits, for good or bad, would reassert themselves. The sinners were more numerous than the saints.

The first stage in the conflict was interference by the Scots to put down the 'impious tolerance' (in other words, independency) represented by the army. The Scots were beaten at Preston. Cromwell's army had now settled at least for a time with Scottish presbyters as well as with English bishops. The next stage was therefore the extrusion of the English presbyterians from parliament. There

---

[1] Gerrard Winstanley, a Lancashire man, is the best-known leader of these minority groups. With a few supporters he began to cultivate some waste land near Walton-on-Thames. He and his fellow 'diggers' asserted as an 'undeniable equity that the common people ought to dig, plow, plant, and dwell upon the commons, without hiring them or paying rent to any'. In 1652 Winstanley submitted to Cromwell a plan for a 'Law of Freedom' in which there would be no lords of manors, lawyers, landlords, or tithes.

was left a 'rump' of sixty members.[1] The 'rump' of Independents had to accept the decisions of the army; the army decided upon the execution of the king. Charles could no longer save himself by bargaining. As Cromwell put it, whatever the king might promise 'all our security should have only been in a little paper'.

The king's trial was illegal; the court which tried him was illegally constituted, and did not include any of the English judges. There was, in fact, no means of bringing the king before his own courts. The execution of Charles (30 January 1649) was probably a political mistake. Although Cromwell had said, 'We will cut off his head with the crown on it', it was impossible to execute the monarchy, and Charles had sons who were out of reach of the headsman. Public opinion, presbyterian as well as anglican, was shocked at the act, and the royalists exploited the sense of uneasiness by publishing a book – *Eikon Basilike* – in which the king recounted his sufferings.[2]

There was no real substitute for the king. In March 1649 two acts declared England to be a Commonwealth and Free State with a parliament of one chamber. The parliament was only the 'rump'; there was no legal way of ending it because new elections would give the royalists – the supporters of Charles II – a majority. Finally Cromwell and the army settled the matter in April 1653 by turning out the 'rump'. Meanwhile the royalist cause in Ireland had been defeated by Cromwell, and in Scotland, where the abolition of the Stuart monarchy had never been accepted, the English victory at Dunbar (1650) was decisive even before the 'crowning mercy' of the defeat of a futile Scottish invasion at Worcester exactly a year later.

Thus the last stage was reached. Nothing was left of the traditional government of England. Cromwell and his army held power by force. Oliver Cromwell[3] was now beginning his fifty-fifth year.

[1] A few members came back and a few more were elected; after the expulsion of the royalists and presbyterians, the average attendance in the commons was about fifty.

[2] This book, which went through nearly fifty editions in a year, was not written, as was generally supposed, by the king. The author was Dr Gauden, bishop of Exeter.

[3] He might have been called Williams or even Smyth, since he was the great-grandson of one Richard Williams, whose father, a Welshman from Glamorgan, had married Thomas Cromwell's sister. Thomas Cromwell's father had also been known under the name of Smyth. Richard Williams rose to fortune under the

Even those who thought him bad could not deny his greatness. His vigour was immense. He was a little under six foot in height, massively built, and athletic. A contemporary said of him that he had as much 'vivacity, hilarity and alacrity, as another man hath when he hath drunken a cup too much'. He could talk Latin (although 'scantily'), and had been for a year at Cambridge. In his high days he encouraged learning and protected the universities. Cromwell was not a puritan in the narrow sense. He liked music and dancing; his refusal to remove the 'pagan' statues from the gardens of Hampton Court scandalized many of his supporters; the mixed dancing which went on at the marriage of two of his daughters in 1657 was even more shocking.[1]

Cromwell believed in toleration and distrusted the use of force in government. He could be cruel, though it is doubtful whether any other general of his age would have disapproved even of his most ruthless acts. In social questions he was conservative; in politics never anxious for innovation. The best explanation of his career is in his own saying that 'no man rises so high as he who knows not whither he is going'. To this may be added the judgment of a modern historian that Cromwell failed to see the incompatibility between constitutional government – the will of the majority expressed through parliament, and the rule of the godly – the will of a self-elected minority.

Cromwell's power rested upon the army alone; outside it there was no traditional loyalty to which he could appeal. After an attempt at a nominated assembly the army gave up the experiment of parliamentary government without a Head of the State and went back to a carefully circumscribed form of monarchy under the title of a Protectorate. As Lord Protector Cromwell summoned two parliaments. He dissolved the first because it was insubordinate. Nearly a hundred members were excluded from the second parliament before

---

protection of Thomas Cromwell and appears to have taken his name. Oliver Cromwell, like Bismarck, had spent some time, before concerning himself with politics, in looking after a none too prosperous family estate. Like Bismarck also he had passed through a period of religious depression ending in conversion. It is possible that at one time Cromwell thought of emigrating to America.

[1] Another daughter made a remark this year which, in the words of a contemporary, was extremely 'ill taken'. She was asked why the wives of most of the major-generals were not at court. She answered that they would be found, 'I'll warrant you, washing their dishes at home as they used to do'.

it met; the country might remember that Charles I had tried to remove only five members.

Thus in 1656 a return to settled institutions seemed as far off as ever. The restoration of kingship might have offered a way of escape from military government and from the likelihood of civil war on Oliver Cromwell's death. Cromwell, who already signed himself 'Oliver P.', would probably have accepted the crown, but the army would not hear of such a plan. None the less Cromwell was king in all but name during the last few years of the Protectorate. He wore purple and carried a golden sceptre on ceremonial occasions.

Cromwell died on 3 September 1658.[1] He had nominated his son Richard as his successor. Richard was an amiable, sporting country gentleman, neither anxious to rule nor capable of ruling. He carried no weight with the army, who forced him to resign. The army had no candidate to take his place. Hence all that was needed for the restoration of Charles II was a general with sufficient military force to overcome the resistance of the extremists. Sixteen months after Oliver's death General Monck, in command of an English army of 7,000 men in Scotland, marched southwards into England. Monck was popular, and had taken care to remove any likely opponents among his own officers. As he moved south he was joined by Fairfax, the first parliamentary commander of the 'New Model'. A sufficient number of old parliamentary soldiers came over to Monck's side; the rest faded out and with them disappeared the last of a series of political experiments in the rule of the godly. A new parliament, elected in April 1660, proclaimed that 'according to the ancient and fundamental laws of this kingdom, the government is, and ought to be, by king, lords and commoners', and that Charles II had suc-ceeded to the throne on his father's death. Charles, at Monck's advice, had made his return easier by offering a general pardon, liberty of conscience, confirmation of all sales of land during the civil war, and payment of arrears to soldiers.[2] On these terms Charles entered London in May 1660. Richard Cromwell left the

---

[1] The Protector's funeral was on a scale as magnificent as that of Philip II of Spain. On 30 January 1661, the anniversary of the execution of Charles I, Cromwell's body was exhumed, taken to Tyburn and hanged. The head was cut off and impaled at Westminster Hall, where it remained until 1684.

[2] These offers were made subject to the consent of parliament. Thereby the king very neatly showed a respect for parliamentary government and kept for himself a means of eluding the strict observance of the terms.

country; he came back in 1680 and lived in pleasant retirement until his death in 1712 at the age of eighty-five.

There may be a moral in this history of the reaction of an easy-going, law-abiding yet turbulent people to large-scale political change and regimentation. If the moral is to be drawn fairly, it must be taken from the history of the reign of Charles II as well as from the history of the Commonwealth and Protectorate. Cromwell was a more honest man, as well as a greater man than Charles II. He also had an English patriotism which Charles could not be expected to share. Cromwell's foreign policy was not 'prophetic'; he still thought Spain more dangerous than France to English interests. On the facts as they appeared in 1654 this judgment was not unreasonable. France was only just recovering from something like a civil war, and the government might seem more unstable than it proved to be. Although to contemporaries the protestant Dutch were more active rivals, Spain was still the greatest obstacle to the expansion of English trade. Moreover Cromwell showed his strategic grasp in realizing the importance of the Mediterranean. He suggested the capture of Gibraltar. In spite of his preoccupation with the defence of protestantism against a catholic crusade, he refused to support Sweden, a great protestant Power, when Swedish ambitions threatened English trade in the Baltic, and his treaty with Portugal prevented a trade war in India.

The attack on Spain in the Indies was only half-successful. Jamaica was easily taken but an attempt to capture San Domingo was a failure and further operations came to nothing because the English forces were ruined by sickness. The West Indies were more important than the American colonies. The colonial settlements were small and poor. The plan of establishing bases in America against Spain had been continued under James I, but efforts at colonization in South America by the Amazon and Guiana Companies had come to nothing. North of the Caribbean Virginia had now established itself by the cultivation of tobacco. The 'Pilgrim Fathers' founded a small colony, named Plymouth, in 1620; the New England Company was established in 1628 and transformed almost at once into the Massachusetts Bay Company.[1] Maryland (named after Charles I's queen) was settled a few years later by the

[1] Only a third of those who sailed on the *Mayflower* were emigrating in search of religious freedom.

catholic Lord Baltimore. Rhode Island, New Hampshire, and Connecticut were colonized to a large extent from Massachusetts. The extension of the area of occupation in North America was due as much to the colonists themselves as to planned development from England. Although there was a considerable response to the opportunity of getting land, the motives of those who went to the American mainland were political or religious rather than economic. Sugar cultivation in the West Indies was a more profitable business. Barbados, which was almost uninhabited when an English ship's captain annexed it to the Crown in 1625, soon became more populous than Virginia.

The colonial policy of English governments in the seventeenth century was directed, in accordance with the ideas of the time, towards securing for the home country a monopoly of trade. There was nothing new about a policy of this kind; the novelty would have been in a recognition of freedom. All governments acted on the view that trade should be regulated with the aim of securing an excess of exports over imports. Such excess tended to be measured, especially by a country possessing neither silver nor gold mines, in terms of bullion which was necessary for providing the basis of credit as well as for waging war. This so-called 'mercantilism'[1] was supported by political writers (as yet they did not call themselves 'political economists') who realized the importance of money without fully understanding the relation between currency and capital. To the popular mind the restriction of imports meant increased employment for Englishmen; a preference given to the English carrying trade was a means of strengthening the national defence. For this reason, parliament in 1651 passed an Act requiring all imports from Asia and Africa as well as from America and imports from Europe not brought in the ships of the country of origin to be carried to England in English or colonial ships.

The Navigation Act of 1651 was not strictly enforced; there were not enough English ships to take the traffic. It cannot be said therefore that the act was in itself one of the main causes of the first Anglo-Dutch war of 1652–4. Ultimately this war between two protestant states – and therefore a war which Cromwell disliked – was due to exasperation on each side at the exclusive policy and high

---

[1] This term, like the term 'feudalism', was not used by contemporaries of the age which it describes.

pretensions of the other. The Dutch had been doing their utmost to exclude English traders from the East Indies.[1] They had refused to 'strike the flag' in recognition of the ancient English claim to sovereignty over the Narrow Seas. They had gained greatly in the carrying trade during the confusion of the Civil War. All doctrines tending towards economic self-sufficiency lead easily to jealousy and envy; the 'mercantilist' system was based on the view that the economic prosperity of one country could be secured only at the expense of other countries. Anglo-Dutch rivalry and, later, Anglo-French rivalry therefore appeared as a struggle for a prosperity which could be seized but not shared.

The victories of the English navy gave Cromwell's government a prestige among contemporaries in Europe which was lost for a generation after his death. The political and constitutional experiments of the years 1650 to 1658 were not less remarkable. They included the union of the three kingdoms of England, Scotland, and Ireland: the redistribution of parliamentary seats and enfranchisement of new towns; the use of parliamentary committees for the management of the kingdom; an attack upon the court of chancery (which was said to have 23,000 cases unsettled two centuries before the time of Lord Eldon); a bold though impracticable attempt to simplify English law without the help of lawyers; the establishment of civil marriage; commissions for the reform of Oxford and Cambridge and the public schools of Eton, Westminster, and Merchant Taylors; the reorganization of the Post Office; the improvement of roads and minor measures such as the relief of prisoners for debt and arrangements for the better custody of idiots and lunatics.[2]

A programme of this kind presupposes a government served by men of ability with a high degree of administrative competence. There are other achievements even more worth recording: the beginnings of toleration – partly indeed as a *reductio ad absurdum* of protestant individualism; the early poetry and prose of Milton; the scientific investigations of Robert Boyle, Christopher Wren,[3] and

---

[1] Dutch hostility in the islands had the incidental effect of turning the activities of the East India Company, which had been founded in 1600, to the mainland of India.

[2] Among other novelties of puritan rule was the introduction of 'teeth brushes' as a new Paris luxury. ('Tooth-soap' was known earlier.)

[3] Wren might have continued his career as a scientist. He did not begin to design buildings until about the age of thirty after his appointment as assistant

their friends in Oxford and London which led to the foundation of the Royal Society[1] in Charles II's reign. It is fair to add that the repressed and repressive elements in the puritan temper have been exaggerated. The puritans objected not to music as such (they encouraged psalm-singing) but to certain kinds of music. The closing of the theatres[2] and the prohibition of masques and of the use of organs in churches had the unexpected effect of encouraging the beginnings of opera in England. It is difficult to make a final estimate of the contribution of the 'rule of the saints' to the manifold tradition of the English people. The age which had recourse to arms in order to find a solution to constitutional problems settled little by its civil war; it did not show signs of weakness of imagination or of failing intellectual powers.

The break in the continuity of government may be said to have opened the way more widely to the individualism which had been increasingly evident in English life for a century and a half. Thus the Civil War, like the Black Death, accelerated social changes already in progress. The old landed class was mainly, though not entirely, on the losing side. The king's demands for money[3] and the fines imposed by parliament upon the losers meant the sale of land on a large scale. Parliamentarians and soldiers bought this land; royalists sold it. This 'upward and downward movement' had been continuous in English society. The new men of the Tudor period had 'gone into land'; younger sons of landowning families had 'gone into business'. Furthermore, owing to the rise in prices, and the many openings for capital, landowners great and small invested in joint-stock and other enterprises or employed new methods in the exploitation of their properties; those who failed to increase their incomes went bankrupt in the attempt to maintain the 'display expenditure' traditional to their class. In 1640 more than half of the peerage was subsequent in creation to 1603; many of these new

---

to the Surveyor-General of Works. Vanbrugh in the next generation first made his name as a playwright.

[1] The first secretary of the Royal Society was a brother-in-law of Oliver Cromwell.

[2] The prohibition was evaded with much persistence, but it was enough to put a stop to the writing of serious drama for actual performance. Under the Restoration the theatre never recovered its large popular appeal. The older plays were also not to the liking of an age which regarded itself as 'refined'. Pepys thought *Romeo and Juliet* the worst play he had ever seen.

[3] The marquis of Worcester spent over £700,000 in the king's service.

peers were country gentry who had enriched themselves in business undertakings.

Behind the political and religious controversies the economic structure of modern England was slowly taking shape. Many later developments are unintelligible in their suddenness if account is not taken of these years of experiment by trial and error. The Bank of England was not founded until thirty-six years after the death of Oliver Cromwell. For this foundation a subscription of £1,200,000 was raised in ten days. Such an effort would have been impossible without a previous extension of banking and an industrial system based upon instruments of credit. The nature of the market and the processes of production had not yet fully imposed a capitalist form upon English economic life, but nearly every new industry and every reorganization of an old industry was on capitalist lines. Manufacture was still mainly in textiles. Fustian[1] had been introduced by refugees from the Netherlands about the same time as the introduction of silk-weaving; cotton was not yet of great importance.

Although there might be factories in the modern sense (ships of war and large guns cannot be made by domestic workers or local blacksmiths), the worker was usually employed in his own home on material supplied by a middleman. This system determined the hours of labour and brought, as a corollary, the employment of the worker's children in his own house from dawn to dusk. The corollary was of ominous significance for the future when these customary hours were to be applied to work with power-driven machinery in a factory. In the seventeenth century, and indeed for many years later, it was assumed as part of the order of things that the poor should work all day long.[2] Puritanism, which tried to get rid of sin, never thought it practicable to abolish poverty.

[1] Like cotton, cashmere, calico, and many other textile names (including the Anglo-Saxon and old Norse silk) this word shows its eastern origin, since it goes back through French, Italian, and modern Greek to Fostat, a suburb of Cairo.

[2] From this point of view puritan sabbath-keeping was no bad thing.

CHAPTER XII

The Reign of Charles II: The Revolution of 1688: The War against Louis XIV

ALTHOUGH MOST OF the great constitutional and political measures of Cromwell's time were annulled in 1660, the restoration of Charles II was not a counter-revolution. To contemporary opinion, looking at events from a legal rather than from a historical standpoint, the return of the monarchy appeared simply as a reversion to the form of government which had existed before the misuse of royal power by Charles I. None the less the position had changed in one important respect and Charles II was aware of the change. Monarchy had been defeated once and might be defeated again. There was now little danger that a system of absolute government would be established in England. Parliament itself had gained in experience. Matters touching foreign policy, trade, and religion were no longer outside its competence. For better or worse, there was no chance of re-establishing the old system of paternal rule. Indeed the only measures of the restoration which might be called counter-revolutionary were those taken against the king's wish by parliament itself in matters of religion. Charles wanted toleration for catholics, and was therefore willing to allow it to non-anglican protestants. Parliament imposed[1] a rigid and formal anglicanism which resulted in the expulsion of one-fifth, or some 1,200 of the beneficed clergy from their livings. These expelled clergy of presbyterian views – the founders of modern nonconformity – were forbidden to preach or even to come within five miles of any town or place where they had preached or held cure of souls.[2]

[1] The legislation which set up this anglican monopoly is generally known as the Clarendon code. In fact, Clarendon, the king's chief minister, wanted something less severe.

[2] The strength of nonconformity in Birmingham may have been an incidental

Charles's attempts to break through this legislation failed. The reasons for the parliamentary persecution of opinion were more political than religious. Laud's policy of religious uniformity had been part of a plan for the reform of abuses in the Church; there was no general effort to raise the spiritual level of the anglican clergy in the reign of Charles II. On the other hand the political fear of catholicism was not unjustified. Apart from the memories of the Elizabethan age, catholicism in Europe was everywhere the religion of absolute rulers. The treatment of protestants by Louis XIV went far beyond anything on the English statute-book. No one knew how many catholics there were in England; they might well be considered a political danger not as potential rebels but as possible supporters of an attempt at the subversion of liberty by a catholic king. Moreover, if Charles's religious views were suspect, those of his brother James were openly catholic in sympathy.

The defence of anglicanism was thus the defence of the privileges and powers of parliament and, as in Charles I's time, ultimately the defence of the interests of the landowning and business classes who dominated parliament. This interpretation, however, must not be made in a narrow sense. The defence succeeded because the interests of all classes were felt to be linked with its success. The victory of catholic absolutism in France was not especially to the advantage of the third estate.

The dispute was not fought out in the grand style, but in a series of intrigues of little credit to either side. The king himself was largely responsible for the ignoble politics of his reign. Charles was a bad man,[1] fond of bad as well as of clever company. Much has been written of the 'inevitable' reaction against the attempt to enforce morality by military order, but the king, who was not in England during the rule of the army, cannot be excused on this plea. No *raison d'état* can palliate the fact that Charles accepted bribes from a foreign sovereign without regard to the interest of his country. It is unlikely that Charles intended to use French money

result of the fact that the villages which later formed the city of Birmingham were more than five miles from any corporate town. The exclusion of nonconformists from public office was one reason why they secured a prominence beyond their numbers in industry and commerce.

[1] He was also a cad. He introduced his most notorious mistress Barbara Villiers to his newly married queen before the whole court, and compelled the queen to appoint the woman to her Household.

and French soldiers for the establishment of absolute rule in England; he merely wanted money to make himself independent of parliament. On the other hand Charles knew that Louis XIV did not pay him without expecting a high return; nothing less indeed than the control of English foreign policy for the furtherance of French plans.

At the beginning of Charles II's reign the conflict of trading interests between English and Dutch flared up in another war. After heavy fighting at sea the English gained New Amsterdam – which they renamed New York – and gave up Surinam (Guiana).[1] Thenceforward Anglo-Dutch rivalry slowly decreased in intensity as the power of Louis XIV began to overshadow all Europe. In 1670 Louis was preparing for an attack on the Dutch as a necessary step in his plan to take the Spanish Netherlands. He therefore tried to isolate any possible enemies. Charles II showed little foresight in agreeing to join the French against the Dutch, but this agreement was not in itself disgraceful. The disgrace lay in a secret treaty by which, in return for no very large sum of money, Charles bargained to announce his conversion to catholicism and, if necessary, to receive 6,000 French troops for the suppression of any domestic opposition. The terms of this secret treaty of Dover were not fully known until 1682; the substance of it was guessed long before and provided good reason for an increasing distrust of the king.

Fortunately for England the Dutch, owing to their courage and to the leadership of the young William of Orange, saved themselves from destruction. Meanwhile Charles had issued a Declaration of Indulgence suspending the operation of the penal laws against catholics and dissenters. Parliament replied by passing the Test Act which excluded catholics from public office. Charles was compelled by English opinion to make peace with the Dutch in 1674, but he continued to receive money from Louis XIV except for a short and sudden change of policy in 1677–8 when he took the momentous step of marrying James's daughter Mary[2] to William of Orange.

[1] During this war England suffered the Great Plague of 1665, and the Great Fire of London in 1666. The latter calamity destroyed over 13,000 houses in addition to churches and other public buildings. There was at this time no regular system of fire insurance.

[2] Mary and Anne were James's daughters by his first wife Anne, daughter of the royalist Clarendon. After the death of his first wife James married the catholic princess Mary of Modena.

This marriage was a form of reinsurance; it might have given the opposition a weapon against the king. In 1678 one Titus Oates invented the story of a catholic plot to kill Charles and to put his brother James on the throne. There was just enough circumstantial evidence – and more than enough unreasoning suspicion – to support the view that protestantism was in danger. The opposition to Charles, under the leadership of the earl of Shaftesbury, used the chance to bring forward a plan for the exclusion of James from the succession in favour of the duke of Monmouth, an illegitimate son of Charles. If Shaftesbury had chosen Mary or Anne, he might have carried his proposal. Monmouth was merely a good-looking nonentity; his candidature would have meant civil war on the death of Charles. Since no one wanted civil war, Charles was able to defeat the exclusionists. He was soon in a position to take the offensive against them. The extremists on the opposite side ruined their cause by a genuine plot to seize Charles and James on their way home from Newmarket.[1] If this wild plot had succeeded, the civil war which most people feared would have broken out. Hence there was for the time a loyal reaction in support of the king.

Charles II died in 1685. He had kept his throne and passed it on to his brother. Apart from the general fear of civil war, it was difficult for the average Englishman to think of any practicable alternative to the king's government. Looking back over two hundred and fifty years a modern historian can trace in the intrigues and confused politics of Charles's reign the beginnings of party government. Contemporaries could not put this modern interpretation upon events as they saw them. The name which Shaftesbury gave to his supporters – the 'Country party' – did not imply any principle; the nicknames applied both to the 'Country party' and to the party of the court definitely implied faction; 'whigs' were rebel Scottish Covenanters, and 'tories' rebel Irish Brigands. Many politicians on either side, like their sovereign, took money from Louis XIV.

James II was perhaps a better man than Charles II,[2] but he was less intelligent and at once hasty and obstinate. He persisted in

[1] Newmarket was already a centre of racing.

[2] It is difficult to hold this opinion in view of the treatment of the west country peasants who supported a foolish attempt at rebellion by Monmouth in 1685. Over 300 were executed; about 800 others were transported to Barbados, and some of them granted as slaves to courtiers.

trying to get relief for catholics and thought that he could do it by an
alliance with the dissenters. One might describe this policy as one of
enlightened toleration. Englishmen did not regard it as such and
their judgment could not remain unaffected by the French king's
revocation of the Edict of Nantes in 1685 or by their knowledge of
James's own character. James II, like Charles I, strained rather
than transgressed the limits of his power against the interpretation
put upon the prerogative by parliament. James's method was to
push to an extreme his undoubted right to suspend laws or to
dispense individuals from the consequences of breaking the law.
The danger was that the king used these prerogative rights not in an
emergency or for a national purpose but as part of a set policy and
for an end of which the nation disapproved.

If James did these things in order to put catholicism on an
equality with anglicanism, what would he do when catholicism was
well established in all the important positions of State? The king
had some success. When he began to apply his policy to the Church,
he was destroying one of the main supports of his throne. The
anglican clergy accepted the doctrine of 'non-resistance' to an
anointed king because the king was the defender of the Church;
if the king himself were delivering the Church to its enemies, non-
resistance became an absurdity. In May 1688 James ordered the
clergy to read in their churches a Declaration of Indulgence – the
second which he had issued – suspending penal laws against catholics
and dissenters. Most of the clergy disobeyed the order; seven of the
bishops petitioned the king against it. The king ordered their trial.
They were acquitted, and for the first time in living memory a
London crowd cheered bishops.

In spite of the king's folly, it is possible that, in order to avoid the
risk of civil war, opinion in general would have been content to
wait until his death. James's two daughters were protestants; the
elder, Mary, was married to the protestant William of Orange.
Three weeks before the acquittal of the bishops, a son was born to
the king. The position was now more serious. A catholic regency
might be followed by another catholic monarch. Hence, on 30 June,
an invitation, signed by representative Englishmen, was sent to
William of Orange.[1]

1 The invitation was smuggled out of the country by Admiral Herbert in the
disguise of a common sailor.

William of Orange landed at Torbay on 5 November 1688. Louis XIV, who might otherwise have stopped him, had not enough ships at Brest; his army was occupied in the Rhineland and was not ready to attack Holland; anyhow, Louis expected William's expedition to fail. A 'protestant wind' from the east kept the English navy, still loyal in an uncertain way to James, to its anchorage at the Nore, while William's ships sailed through the Straits of Dover; the wind changed after the Dutch had reached Torbay, and held up the English off the Isle of Wight. Once William had landed, the determination of the English people not to have another civil war settled the matter. They could avoid civil war only by getting rid of James and agreeing upon the method of doing so and upon the steps to be taken after he had gone. Agreement could be reached most easily on the theory that an attempt at arbitrary power was an innovation upon the traditional rights of Englishmen. James himself was allowed and even encouraged to escape to France. Then parliament settled how to describe what had happened. 'James, having endeavoured to subvert the constitution of this kingdom, by breaking the original contract between king and people, and by the advice of Jesuits and other wicked persons having violated the fundamental laws, and having withdrawn himself out of the kingdom, has abdicated the government. . . . The throne is thereby vacant.' To this description of events was added the opinion that 'it hath been found by experience to be inconsistent with the safety and welfare of this Protestant kingdom to be governed by a Popish prince'.

The narrative of events was inconsistent and untrue. James had not abdicated; the throne was not vacant. There never had been an 'original contract' between king and people. None the less, although few of James's subjects could accept all this stylized version of the expulsion of their king, most of them were able to accept enough of it to justify their allegiance to James's daughter Mary. Mary refused to reign without William; William refused to be a prince consort. It was therefore necessary to accept both William and Mary.

The conditions upon which these sovereigns were allowed to reign were laid down in the conservative form of a Declaration of Right. The Declaration (which was embodied in an act of parliament) asserted that certain things were illegal, although there was no doubt of their formal legality, but the monarchy was not deprived of all executive authority. The 'tradition' allowed the sovereign certain powers, and indeed required him to use them, since without their use the machinery of government would have broken down. The point was to get rid of the suspending power and to prevent the use of the dispensing power 'as . . . exercised of late'. The coronation oath was modified in the sense that William and Mary promised to govern 'according to the statutes in parliament agreed on'. The problem of toleration was settled by allowing freedom of worship to all but catholics.[1]

Although care was taken at the time to avoid anything revolutionary, the political acts following the landing at Torbay became known to posterity not merely as the 'Revolution' but as the 'Glorious Revolution'. There was a revolution; the extent of it could be measured only after the lapse of time. The revolution was 'glorious' because it was successful. The modern constitution, even the constitution which was so much reverenced in the eighteenth century, was not established in 1688–9. The success of the revolution lay in the opportunities which it gave for peaceful change.

For a quarter of a century after the accession of William and Mary, England was almost continuously at war with France. William of Orange had risked his English adventure only because he needed English help in resisting Louis XIV. The combination of English and Dutch naval power, which Louis had so long prevented, now turned the scale against France. The first stage was none too easy. The English and Dutch fleets had the worst of a battle off Beachy Head in 1690. Almost at the same time the victory of the Boyne[2] over James II meant that catholic Ireland would not provide a base for a French invasion of England. In 1692 Louis planned a direct invasion from northern France. The French fleet was defeated off Cape La Hogue. Henceforward William could concentrate on the land war. In 1697 Louis XIV signed the peace of Ryswick, in which he gave up most of his conquests since 1678, and recognized William as king of England and Anne as heiress to the throne.

William died in 1702, seven years after the death of his wife, and

---

[1] In practice, catholics were permitted the freedom which they were not allowed by law, but they were exposed to prosecution by petty informers. Dissenters and catholics alike were still disqualified from public office.

[2] In this battle a mixed force of English, Scottish, French, Dutch, Danish, and Irish protestants fought English, Scottish, French, and Irish catholics.

E

at a moment when the work of resisting Louis had to be done over again. Fortune had put in Louis' way a temptation which he was not wise enough to resist. At the time of the peace of Ryswick it was clear that Charles II of Spain would soon die and that he would leave no direct heirs. Among the nearest claimants to the succession was Philip, grandson of Louis XIV. The prizes at stake included the Spanish Netherlands, Gibraltar, the Balearic Islands, Sicily, Milan, Naples, and the immense Spanish inheritance in South and Central America. If these territories went to a member of the house of Bourbon, French naval and colonial supremacy might be assured throughout the world. Attempts were made to settle the Spanish succession by treaties partitioning the Empire, but Charles died in 1700, leaving everything – as Spanish interests inclined him to do – to Philip. Louis accepted the inheritance on his grandson's behalf. Acceptance need not have meant immediate war with the English and Dutch. Louis, however, thought that he would have to fight sooner or later. He decided to establish his position at once. He forbade the importation of English goods into France and ordered Philip to do the same in Spain. He also made the mistake of recognizing James's son, the 'Old Pretender', on his father's death in 1701. A few months earlier, on the death of Anne's surviving son, the duke of Gloucester, parliament had passed an Act of Settlement ordering the succession to the Electress Sophia[1] and her children.

It was hardly possible for England not to resist these evident signs of French aggression. Their resistance was directed by John Churchill, duke of Marlborough, a soldier of genius whose humanity, personal charm, and diplomatic skill also succeeded in keeping together a difficult coalition. The most serious threat came, as always, from the Low Countries. Marlborough's strategy was based upon a threefold plan of driving the French from the Spanish Netherlands, taking the 'barrier fortresses' and then, if necessary, invading France. The campaign of Blenheim was no exception, since a French advance on Vienna would have broken the coalition which Marlborough did so much to maintain.

The success of this strategy was not affected by the failure of the secondary plan to keep the French out of Spain. Even this secondary

---

[1] The Electress Sophia's mother was Elizabeth, daughter of James I, who had married Frederick, Elector Palatine. See above, p. 96.

plan brought the capture of Gibraltar[1] in 1704 and Minorca in 1708. In this latter year the war might well have ended. The Netherlands were secure; and the French too exhausted to attempt any more grand offensives. The tories in England thought that English security had been obtained and could be preserved by sea-power without the expense of more fighting on the Continent; the whigs wanted to go on until Philip had been expelled from Spain.[2] In 1710, after winning a general election, the tories opened negotiations with Louis. They conceded the Spanish throne to Philip; the rival candidate, Charles, archduke of Austria, became Emperor in 1711. They kept Nova Scotia, Newfoundland, Gibraltar, and Minorca, and regained trading factories in Hudson Bay lost during the war. They secured the right to supply slaves to the Spanish American colonies and the transfer of the Spanish Netherlands to the Austrian Habsburgs. The allies of England did less well; to the discredit of the English government the Catalans, who had opposed French claims, were left to the mercy of Philip.

This settlement finally made at Utrecht in 1713 had an importance beyond the partitioning of territory. English sea-power was secure in the western Mediterranean and in the north Atlantic. Spain had ceased to be a Great Power in spite of her great resources. Antwerp was not in the hands of a state with a navy. The long period of war had permanently weakened the Dutch. The English colonies in America were free to develop without immediate danger from France. The prestige of English arms was high in Europe. English political institutions had shown themselves more impressive than those of France, with the result that, while Frenchmen became increasingly critical of their government, nearly all Englishmen praised the English constitution even if they could not yet agree upon the person of their sovereign. The struggle for world-empire between England and France had still to be fought to a finish. France was richer and more populous than England, but every year during which the English could build up their resources behind the shelter of their naval power made ultimate success more likely.

[1] Gibraltar has thus been longer in English than in Spanish possession. The Spaniards took it from the Moors in 1462.

[2] For the first time in English history public policy in a question of war and peace was directly influenced by a man of letters writing in opposition to the government. Swift's work *The Conduct of the Allies* (1711) had a direct effect upon opinion in favour of the tory policy of peace.

Henceforward, also, these resources were not those of England alone. Throughout the eighteenth century the English failed to conciliate Irish feeling – much harsher terms may indeed be used to describe the reasons for this failure – but they were saved from what might have been a serious Scottish problem by the good sense of the English and Scottish negotiators of the Union of 1707. There were solid reasons on each side for the Union. The Scottish parliament had not passed an act corresponding to the English Act of Settlement; hence the English wanted to avoid a disputed succession at the death of Anne. The Scots – excluded by the Navigation Acts from the English colonial trade – hoped to share English prosperity.

A Scottish attempt to find a market in America outside the English and Spanish monopolies had been a tragic failure. An expedition to the isthmus of Darien (Panama) in 1698 ended in the deaths of most of the settlers from disease and the surrender of the remainder to the Spaniards. The English in the West Indies had given no help because William III did not wish to quarrel with Spain, and the East India Company was jealous of Scottish encroachment. After this disaster the only solution for Scottish merchants and traders was union with England on terms which would admit them to the benefits of the colonial trade. Upon this foundation and in spite of English contempt for the Scots and Scottish dislike of the English, the union was concluded.

Each side gained from the terms. Scotland, the smaller kingdom, lost neither its identity nor its national pride with the disappearance of a separate political sovereignty. Economically the country prospered beyond Scottish expectation. Glasgow, for example, a town of about 12,000–13,000 people in 1714, nearly quadrupled its population within seventy years and won from Bristol and Liverpool the larger share of the tobacco trade.[1] It would also be unwise to write down the contemporary achievement of the Union as a sordid bargain for material ends. There would have been far less bloodshed and misery in Europe from 1707 to the present day if the good sense which regulated Anglo-Scottish relations had been applied to other territorial and political questions upon which feeling ran high.

[1] Glasgow raised two regiments against the Young Pretender in 1745. After the failure of the '45 rebellion, the English and the Lowland Scots collaborated in improving the material condition of the Highlands. Before the accession of George III Pitt was able to enlist Highland regiments to take part in the conquest of Canada.

CHAPTER XIII

England in the Eighteenth Century

ON THE DEATH of Queen Anne, in August 1714, George, Elector of Brunswick-Lüneburg,[1] and son of the Electress Sophia, succeeded to the throne in accordance with the terms of the Act of Settlement. If Anne had lived a few weeks or even a few days longer, the succession might have been disputed in favour of the Old Pretender. Bolingbroke, the leader of the 'Jacobite tories', had driven his rival, Harley, leader of the 'Hanoverian tories', from office on a Tuesday; the queen died on the following Sunday. It is, however, likely that a move on behalf of the Pretender, a declared catholic and pensioner of France, would have been as futile as the Jacobite rebellions of 1715 and 1745. The Union with Scotland had lost the Stuarts their chance of strong support except perhaps in the Highlands. Elsewhere the temper of the age was unfavourable to romantic adventure.

Every historian has noted the predominance of material interests, a self-confidence, checked to some extent by sound judgment and a sense of limits, as features typical of England in the eighteenth century at least until the outbreak of the French Revolution. The full effects of the settlement of 1688 were now felt in English political life. No one element of power had been allowed to obtrude or to upset the balance. The admirers of the English constitution attributed to it something of the elegance of proportion proper to an eighteenth-century country house. On a closer view this equipoise of legislative, executive, and judicial power was less complete. The salons of the house might be in perfect

[1] The Electors' territories were, like those of most German princes, a mosaic of small acquisitions. They were governed from Hanover and to Hanover the electoral title was loosely applied.

harmony, but there were backstairs and interconnecting passages of a less symmetrical construction and dating from an older building.

The character of these necessities of service may be summed up in the word 'influence'. 'Influence' was of the nature of the compromise between monarchy and aristocracy reached at the revolution. The king had been left with a sphere of action defined more negatively than positively. He was still expected to frame policy and to choose men who would carry it out. The sphere of parliament was also undefined, but the king was under the practical necessity of getting parliamentary approval for his policy. Parties were still loose agglomerations of groups, or rather, party divisions did not cover the whole field of policy. They could not do so until parliament assumed full control of government and had the responsibility of power as well as opportunities of criticism. Until this time parties were regarded as due to exceptional circumstances and as factions if they continued into normal times. Most people thought that the Crown had first claim upon the support of right-thinking men.

If therefore the king had to choose ministers who would obtain parliamentary support, he was not expected to choose them only from one party. George I and George II always chose whigs; they did so not because the whigs were a party in the modern sense but because the term 'whig' was a guarantee of loyalty to the Hanoverian succession, while the tories were tainted with Jacobitism. On their side the king's ministers were under no obligation to agree among themselves. Each was responsible to the king for his own department. If ministers appointed by the king ceased to agree with his policy, they were not expected to resign; their resignation might even be taken as a kind of conspiracy or at all events as a failure to fulfil their duties as the king's servants.

It was in the logic of the revolutionary settlement that this situation should ultimately be resolved in favour of ministers and parliament and to the detriment of the king's power. The development of the Cabinet, the emergence of a Prime Minister, the conception of party in the terms extolled by Burke were essential to the functioning of the 'balanced' constitution. The Cabinet, obviously, had to exist before the Prime Minister; it is significant that each of these new features caused considerable disquiet and was then accepted as necessary.

As early as Charles II's reign proposals were made for the improvement of the conduct of business by the Privy Council. One problem was to find a method of getting the consent of councillors holding different views to the advice which ministers holding roughly the same opinions wished to give the Crown. In the reigns of William and Mary and of Anne the term Cabinet Council was used colloquially for the small body of privy councillors whom the sovereigns called regularly for consultation, especially on foreign affairs.[1] Under Anne membership of this Cabinet was becoming fixed in the sense that certain high officers of State had a right to be called. George I continued the Cabinet, and indeed could hardly do otherwise.

Furthermore, the process of specialization, or rather of elimination, continued. Already in Anne's reign there had been regular but informal meetings of the chief ministers to discuss policy and to prepare the business to be laid before the Cabinet. This working body, the 'Efficient' or 'Effective' Cabinet became differentiated from the larger or 'Nominal' Cabinet. The distinction was not lasting because the larger Cabinet faded away, but while it lasted it facilitated the rise of one leading minister.

It was not the practice of the sovereign to attend the working Cabinet. George I and George II did not willingly give up any of their customary rights; neither of them realized that the position of the sovereign would be greatly weakened if he could be presented with a unanimous decision reached in his absence and voiced by a Prime Minister. In fact the king's ministers were not able to treat George I or George II in this way. Nevertheless the Cabinet, meeting without the king, was likely to fall under the influence of a leading minister; the king had an interest that it should do so because he wanted his policy to be made acceptable to parliament.

This leading Servant of the Crown had no official title; the term 'Prime Minister', as the alternative 'Premier' shows, was borrowed from France, where there was no parliamentary system. In Anne's reign it was sometimes used in the plural to describe the most important ministers.

Walpole's enemies called him a Prime Minister because they wanted to imply that it was unconstitutional for one man to take a more prominent part than his colleagues in advising the king. Walpole was never asked to 'form a ministry'; he never 'led' a party

[1] It is of interest that in Anne's reign the Cabinet met on Sundays.

with a majority in the house of commons. His resignation in 1742 did not bring with it the resignation of all his colleagues.

Nevertheless Walpole was a Prime Minister in the sense that his grasp of business, his ascendancy in the house of commons and reputation in the country gave him a primacy which his colleagues recognized. The colleagues of Chatham in the great days of his power would not have dared to think of themselves as his equals. Finally, in name as well as in fact, the younger Pitt was acknowledged as Prime Minister even when he was a young man of only twenty-four.

There was a special reason why the leading minister – the Prime Minister – tended to be the First Lord of the Treasury. In the absence of organized and disciplined parties the safest way was to make sure of a majority by buying it. The parliamentary representation of Great Britain was based upon an ancient system of franchises and an out-of-date distribution of seats. In England 403 seats were allocated to 203 cities and boroughs; in 1760 only 22 of these boroughs had more than 1,000 electors apiece, and most of them had less than 400. Voting was open; borough electors were ready to sell their votes, and county electors found it in their interest to vote as their landlords desired. The Crown, through the Treasury, controlled about 30 boroughs, where appointments to customs posts and the like could secure a majority. The landowners controlled a much larger number; about the middle of the eighteenth century 51 peers and 55 commoners decided or influenced the election of 192 members to parliament. Less than 3,000 voters – half of them 'faggot' [1] voters created by landlords – returned all the Scottish county members.

The line of least resistance for ministers was therefore to get the support of the borough-owners by the gift of Crown patronage; administrative offices (many of them sinecures), pensions, naval and military commands, Church preferment. The upper class, to whom or through whom most of this patronage flowed, thought of it as their right; it was even considered that impoverished peers had a claim to royal help for the maintenance of their station. In a society graded hierarchically the claim did not seem absurd and to an age with modest standards of professional efficiency, appointments to

[1] A 'faggot' voter was a person to whom property was transferred temporarily, often by splitting a holding, in order to qualify him for the franchise.

office without reference to the abilities of the holder were not regarded with alarm. There was always someone of lower station to do the work. Moreover, in return for the public money dispensed to them the nobility and gentry undertook reasonably well and without payment almost the whole of the local government of the kingdom outside the corporate towns.

This system was never 'closed'; on the largest issues place-men could not be relied upon to vote with the administration. In any case the gradual development of party alignment based upon principle made the use of 'influence' appear scandalous, at least to the party not in office. The change of attitude was hastened by the *maladresse* of George III. George III did not try to govern unconstitutionally. He merely expected parliament to support the ministers of his choice, and, to this end, used on a lavish scale the 'influence' available to him. Some 250 members were at one time paid for their support. George had certain advantages. The tories were no longer opposed to the dynasty; the whigs had fallen into coteries and there was as yet no Prince of Wales around whom malcontents could gather.

George III was neither a wise nor even a clever man. He could not get anyone of first-class ability, still less a united Cabinet to accept his dictation and to hold the position in parliament. He had a good deal of success. He could outdo any one group in buying support; ministers might go but the king was always there. In 1770, with the appointment of Lord North,[1] the king seemed to have attained his purpose. He had freed himself from the control of the whig magnates. In so doing he had become a politician among politicians and involved the Crown in responsibility for every great failure. Failure came with the loss of the American colonies. An opposition group, supported by the magnificent oratory of Burke, set up as an alternative to the manipulation of the system of influence by the king the rival theory of parliamentary government through ministers representing a party with a majority in the house of commons.

King, Cabinet, Prime Minister, and parties now began to take their modern alignment, but the process of development had not come to an end. Royal influence of the traditional kind, often with little more than nuisance value, continued under George III,

[1] Lord North was one of the few leaders of an administration who could speak three foreign languages: French, German, and Italian.

George IV, William IV, and even under Victoria before constitutional monarchy reached its present form. Ministerial responsibility was tidied up a little earlier. The younger Pitt enforced the resignation of a Lord Chancellor who opposed him in parliament. In 1801 Addington refused to allow an ex-minister to sit in the Cabinet. Henceforward no one challenged the view that office-holders alone could attend Cabinet meetings, yet even in 1850 Peel did not go beyond the view that the work of choosing a ministry was left 'almost exclusively' to the Prime Minister. No ministry between 1783 and 1830 resigned merely as the result of defeat in the house of commons. Finally, the proper functioning of representative government was impossible without reform of the franchise and the redistribution of seats. There was a general feeling to this effect in the middle and later years of George III's reign. Nothing was done because the events of the French revolution alarmed opinion. There was no knowing to what extremes large-scale political change might lead.

The contemporaries of George I and II did not look at political change or any other kind of change with favour. They hoped that they had attained stability after a long period of confusion. John Locke, whose philosophy was a justification of the revolution of 1688, based government on a contract between ruler and subjects for the defence of property. The setting in which property was held during the first half of the eighteenth century made for social and political conservatism. At the apex of society was a landowning nobility, living more in magnificence than comfort, highly civilized for their age,[1] and more closely linked than before or since with the most original, tolerant, and interesting ideas of their time. They were expected to be patrons of art and letters; the system of patronage had grave drawbacks, but it secured the production of unremunerative work which otherwise could not have been produced at all. Although they took an increasing share in the national

[1] Judged by modern middle-class standards the aristocrats of the early eighteenth century were dirty and evil-smelling: their clothes were unhygienic and inconvenient. They had neither good dentists nor good oculists. Their medicine, in spite of the fortunes made by a few good or fashionable doctors, was mostly an affair of quacks, and their surgery worse. They ate and drank too much. Their manners towards women were a mixture of peacock ceremonial and barbarism. These and many other such facts should be remembered in reading panegyrics on the grace of living two hundred years ago.

income from investments and indirectly from trade and manufacture, these magnates drew their private wealth mainly from agriculture. Here they showed a sense of enterprise and enlightenment which was not found in any department of State or indeed in the aristocracy of any other European country. They continued the improvements begun in the later seventeenth century. They introduced better breeds of cattle and sheep, a better rotation of crops, new agricultural implements, and new methods, such as the use of turnips (hitherto a garden vegetable) for cleansing the soil. They paid for these innovations mainly out of profits, and over a long period of unusually good harvests enriched themselves by the sinking of capital in their land. For all their pride of place they did not harden into a caste. The 'upward movement' of the past two centuries was accelerated. Bankers, clothiers, merchants from London, Liverpool, and Bristol, fortune-finders from India (such as Chatham's grandfather, who bought a diamond for £20,000 and sold it to the duke of Orleans for £135,000)[1] were accepted into their ranks if they bought estates and behaved as large landowners were expected to do.

The country gentry, a class with almost as wide variations in income and culture as the middle class of today, were equally proud of their station. They enjoyed immense local esteem and real authority as justices of the peace. They had their position in politics and in the receipt and dispensing of patronage. They could satisfy their love of field sports which, incidentally, owing to the mildness of the English climate, kept them on the land in the winter. They had also the simple but satisfying diversions of the local county towns. Here, as in their sports, they touched the growing middle class, but this class, outside London, the seaports, the cloth towns, and a few other centres of manufacture, was still small and, except in fiscal questions, politically self-conscious only or mainly to the extent of requiring liberties for dissenters.[2]

The condition of the labouring class is less easy to define. Town workers were still in a minority. The population of England and Wales was about five and a half million in 1700 and about seven

[1] The stone was found in an Indian mine by a slave. The slave concealed it in a wound in his leg, but it was stolen from him by an English sea-captain who sold it to the native merchant from whom Pitt bought it. In 1791 the diamond was valued at £480,000.

[2] The novels of the century show the middle class at its best and worst; healthy, unsophisticated, modest, hard in bargaining but not merciless to inferiors.

million in 1760. Henceforward there was a more rapid increase. This increase, especially after 1760, was mainly in the towns; it was not nearly enough to turn the balance from agriculture to other industries. The real wages of the country labourer are difficult to establish. It is significant that in some areas they were supplemented at an early date by grants out of poor rates. On the whole, up to 1760 standards of living were probably a little better than in the seventeenth century, except in those areas, especially in the Midlands, where the open fields and common lands – the medieval 'waste' – were being enclosed. These enclosures, mainly for arable, had continued throughout the seventeenth century. They became more widespread from about 1730 and were most frequent during the period 1760–1800. They went on until about the middle of the nineteenth century. Without them agricultural production could not have been increased or methods improved to any large extent. Ultimately all classes gained from the addition to the national wealth, but the price paid was high. Enclosures were carried out by act of parliament. The procedure at every stage was weighted in favour of the large landowner. Compensation paid to the cottiers was of little use to them, since it could not buy the advantages which they had lost. The enclosure of common land deprived many thousands of small grazing rights which had kept their families just above subsistence level. In any case agricultural improvements which brought an economy in labour would have caused a problem of rural unemployment. It is not to the credit of a parliament representing the landed interest that little or nothing was done to safeguard the position of the country labourers whose long history from Anglo-Saxon times, through Anglo-Norman villeinage and the slow achievement of freedom, ended too often in a drift to unskilled work in the towns.

The landless poor were the worst sufferers from the process of enclosure, but the small freeholders, yeomen holding a hundred acres or less, in the enclosed areas tended to find competition impossible against the larger owners. Many of them could not pay their share of the cost of fencing. They too began to sell their holdings and to join the class of tenant farmers under the greater landlords or to put their energy and money, for better or worse, into the new industrial enterprises. Up to 1750 the openings in manufacture and industry were far less than in the latter half of the century. The various branches of the cloth industry, located mainly in Wiltshire and the western counties and in Norfolk, still employed more labour than any other manufacture. The iron and steel industries, judged by later standards, were on a small scale. The production of iron had declined owing to the exhaustion of the forests from which charcoal was made. Experiments had been made in the use of coal for smelting;[1] Abraham Darby[2] used coke about 1709, but the process was not general until about fifty years later. Except for the manufacture of gunpowder, sulphuric acid was the only chemical product for which there was large demand.[3]

Industrial development was unlikely to be quickened until inland transport became easier. The roads of England in the early eighteenth century were still so bad that the common mode of transport, away from navigable rivers, was by pack-horse. This method was expensive, useless for heavy or bulky goods, and hardly more suited to the carriage of breakable articles like the china which Wedgwood began to make in 1759. Road-making and canal-building were necessary before heavy machinery could be set up or coal carried cheaply to inland factories. The annual output of coal – a test of industrialization – went up from two and a half million tons in 1700 to six million tons in 1770, but the increase was due mainly to domestic use in seaports, especially London. In 1800 the figure had risen only to ten million tons.

The rate of scientific discovery and invention was another limiting factor in the expansion of industry. The discoveries of the age of Newton had been mainly in the fields of mathematics, physics, and astronomy. Astronomy and mathematics had long been recognized as of practical importance in connexion with navigation and map-making; Greenwich Observatory had been founded as a State institution in 1675. The bearing of pure science upon manufacturing processes was less generally understood, and the possibilities of

[1] The problem was to keep the sulphur in the coal from getting into the iron and making it brittle.

[2] Darby brought Dutch workmen to Bristol about 1704 and started a brass foundry. He moved in 1709 to Coalbrookdale in Shropshire. His grandson Abraham Darby built in collaboration with John Wilkinson the first iron bridge. Wilkinson was such an enthusiast for iron that he was buried at his own wish in an iron coffin.

[3] A considerable element in this demand was the employment of sulphuric acid in the manufacture of Glauber salts, a universal medicine in an age of over-eating and over-purging.

discovery undervalued.[1] From the point of view of business a new invention was not always attractive in its early stages. Newcomen's steam engine was working before 1720, but it was employed only at a pit mouth to pump up water. It consumed so much fuel that, until Watt (about fifty years later) designed something better, the use of steam power at a distance from a coal mine was uneconomical. The early machines often went out of order; there was no one to repair them or to provide spare parts of accurate measurement. Manufacturers regarded machines rather as instruments for saving labour than as the means of greatly increased production.[2] Workmen held the same view and drew from it the corollary that every new machine caused unemployment.

There was little general encouragement of inventors. Capital was not easily available, especially after the speculative crisis ending in the so-called 'South Sea Bubble' of 1720, when the South Sea Company persuaded an over-credulous public to invest – and lose – large sums in a wild scheme for liquidating the national debt. Industry, unlike agriculture, was not in itself a gentleman's occupation, although a duke might share in the profits. The great landowners, who were hard-headed enough to watch for improvements in methods of farming, did not much concern themselves with the coking of coal or the puddling of iron. There was neither social prestige nor cultural merit about the invention of the steam engine. Although the universities, especially Cambridge, had not altogether lost the scientific impulse of the later seventeenth century, they too were not interested in the application of science to industry. School education, except in the dissenting academies, was unconcerned with the physical or biological sciences.

There could be no question of a 'popular interest' in science. Village schoolmasters might teach the rudiments of reading, writing, and arithmetic. Charity schools in towns under the auspices of bodies like the Society for Promoting Christian Knowledge gave a little better education, but the age did not consider that the poor needed to learn anything not directly useful in their state of life. As a consequence the public attitude towards practical measures

---

[1] Electricity was only an amusing toy, although a few people, including John Wesley, were interested in its therapeutic possibilities.

[2] It has been pointed out that the use of the term 'iron horse' in the nineteenth century to describe the locomotive shows how long this attitude lasted.

based upon scientific knowledge was often superstitious and absurd. When the inaccurate Julian calendar was reformed in 1752, thousands of people believed that eleven days had been taken out of their lives.[1]

The upper class, concerned with politics, government, and the pleasures of living, took the miseries of the poor for granted. Certain scandals, such as the devastating effects of cheap gin in the first half of the century, were remedied by law. Other scandals – for example, the exploitation of pauper children in industry – were more hidden from view and even condoned as saving the children from the vice into which the poor were supposed to rush if they had any leisure. With few exceptions, such as Hogarth,[2] the most imaginative minds of the age accepted the tone of polite society or, if, like Swift, they rebelled against it, their rebellion was not directed against remediable social evils. Pope might have had more to say if he had turned away from elegant drawing-rooms. There was much sentiment about the poor, or rather about the virtuous poor, but even their tragedies were introduced into fine letters with an air of apology and resignation. Goldsmith's poem on *The Deserted Village* did not influence public opinion to safeguard the rights of the poor in enclosure acts.[3] Gray's *Elegy in a Country Churchyard* treats the poor with a charming tenderness and points a moral from their virtues; there is no stirring of conscience about the years of misery in the repressed lives of the 'village Hampdens'. There were individual philanthropists, such as Oglethorpe[4] and John Howard, who exposed the fearful condition of prisons, or Thomas Coram, who endowed the Foundling Hospital. Not until Blake was there any sharp and deep expression of general responsibility for social evil.[5]

The established Church and the older dissenting Churches – presbyterian, baptists, congregationalists – did not encourage doubts about the rightness of the social order. The decline in sectarian

[1] The grounds upon which the house of lords threw out in 1753 a proposal for a census were equally obscurantist.

[2] Hogarth's *Gin Lane* did a great deal to focus attention upon conditions which in fact were obvious to any Londoner.

[3] This poem was published in 1770. During the next ten years there were more enclosure acts than in any previous decade.

[4] Oglethorpe founded the colony of Georgia primarily as a place in which discharged debtors and other social failures might find a fresh start.

[5] 'The harlot's cry from street to street
Shall weave old England's winding-sheet.'

violence was to the advantage of religion as well as of politics, but the whig attempt to make the Church of England a moral temple of the 'Glorious Revolution' had a deadening effect upon the clergy. The Church of England produced the Wesleys, although it failed to keep their followers. Neither John nor Charles Wesley were revolutionaries or levellers. To the upper class of the time they were eccentric gentlemen with a zeal which might do good and was unlikely to do harm. The hostility of the clergy to the methodist movement[1] was due less to questions of doctrine than to dislike of intrusion into their parishes and to a feeling of unseemliness about the emotional character of methodist preaching. The importance of this preaching was that so much of it took place in the open air to audiences, including the very poor, whom the Church had neglected. John Wesley's sermons were addressed to people whose clothes would have kept them out of most parish churches. It is difficult to overestimate the effect of such an appeal. Some historians have thought that the methodist movement saved England from social and political revolution. An opinion of this kind must be conjectural; what is certain is that the movement gave to large sections of English society a new self-respect based upon their individual significance in the scheme of the universe.

[1] The term 'Methodist' was first applied to the Wesleys and a few friends at Oxford who founded a society to follow the method of study (which included religious observance) prescribed by the statutes of the university. The Wesleys themselves were accomplished scholars who began at the university a lifelong practice of talking to one another in Latin. Dr Johnson spoke favourably of John Wesley's conversation.

CHAPTER XIV

Walpole: Chatham:
The Loss of America:
The Defeat of Napoleon

IN 1721, eight years before the Wesleys had founded their Oxford society, Robert Walpole began his long tenure of power. Walpole was a country gentleman, coarse-grained, masterful, and clear-headed. Although his judgment of men and affairs was pitched too low, he kept England out of war – not always honourably, restored the finances and to some extent simplified the fiscal system of the country. Walpole did not regard himself as an innovator, yet in one respect he fixed the character of English politics. Throughout his years of office he sat in the house of commons and established his ascendancy over his colleagues by his management of the house. He thus made the commons the centre of government and not merely of criticism and surveillance of the administration.

Walpole used 'influence' to the full. The career of the duke of Newcastle showed that influence alone was not enough to get the support, still less the confidence of parliament. Newcastle was an arch-jobber. He enjoyed the manipulation of patronage as much as he disliked the responsibilities of government but for all his know-ledge of the back stairs he was discarded at a time of serious crisis – the beginning of the Seven Years War – because public opinion compelled the king to take William Pitt in his place.[1]

The Seven Years War (1756–63) decided that England and not France should control North America and India. The first stage of this contest had begun some sixteen years earlier. The real issues were then overshadowed by considerations affecting the balance of power in Europe. In 1739, against Walpole's advice, England

---

[1] Even so Newcastle came back in 1757 to control patronage, while Pitt directed the war.

had gone to war with Spain over the old question of the Spanish monopoly in the New World. This Anglo-Spanish war had developed into a war with France because the French could not allow England to seize any of the Spanish American colonies. The war had spread beyond the three maritime Powers because Frederick of Prussia (and, for that matter, two other German princes) had broken their agreement to recognize Maria Theresa as heiress to all the dominions of the Austrian Habsburgs, on the death of her father, the Emperor Charles VI. The treaty of Aix-la-Chapelle (1748) which ended the war was hardly more than a truce. In India it was not even a truce.

The East India Company was steadily increasing in wealth. Import of coffee and tea,[1] raw silk and calicoes had risen every year; the rise in tea between 1706 and 1750 was from 54,000 to 2,300,000 pounds.[2] The Company had 'presidencies' at Bombay, Calcutta, and Madras, and some fifteen 'factories'. Bombay had come into English possession as part of the dowry of the Portuguese wife of Charles II. The Portuguese and Dutch had ceased to be serious rivals. The French had factories in Bengal, at Pondichery, and on the west coast. In 1741 the French appointed Joseph François Dupleix as governor of Pondichery. Dupleix broke the long-standing agreement between French and English that an Anglo-French war should not extend to India. After the peace of Aix-la-Chapelle hostilities were continued indirectly through support given by French and English to rival Indian rulers. Intrigues of this kind, in which Dupleix again took the initiative, were easy at a time when the authority of the Great Mogul had weakened. Dupleix's plans were wrecked by Robert Clive who had come to India as a writer in the Company's service and soon showed his military ability. By 1752 Clive had restored the Nawab of the Carnatic whom Dupleix had expelled. Two years later Dupleix was recalled, but his policy was continued, with more success, in Hyderabad.

Anglo-French rivalry in America was on a larger scale. The English colonies in George II's reign stretched from Nova Scotia

---

[1] Coffee-drinking became fashionable in England after about 1670. Tea-drinking grew in popularity about seventy years later.

[2] In order to get the figures of Indian trade in a right proportion it is necessary to remember that the maximum number of ships employed annually by the Company during this period was about 20, and that they were all under 500 tons.

to Georgia. The French held Louisiana; Florida was still in Spanish hands. French policy – more unified in design and execution than that of the English government and of the disunited seaboard colonies – aimed at linking up the Mississippi and St Lawrence territories through the valley of the Ohio. If this policy were successful, the English colonies could be taken in the rear. A good deal of success had been obtained before 1755. The French had established a strong point at Fort Duquesne (the modern Pittsburgh); the English had failed to drive them out.

War between England and France actually broke out on a Continental question. Newcastle had hoped to build up a coalition which would keep the French occupied on land, but he failed to prevent the 'diplomatic revolution' whereby France joined Austria against Prussia. When Pitt succeeded Newcastle he too tried to engage France in Europe while he attacked her in America. Unlike Newcastle, he put into his actions an energy, speed, and foresight which at once changed the situation. His majestic ways and splendid oratory held parliament. He chose excellent commanders and set them to work in favourable conditions. Above all, his own nobility of mind, even his imperiousness, strengthened the whole nation. By the end of 1760 Montreal and Quebec had been captured. The French fleets of Toulon and Brest – intended for the escort of an invading army – had been destroyed off the coast of Portugal and in Quiberon Bay. Clive had retaken Calcutta, which had been lost in 1756, and defeated the Francophil ruler of Bengal at Plassey. Eyre Coote had driven the French out of most of the Carnatic; in January 1761 he forced the surrender of Pondichery. Spain made the mistake of joining the French side in 1761. In January 1762 England declared war against her, and within ten months occupied Havana and Manila.

Pitt would have fought a war à l'outrance with the French. George III, who wanted ministers of another type, supported the opposition to further expenditure of life and treasure once English maritime and colonial interests had been secured. Pitt and, some months later, Newcastle therefore resigned. In 1763 peace was made on terms[1] which Pitt denounced as ruinous. He objected

[1] The French surrendered Canada and the right to fortify their factories in India; most of their West Indian islands were returned to them, although there was some controversy in England whether the cotton-producing island of

above all to the retention by the French of fishing rights in the
Newfoundland fisheries, since their exercise provided France with
thousands of trained sailors.

Within twenty years of this victorious war, England had lost her
American colonies. This loss was due in some part to George III's
narrow judgment of men and affairs. It is, however, more just
to say that the king's mistakes were the occasion and not the cause
of the American Revolution. The ultimate cause can be summed
up in one word: distance. In an age of slow and difficult communications, when Boston was, on an average, six weeks' sailing distance
from Liverpool, the colonies were bound to develop a sense of their
independent existence. Their white population had increased from
about 200,000 in 1700 to 2,000,000 in 1770; in this latter year
most of the colonists were American-born. There was no 'steady
stream' of immigrants. Ever since Stuart times most of the new-
comers from England had little incentive to maintain a tradition
of loyalty; large numbers had not come from England or Scotland,
but were German, Dutch, or French protestants or Irish catholics.
The isolation of the colonists from England was increased by
their isolation from one another. Each colony was absorbed in
its own domestic problems; such problems were unlike anything
familiar to politicians in Great Britain. The leaders on either
side of the Atlantic had never met. Washington had never been
to England; Chatham,[1] Burke, and Lord North never went to
America.

The grievances of the two parties need not be set out in a balance-
sheet. The English complained, with some reason, that the colonists had taken little part in the defence of their own territories
against the French and that there had been much scandalous
trading with the enemy at sea. The colonists realized that after the
French defeat they had less need of an English garrison, but they
still wanted protection against the Indians. In 1763–4 they had to

Guadeloupe was not more valuable from an economic point of view than Canada.
Havana was exchanged for Florida and Manila given back to Spain in return for
a ransom. The interests of England's Continental ally Prussia were not much
considered (a fact which Frederick the Great did not forget), but Frederick
would not have been satisfied with anything less than Hanover.

[1] On his resignation in 1761 Pitt accepted the title of Baroness Chatham for
his wife. In 1766, when ill-health made it difficult for him to attend regularly at
the house of commons, he was raised to the peerage as earl of Chatham.

meet a great Indian rebellion.[1] Once again they left most of the defence to the small English garrison.

Hence arose the difficult question: Who was to pay for this garrison? The English government, with a public opinion demanding economy after an expensive war, did not feel justified in providing the whole sum. The colonists offered nothing. They considered that they were hampered enough by the Navigation Acts and by restrictions upon the development of American manufactures. The Navigation Acts had not been strictly enforced for many years. The English government now began to take measures for their enforcement. The colonists objected, but had no legal case and indeed could not complain without admitting that they had been breaking the law for a long time past. The imposition of stamp duties on official documents by Grenville's administration in 1765 was not an act of tyranny. To Englishmen it was not even a novelty; stamp duties had been paid in England for seventy years. The duties levied in the colonies were not expected to bring in more than £100,000, or a third of the cost of colonial defence. The colonists, however, had never paid a tax of this kind. Moreover they could now make a stand on the general principle that they were being taxed without their consent.

The English government, which was still acting within its legal rights, failed to realize the intensity of colonial feeling. Grenville was forced to resign, but American taxation had nothing to do with his resignation. The Rockingham administration repealed the Stamp Act in 1766 only because they were not strong enough to enforce it.[2] They accompanied repeal by a declaratory act that parliament had a right to tax the colonies. In 1767 Townshend, chancellor of the exchequer in the administration of Pitt and Grafton, imposed a number of import duties for revenue purposes and showed that he intended to collect them. The Stamp Act had affected legal and commercial documents and newspapers

[1] The Indians had been treated more wisely and with more uniformity by the French than by the English colonists. In 1763 Grenville wanted to deal with the whole Indian problem (which had become more serious with the extension of colonial territory) on broad lines and to give assurances that Indian territory would be respected. The rebellion broke out before those plans could be put into effect.

[2] Horace Walpole wrote of the Act: 'Nothing of note in Parliament but one slight day on the American taxes.'

(which were printed on stamped paper). It therefore annoyed, in particular, lawyers, merchants, and printers. The import duties annoyed everyone. In view of the colonial agitation all the taxes except that on tea were repealed in 1770; this one duty was maintained as an assertion of principle.

The colonists would not recognize the principle. They boycotted the imports of tea. The boycott affected the East India Company; the English government then tried to satisfy both the colonists and the Company by allowing the import of tea free of the entire duty charged in England. The colonists would thus have to pay only the small American duty. In 1773 rioters at Boston threw into the harbour a quantity of tea on an East Indiaman. The whole colony of Massachusetts supported their action. The English reply was to substitute a nominated council for the democratic assembly of Massachusetts. One colony alone would not have been able to resist a measure of this kind but the other colonies could not allow action to be taken against them singly. They called a Continental Congress in 1774; although they did not as yet declare their independence, they repeated their claim not to be taxed by the English parliament and went as far as demanding the withdrawal of the English garrison. The English government could not accept these demands and the colonists could not withdraw them. Therefore war broke out in 1775. In the winter of this year the Americans fought under a flag of their own and in July 1776 a Congress at Philadelphia declared American independence.[1]

War with America might have been avoided at this time if the government of George III had given up not only the attempt to make the colonies pay for their defence but also the assertion of the right to tax them. The Americans might have been defeated if English generalship had been more skilful and if Franklin's able diplomacy had not brought into existence a European coalition against England. Nevertheless the later American term 'manifest destiny' may well be used in a judgment upon these events of immense historical significance. Even if England had resigned all right to tax the colonies, separation would have come sooner or later; possibly without war, though it is unlikely that an English

[1] Another important colonial grievance was the passing of the Quebec Act of 1774 which annexed to Canada the country between the Mississippi and Ohio and the Great Lakes, and also recognized French law and endowed the catholic church.

government would have agreed to peaceful separation. If the Americans had been defeated, the war would still have made them a nation, or rather it would have made them understand that they already were a nation. The English government would have been left with colonists angry under a sense of intolerable wrong and waiting only for a more favourable chance to reassert an independence which could not long have been denied to them.

If the Americans had been compelled to look for an opportunity in the later embarrassment of England, they would have found it during the Revolutionary and Napoleonic wars with France.[1] From 1793 to 1814, with fourteen months' interval after the treaty of Amiens, England was at war. For most of this time she was fighting a military genius who had defeated the lumbering and inefficient armies of Austria and Prussia and was strong enough, until 1813, to beat down every coalition of land forces against him. The length and violence of this war were unexpected. At the outbreak of the French Revolution the younger Pitt had been Prime Minister for nearly six years. Pitt was as masterful as his father, but in a different way. He had plans of financial and administrative reform and believed that he could look forward to a period of peace in which to carry them out. Pitt had been convinced by Adam Smith's *Wealth of Nations* that trade would expand more easily under a relatively free fiscal régime. The first practical result of his policy was a commercial treaty with France in 1786. Even during the earlier stages of the French Revolution he assumed that France would be prevented by internal trouble from undertaking aggressive action.

English opinion in general, forgetting the history of the Commonwealth, was slow to realize that the revolutionary government might be as strongly nationalist and more efficient than the monarchy which it had overthrown. The French advance into the Low Countries and the arrogance of revolutionary diplomacy almost compelled Pitt to go to war, yet national unity, even against a 'traditional' enemy and in the 'traditional' policy of keeping France out of the Low Countries, was not complete until it was clear that

[1] In 1812 the United States went to war with Great Britain over the question of maritime rights. They had similar grievances against France, but English interference with American shipping was greater because the English had more ships than the French with which to enforce a blockade. The English also searched American ships for deserters.

Napoleon was aiming at the conquest of England. The poetry of
Wordsworth is typical of the change in English opinion; at first,
a sense of exultation at the achievement of liberty in France; and
later, the discovery that popular control of national power might
mean, not the peace of nations, but the repudiation of treaties,
territorial aggression, a pitiless exploitation of conquests, and, finally,
military despotism.[1]

The history of this war with France can be told only with reference to a large-scale map. As so often in the wars fought by the
English, the first stages were full of mistakes and failures. For a long
time the strength of France was underestimated in the belief that
economic strategy, such as the capture of West Indian islands,
would win the war. In spite of these early mistakes Pitt was justified
in his boast after Trafalgar that England had saved herself by her
exertions and would save Europe by her example. The persistence
with which the English continued the war, while Continental
coalitions broke down, allowed time for the inevitable weakening
of France and the recovery of confidence elsewhere. The domination of continental Europe by a single nation had proved impracticable for Charles V, for Philip II, and for Louis XIV. It was
even less possible when 'Europe' stretched out over vast spaces of
Russia and when English sea-power had behind it the resources not
of a small and relatively poor kingdom but of an Empire.

The exertions of the English in keeping the mastery of the sea
saved them from invasion and compelled Napoleon to try to ruin
England by cutting off her trade with the Continent.[2] This plan
brought a feverish wealth to certain industries and individuals
in France; it could not be enforced for long against the demand
for English and colonial goods. One of the reasons for Napoleon's
expedition to Russia in 1812 was the refusal of the Tsar to exclude
all trade with England. The Russian victory, which was more than
a victory of the Russian climate, made possible the formation of a
coalition too strong, and too angry, to make peace with Napoleon.

[1] The repressive measures in England during and after the French war should
be considered in the light of these facts. 'Democratic' control was regarded not
merely as a danger to liberty and property but as chauvinist and aggressive.

[2] Napoleon also wanted to give France a start in production by power-driven
machinery. In fact Napoleon himself could not do without English goods. The
greatcoats and boots of the Grand Army of 1812 were largely of English manufacture and were obtained by smuggling at Hamburg.

Thus, although English resistance to Napoleon is only part of the story, it is far more than a single chapter in it. There were moments when England was in the gravest danger. In 1797 her Continental allies had made peace. The Dutch fleet was at French disposition.[1] Ireland was on the point of rebellion. The fleets at Spithead and in the North Sea mutinied. If at this time the French had agreed to reasonable terms, they might have made peace to their advantage and given Napoleon a better start for his imperial career. Nevertheless English recovery at sea was both quick and lasting. The trouble in the fleet had been due mainly to grievances which should have been redressed years earlier; the sailors who had mutinied in the spring won in October the battle of Camperdown against the Dutch. The Irish rebellion was not supported by France. The English fleet, which had left the Mediterranean in 1796 because French invaders had closed the Italian ports and Spain had joined France, came back with Nelson in 1798 and won a great victory at Aboukir Bay.

There was a second period of grave danger after the short-lived treaty of Amiens (1802). In 1803 Napoleon made preparations for the invasion of England from the north coast of France. One of his difficulties was that there was no French port nearer than Brest large enough to take first-class ships of the line. Brest was blockaded by the English; so also were Rochefort and Lorient, where a smaller French fleet was stationed. Another English fleet based on Gibraltar watched Toulon and the entrance to the Mediterranean. Early in 1805 Napoleon planned that the Brest, Rochefort, and Toulon fleets should slip the blockade, unite in the West Indies (where the Spanish fleet would join them) and come back to hold the Channel for an invasion.

This plan failed. The Brest fleet could not get out because the blockade was too close. The small Rochefort fleet went to the West Indies, did not find the Toulon fleet, and came home. The Toulon fleet, followed by Nelson to the West Indies and nearly caught there, did not achieve anything, and turned back with Nelson again close behind it.[2] Nelson sent warning by a fast ship that it was

[1] So also was the Spanish fleet but it was defeated early in the year at the battle of Cape St Vincent.

[2] In July 1805 Nelson wrote in his diary that he had set foot on shore for the first time since 16 June 1803.

coming. Villeneuve, the French admiral, was able to reach Ferrol, but he was headed off from Brest by Calder, and knew that the strategic purpose of his Atlantic crossing had been defeated. He therefore took refuge in Cadiz. Napoleon ordered him to sail thence with the Spanish fleet to protect the French in Italy. Nelson met the two fleets at Trafalgar on October 21.

Napoleon could not replace for a long time the twenty ships of the line which the combined French and Spanish fleets lost at Trafalgar. English sea-power was therefore free to support land operations. Herein lay the importance of the operations which began in the Spanish peninsula during the autumn of 1808. Napoleon was unlikely to commit his whole force in Spain, where he had expected little or no resistance. He could, however, be weakened there by an inferior force using sea communications. After clearing Portugal, Wellington advanced into Spain every year between 1809 and 1812 and diverted the French from the suppression of Spanish guerrilla resistance. He fell back again as the French attacked him in strength. In 1810, when the counter-attack was strongest, he established himself in the lines of Torres Vedras – a triangle of land between the estuary of the Tagus and the sea and covering Lisbon. Only 2,000 yards separated the rear of his position from the French on the south bank of the river where the road from Madrid to Lisbon reached the estuary.[1] In June 1813 Wellington broke the French strength at Vittoria; within five months he had begun the invasion of south-west France.

There was thus a dramatic fitness that the last victory of Waterloo[2] should have been due mainly to the steadfastness of the English.[3] The battle was not won until after the Prussians had come up at the end of the day, but it would certainly have been lost if the English had not held out for long hours of fighting, as they had already held out during nearly twenty years of war.

[1] Owing to the nature of the country there was no direct road down the Tagus valley.

[2] It must remain a matter of speculation whether Napoleon would have lost Waterloo if his troops had been quicker in assembling and if he had not decided to wait several hours in the morning for the sodden cornfields to dry, after a night of thunder and rain, before bringing his artillery into position.

[3] Wellington's army of 68,000 was slightly smaller in numbers and considerably weaker in artillery than that of Napoleon. About a third of Wellington's infantry were British; the greater part were Dutch, Belgian, and German. Some of these Allies behaved badly. Four brigades of British infantry from the Peninsula had been sent to America.

CHAPTER XV

England in the Nineteenth Century

AFTER THE VICTORY of Waterloo contemporary opinion was not optimistic about the condition and prospects of England. Since 1783 the National Debt had increased from £231,000,000 to £861,000,000. Taxation was high. There was social unrest in town and country. Many people feared that a rapidly increasing population might outgrow the means of subsistence. No one foresaw the advance in general prosperity during the next fifty years because no one, or at most only a few scientists and engineers, could envisage the rate of material progress which technical invention would make possible or the liberation of mind which would follow material progress.

Already there was a considerable development of power-driven machinery, especially in the mining and cotton industries. The first steam engines were used for the heavy work of pumping water from mines.[1] The new power was applied early in the cotton industry, because the technical problems set to the inventor were not over-difficult and the demand for cotton goods outran the supply of labour.[2] As yet, however, the other main industries of the country, including agriculture, were carried on much as in 1760.[3] Foreign trade, with the exception of cotton and timber, was still small in bulk compared with its value. There was thus little to suggest the cumulative effects of the new discoveries. Even after the improvement in communications owing to canal-building, it was not obvious that better means of transport would mean still cheaper coal; that cheaper coal[4] would mean more iron, and cheaper

---

[1] See p. 134

[2] It is well known that water-power was employed before steam. There was no steam-loom factory in Manchester in the year of Trafalgar.

[3] On the other hand the knowledge spread by the great 'improving' landlords was slowly producing an effect on methods of farming.

[4] Cheaper coal in country districts also meant that poor families could have more hot meals.

iron more machinery and therefore better methods of coal-mining.

The introduction of railways, or rather the introduction of the locomotive engine and the use of railways – long employed in collieries – for general carriage, changed the outlook of the population towards machines. People saw machines and found them useful. The railways themselves made large demands on the heavy industries; they benefited agriculture by opening new markets for perishable goods[1] and by the cheap transport of manure. Moreover railways showed that material progress might imply more than progress in material things. Children formerly out of daily reach of towns could go to school by train. Cheapness of travel (especially after the railways were compelled to run at least one passenger train a day from terminus to terminus at the rate of a penny a mile) secured that for the poorer classes migration from home did not mean something like permanent exile. Railways also changed the economic structure of the country. They increased the separation of ownership from control in business and industrial enterprises. They offered a safe investment of a kind possible hitherto, with few exceptions, only in land or in government securities.

These things could not be realized at once. The railways were regarded at first as a new kind of turnpike[2] road upon which all comers could use their own engines. The next stage was a charge for the hire of locomotives. As late as 1837–8 a committee of the house of commons thought that the right of private persons to put their own engines on the lines might be extended to the post office. This recommendation was reversed in the following year, but even those who wanted a 'planned development' of a railway system for the country underrated the volume of traffic. One scheme proposed six lines of rails for traffic in and out of London.

Railways were not laid out under government direction. Parliament never initiated a railway bill and did not prevent a good deal of wasteful competition. It was unlikely that parliament would

[1] Railways had over canals the advantage which motor traffic today has over the railways; they provided a closer network and were more accessible to customers. Canal transport was too slow to carry perishable goods for more than short distances.

[2] The turnpike roads (i.e. roads upon which tolls were levied at certain bars or 'turnpikes') dated from the latter part of the seventeenth century. Many of the toll-houses can still be seen along the older main roads of the country.

consider it even feasible to direct the development of railways or that the country would regard such direction as free from the temptations of jobbery. The tendency of nearly all political thinkers as well as of practical men of affairs was to get rid of official control. State control was thought of in terms of the old and inefficient machinery of government because the reform of public administration had lagged behind other improvements. Under the system of 'influence' there could be no proper scrutiny of candidates for official posts. The notion of government paying for itself by means of fees still prevented fair grading of salaries and maintained a body of vested interests opposed to reform. Administrative methods were unbelievably complicated; some of the public accounting in the Exchequer was done in Roman numerals until George IV's reign. There was no annual balanced statement of the national accounts before 1822. The only social service undertaken by the central government in 1815 was the post office. Even this service had been partially farmed out between 1720 and 1769.

The post office was an example of the difficulty of reforming an administrative department. When Rowland Hill – a schoolmaster – published in 1837 a pamphlet on Post Office Reform the charge of sending a letter from London to Edinburgh was $1s.\ 2\frac{1}{2}d.$; the cost of transporting it was one-thirty-sixth of a penny. Time was wasted in collecting on delivery the charge for every letter. Hill's suggestions for a uniform penny postage and for postage stamps were opposed by the post office, but the calculations upon which Hill worked ought to have been made years earlier by the postal authorities. The reasons for the distrust and impatience of official control were therefore practical. Manufacturers and business-men who were learning the 'pursuit of rational ends by rational means', or inventive thinkers, like Bentham, who spent his life in trying to free society from the weight of prejudice and tradition, were bound to distrust government interference and to try to get every social activity, including the administration of the poor law, out of official hands. This attitude has been summed up as one of *laisser-faire*.[1] The term may serve if it is not taken to mean an indifference to the reform of political institutions or complacency over social evils.

There was 'complacency' in England, mainly after 1860, and with reason, in view of the astonishing results of fifty years of effort,

[1] A chance phrase used by a French economist in the eighteenth century.

but it was not complacency over clearly demonstrated social evil. Standards of comparison in this matter should be with the eighteenth and not with the twentieth century. Against the background of an earlier age the Victorian era appears as a vast and unexpected awakening of conscience and an attempt, however imperfect, to apply the Christian ethic to modern conditions. Many things which today seem intolerable were accepted as without remedy. Such things should have been thought intolerable at the time, but a growing sense of responsibility for, and capacity to deal with social misery, was one of the novelties of the age. Thus the bad housing of the poor was nothing new; there was something new in the fact that parliament should set up an inquiry into the housing and general conditions of the working class on the assumption that measures of improvement were possible. The slums between Westminster and the City had existed for centuries – the desire to avoid passing through them had been one reason for the use of the Thames as a highway for passenger traffic. The Factory Act of 1802 limited the employment of pauper apprentices to twelve hours a day; the act of 1819 extended this limitation to all children under sixteen employed in cotton mills.[1] The significance of these acts is not that they fixed what was obviously too long a working day but that until 1802 no law had protected a child from exploitation in factory work.

The early factory acts were largely evaded because there was no inspection to secure their enforcement. Here again the lack of administrative technique was not new. There was no profession of factory inspector just as there were no building regulations to prevent the erection of back-to-back houses without sanitation or water-supply, and no public authorities competent to secure the retention of open spaces for recreation in towns. There could be no good water-supply or drainage system until the invention of cheap pipes and of the traps and gullies unknown to the plumbing of the eighteenth century. Liverpool in 1847 was the first city to appoint a medical officer; the appointment was not made on the initiative of a State department but as the result of the efforts of a few public-spirited citizens sensible enough to see that their own interests as well as those of the poor were affected and that the measures necessary to prevent epidemic diseases could not be left to hap-

[1] The employment of children under nine was forbidden.

hazard charity.[1] Private charity could not cope with the large-scale problems resulting from the displacement of hand-work, especially in the various branches of weaving, or with the problem of immigrant Irish labourers[2] accustomed to the lowest standards of life, but there was no machinery of State competent to deal with either of these causes of misery.

The ultimate test of the physical level, though not of the happiness of a society, must be its mortality rates. On this test the remarkable feature of the nineteenth century is the increase of the population. The figures for England and Wales are roughly nine million in 1801, twenty-one million in 1851, thirty-two million in 1901. During the early years of the century contemporaries attributed this increase to the employment of children in cotton mills (the larger the family, the larger the income) or to the subsidy of agricultural wages out of poor rates. The increase was, however, due less to a rise in the birth-rate than to a fall in the death-rate, especially in the death-rate of babies and young children. From about 1790 to 1830 the birth-rate was more or less stable. Then came a fall, a rise between 1850 and 1870, and another fall. Even if in some respects life was less worth living, conditions of food, housing, clothing, and general health tended to prolong existence beyond the limits known to earlier generations.

The facts are still not fully investigated, but evidence of the relation between wages and the cost of living also seems to point towards improvement. In the country the average labourer was probably not worse off in 1830 than in 1790; the average manual worker in the towns, when in employment, was possibly a little better off. Money wages and prices rose between 1850 and 1870: the rise in wages was about 10 per cent higher than the rise in prices. This tendency for 'real wages' to increase lasted until 1900, when 'real wages' were about double the figure for 1850. Between 1900 and 1914 there was a rise of more than 10 per cent in the cost of living; wages also increased, but at a slower rate.

[1] The analysis may be pushed a stage further. Although the fact of infection, attributed to atmospheric impurity, had always been known, the spread of disease by micro-organisms could not be established scientifically until there were microscopes for their detection.

[2] The scale of this immigration is still not realized. In 1871 nearly one-eighth of the population of Scotland was of Irish origin - one-sixteenth was Irish-born. In 1841 the Irish-born population of English and Wales was just under 300,000, and in 1871 over 560,000.

Averages, especially for the period 1815–50, do not reveal the plight of the lowest-paid workers or of the unemployed. As late as 1901 Rowntree's investigations at York disclosed that 43·4 per cent of the wage-earning class, or about a quarter of the population, lived on incomes insufficient to meet bare physical needs.[1] None the less the amount and area of misery had diminished as the years passed. Conditions of labour had also improved. Since this improvement was due largely to the collective bargaining of the trade unions it was mainly in hours of work; housing conditions could not be improved by strikes. By 1850 the textile industries had secured a ten-and-a-half-hour day and a sixty-hour week. Twelve years later the engineering industries obtained a nine-hour day. The general aim was an eight-hour day; this aim was reached between 1885 and 1900 in many industries. After 1870 there was a continuous increase in the social services. Elementary education was free after 1870 to the children of parents who could not afford to pay fees, and free to all after 1891. Hospital services improved, indoor and outdoor entertainments were cheaper; there were more open spaces in towns and easier means of getting to them. Old age pensions were begun on a small scale in 1909; two years later a national insurance scheme covered sickness for all workers and unemployment relief for a large number.

At the end of the century the better-paid and better-organized manual workers were gaining a sense of their power and some knowledge of practical political action. This experience came through the trade unions. Working-class movements in the early part of the century had failed because their organization depended too much upon immediate enthusiasm. Political and economic action by working men had been difficult before the repeal in 1824–5 of the laws against 'combinations'; the legal status and degree of freedom of trade unions remained uncertain for another fifty years. In 1875 an act passed by Disraeli's government laid down that a combination of persons might lawfully do anything, for example, peaceful picketing, which was not punishable if done by an individual. Nevertheless after 1825 there existed a legal distinction between trade union action and conspiracy;

---

[1] A less detailed investigation by Charles Booth in 1888 gave a slightly higher figure – 30·7 per cent – for the proportion of the population of London living on or below the 'poverty line'.

the politics of the working class were no longer equated with mob violence.

It was indeed inevitable that working-class aims should first be expressed in grandiose plans put forward without solid backing or realist calculation of the prospects of success. The chartist movement is an example of this political immaturity. Chartism arose out of disillusion at the results of the reform act of 1832; the new poor law which was the first general[1] social measure of the reformed parliament was a chilling response to hopes of a less harsh attitude. The 'People's Charter', first presented to parliament in 1839 in the form of a large petition, asked for universal male suffrage, equal electoral districts, the abolition of the property qualification for members of parliament, vote by ballot, and the payment of members. Most of these demands have since been accepted. There was little chance that any of them would be granted by the upper and middle classes in 1839, especially when they were intended as the means of establishing the working class in political power.

The chartist leaders were themselves divided; some were mere cranks who edged their way into the movement. The wiser among them could not prevent their followers from falling under the attraction of an Irish demagogue, Feargus O'Connor,[2] who produced a bogus scheme of land settlement. Throughout its tragic history chartism secured the loyalty of thousands of poor men; it was never a serious threat to the established order – only a small minority of chartists believed in revolutionary action – and cannot be said to have accelerated a single measure of benefit to the working class.

The relatively small number of skilled workmen did not support chartism in its later stages. They concentrated on their own organizations and, through the efforts and ability of a few leaders from their own class, built up strong craft unions as a preliminary to societies on a wider basis. The first Trade Union Congress met in 1868. In 1871 the congress elected a parliamentary committee. The reason was not merely that the extension of the franchise in

[1] The Factory Act of 1833, though of great importance (since for the first time it provided for inspectors to enforce its regulations), applied only to textile factories.

[2] O'Connor was neither a working man nor (as he claimed) of ancient royal Irish descent.

F

1867 had nearly doubled the electorate of England and Wales. Parliamentary action was necessary to assist in raising the condition of the great majority of unskilled workers and sweated labour still outside the trade unions.

In order to be effective this action had to be based upon a positive programme, with a theory separating the working-class movement from the 'half-way' programmes of social reform advocated by the radical wings of the liberals and conservatives. Some of the early trade unionists and chartists had advocated an extreme but doctrinaire form of socialism and had made use of Ricardo's theory of rent to denounce unearned increment. After the collapse of chartism and the failure of the European revolutionary movements of 1848 the English trade unions had concerned themselves little with theory; socialism, as such, was almost reintroduced into England about 1880; the revival was due not to Marx[1] but to the American, Henry George. George was not a socialist; his book *Progress and Poverty* (1879) was an exposition of the 'single tax' theory, i.e. a levy on unearned increment from land. The immense increase in urban land values in England was indeed obvious and the taxation of unearned increment from this source was as much a part of the radical as of the socialist programme, but it provided a starting-point from which trade union politicians could follow the broader programme expounded by the Fabian Society. *Fabian Essays in Socialism*[2] (1889) had a very wide circulation; the new ideas were given greater publicity by a journalist, Robert Blatchford. Blatchford's own book, *Merrie England* (1894), sold over a million copies and his Sunday paper, *The Clarion*, was one of the first examples of clever and continuous political propaganda covering every field of the average man's activities.

The third extension of the franchise in the nineteenth century added (1884) over a million and a half voters to an electorate in England and Wales of about two and a half million. The attempt

[1] French exiles in London after the suppression of the Commune in 1871 had some effect in forming socialist opinion. Marx, although he lived long in London, had a very small direct influence upon English working-class organization or theory. Hyndman, who founded the Social Democratic Federation in 1881, had read Marx in a French translation. William Morris, the founder of the Socialist League, never read him, but Morris's socialism was much more an attack upon the ugliness of industrial civilization than a reasoned economic programme.

[2] The authors included Bernard Shaw, Sidney Webb, Graham Wallas, and Mrs Annie Besant.

to win these votes for the return of a labour party distinct from the radical wing of the liberals was not at once practicable. The Independent Labour Party, founded in 1893, was more of a co-ordinating and propagandist body than a fighting organization. Such an organization in the full sense of the term was not established until 1900. The Trade Union Congress was then mainly responsible for its existence and for a political levy for its expenses. This 'Labour Representation Committee', with Ramsay Mac-Donald as its first secretary, came into being too late to have much effect upon the general election of 1900. In 1906 its supporters won twenty-nine seats and could designate themselves as a party.[1]

Such are the bare facts and dates marking the emergence of a new class, or as writers in the eighteenth century would have put it, a new 'interest', as one of the competitors for political power. They are facts which had little prominence at the time. Contemporaries could not be expected to see the importance of the trade union movement of the middle years of the century, just as the contemporaries of Edward I did not realize the significance of the summons of the third estate to parliament. Furthermore the labour movement itself can be understood only in the general setting of English life; *Fabian Essays in Socialism* were written for an environment which differed as much from that of chartism as the environment of Pope had differed from that of Milton. The change for the better in the nineteenth century as in earlier centuries had come about for many reasons; no one class or party can take the whole responsibility for retarding it or the whole credit for bringing it about.

[1] Twenty-four other 'Labour members' were elected in 1906. The 'Labour Representation Committee' and the trade union movement in general had a special motive for securing direct parliamentary representation after 1901 when a decision of the court in the Taff Vale Case laid down that a trade union was liable to pay damages for wrongs done by its agents. The decision was upheld by the house of lords, and, in the case at issue, the Amalgamated Society of Railway Servants paid £42,000 in costs and damages.

CHAPTER XVI

Free Trade: Sir Robert Peel and Lord Palmerston

IF CONTEMPORARY OPINION were regarded as evidence of the absolute importance of events, the reform act of 1832 would be the greatest political measure of the nineteenth century. There was something revolutionary about an act of parliament which enfranchised new towns, increased the electorate by 50 per cent and at least in the boroughs cut at the roots of the old system of influence. The popular agitation which forced the surrender of vested interests came near to revolutionary excitement and the consequences of parliamentary reform extended far into other established institutions. The first reformed parliament after 1832 remodelled the municipal corporations of England and did away with the bumbledom and oligarchical control which prevented the improvement of towns. The worst financial abuses in the Church of England were remedied between 1835 and 1840 by a redistribution of the incomes of the richest episcopal sees and the prohibition of pluralities. The reform of the poor law was on harsh lines, but the abolition of the system – never universal – of subsidizing agricultural wages out of poor rates was ultimately in the interest of the country labourers. Without the creation of new units of administration under a central authority the relief of the poor could not have been freed from local abuses and disastrous variations of scale. The fault lay not in the plan of poor law reform but in the niggardliness with which relief was given, and in the unimaginative attitude of mind which talked of 'pauperism' in terms of disgrace, and not of very poor men, women and children.

The excitement of the reform bill was soon forgotten. The country became accustomed to greater changes. These changes were least in the outward setting of politics. The social composition of the house of commons altered little for two generations. In 1833

217 members of parliament were sons of peers or baronets; in 1860 the number was 180, and in 1880, 170. The disappearance of the pocket borough increased the number of contested seats and reduced, although it did not at once eliminate, the more obvious forms of bribery. Political appeals to the electorate were not made in any new way. Party organization hardly existed in the constituencies. The Carlton Club, founded in 1832, concerned itself after 1832 with the registration of voters. The radicals set up a registration office in 1835. The conservative central office began in 1852 to keep a list of approved parliamentary candidates. Party caucuses came into existence only after 1868, and then almost by accident as a means of organizing votes in order to win two seats in three-member constituencies. In 1868 local conservative committees were linked up in a national union; there was no liberal federation until 1877. Politicians of the first rank did not address meetings outside their constituencies or appeal to the whole country with a programme. Peel's Tamworth Manifesto of 1834, which is generally regarded as the first programme of this kind, took the form of an address to his own constituents. It was a statement of principles and did not mention the name of a political party or discuss in detail any proposals.

Nevertheless Peel himself changed the character of English politics. For the first time the Prime Minister was the son of a manufacturer. Peel was conscious, one might almost say self-conscious, about his origin[1] and felt a certain contempt for the magnates of his own party. He led them by right of intellectual power and administrative grasp. Peel lacked the imaginative insight of the greatest statesmen, but he always knew the next thing to be done. As home secretary he established the metropolitan police force and thus solved the problem of maintaining public order without military control. His reform of the criminal law removed the savage penalties which had accumulated during the eighteenth century; the reform of prison administration at last did away with the worst abuses.

Peel was twice Prime Minister; his first period of office lasted

[1] Melbourne, whom Peel twice displaced, is generally regarded as a typical whig aristocrat. He was a sensitive, fastidious man, distinguished in mind though narrow in his sympathies, but he was not a member of one of the great whig families. His grandfather, Sir Matthew Lamb, was the son of an attorney of Southwell.

only a few months. In his second term (from 1841 to 1846) he cut down by more than half the number of articles subject to import duty and lowered the rate of tax on nearly all the remainder. He made good the loss of revenue by an income tax. He thought that this tax would be a temporary measure because increased consumption resulting from greater freedom of trade would balance the remission of duties. He was wrong about the temporary nature of income tax, but right about the results of free trade. From a party point of view, however, the last of Peel's reforms – the repeal of the corn laws – appeared to be a disaster.

The occasion of repeal was the failure of the Irish potato crop and of the English harvest in the autumn of 1845. Peel had admitted, however, before this time that he could not answer the arguments against protection. Since 1842 these arguments had been popularized by Cobden and the Anti-Corn Law League often in the crude form of an attack on landlords. The landlords in return had attacked factory abuses. In his refusal to continue the protection enjoyed by the landlords since the corn law of 1815 had shielded them against foreign competition Peel broke the unity of the conservative party. As so often, the importance of repeal was exaggerated by each side. A bad harvest in England generally meant a bad harvest in northern Europe, and therefore a fairly high price for imported corn. Owing to the rise in world prices after the discovery of gold in California and elsewhere the price fell very little.[1] Bread was not much cheaper; agriculture was not ruined. Disraeli, the leader of the attack on Peel, dropped protection before he became Prime Minister and during his last tenure of office did nothing to prevent the ruin which came to agriculture not directly from the repeal of 1846 but from the competition of American wheat after 1875.

The break-up of the conservative party which Peel himself had founded on the ruins of the old toryism resulted in an instability of parties for some twenty years. The old whig party, which had regarded the reform act of 1832 as the last stage in political evolution, was also without a programme. Hence majorities were small and composite, and the leading men in the house of commons could themselves change sides without discredit. Gladstone, who had

[1] The quinquennial average price of wheat was 54/9 in 1841–5 and 54/8 in 1870–5. In 1884 the price fell to 35/8 and in 1894 to 22/10.

supported Peel in 1846, joined Palmerston's administration in 1859 after voting against the motion which had overthrown the previous government. Reforms of the highest importance were carried through during this period, but their importance was hardly realized by parliament. Gladstone was chancellor of the exchequer from the end of 1852 to the early part of 1855, and again from 1859 until the summer of 1866. His budgets completed the change to free trade. In 1855 the long-delayed improvement of the civil service was made possible by the adoption of the principle of entry by examination. For a few years the examination was only a qualifying test; it then became a limited competition which, after 1870, was open to all. The rise in professional standards also created a demand for improved secondary education. Two royal commissions in 1861 and 1864 investigated the older public schools and grammar schools. The great public schools had already been reformed through the initiative of a few remarkable head masters of whom Thomas Arnold of Rugby is the best known. Although these reforms, together with the recommendations of the Commission of 1861, did not affect the 'class basis' of the schools, they introduced new subjects and new methods of teaching. Men like Arnold had begun to change the relationship between boys and masters, and to substitute more reasonable ideas of discipline based largely – perhaps too largely – on the grant of authority to the boys themselves.

The extension of higher education to women was also the work of a few individuals, such as Dorothea Beale, who became Principal of Cheltenham Ladies' College in 1858. The reform of the universities of Oxford and Cambridge[1] was impossible without State action. The vested interests of life fellows, the autonomy of the colleges, the conservatism of most academic teachers, and the close association of the universities with the Church did not make change easy. Nevertheless the abuse of college funds was abolished and the religious tests limited to admission to fellowship and to theological degrees. In 1871 fellowships were thrown open.

Elementary education was dealt with less completely. It is harsh

[1] University College, London, founded in 1828, as a nonsectarian university of London, was incorporated with King's College as a university in 1836. The university of Durham was founded in 1832 with a grant from the revenues of the cathedral. Owens College, Manchester, was endowed as an undenominational body in 1851.

to say without qualification that the collective exclusiveness and mutual jealousies of church and chapel blocked the way to improvement. At a time when most people thought it unnecessary or dangerous to educate the children of the poor, religious societies had begun the work and had paid for it. No State grant was made until 1833; even then the figure was only £20,000. Technical education also developed slowly although a certain stimulus was given to it by the Great Exhibition[1] of 1851. This backwardness was one of the results of English predominance in manufacture; factory and workshop were regarded as the best schools of training.[2]

There was no falling-off in the inventiveness and progress of English industry. The commercial development of the Bessemer[3] steel process after 1856 changed in a few years the character of the age from one of iron to one of steel. This transformation is perhaps the most important single fact of the first administration of Lord Palmerston. The Prime Minister himself could hardly have been expected to take this view. Palmerston was born five years before the French Revolution. He had sat in sixteen parliaments and had been in office almost continuously since 1807. On domestic questions he was, like most of the great whigs, open to conviction and ready to correct manifest abuses. On the whole, however, the 'condition of England' meant to him not the state of the labouring poor but the place of England in the world. Palmerston's claims for his country were large. He did not practise understatement or express himself in half-tones. His popularity at home came partly from his openness of manner but above all from his plain-speaking to foreigners. The foreigners found such brusque assertions intolerable; their distrust increased when to Palmerston as Prime Minister was added Lord John Russell as Foreign Secretary.[4] Russell had most of Palmerston's prejudices without his common sense.

A good deal of this foreign criticism may be discounted. Palmer-

[1] The building in which this Exhibition was housed and which was afterwards moved to Sydenham Hill as the Crystal Palace was one of the few Victorian attempts at functional architecture.

[2] One reason for the more rapid development of technical education in Germany was the lack of opportunity for this practical training.

[3] Bessemer continued the long tradition of contributions made to English prosperity by French Huguenots.

[4] In the language of Queen Victoria, 'these two dreadful old men', or of Lord Granville, 'the two old boys'.

ston was as a rule a better judge of English interests than the Prince Consort[1] who had fixed in Queen Victoria's mind the opinions which he had learned from his tutor and life-long adviser, Baron von Stockmar. In general the abuse of Palmerston came from the European opponents of 'free government'; the fact that English economic interests were furthered by the extension of political liberties abroad is not an argument in support of despotism.

Palmerston indeed was less concerned than he might have been with the more novel economic factors in foreign policy. The investment of British capital abroad was regarded as a matter for the investors' private judgment. The British Government interfered to protect merchants and trade routes but not bondholders. To Palmerston and his contemporaries the business of diplomacy was primarily to secure a peaceful world. A peaceful world depended upon a balance of power in Europe. Therefore the aim of British policy was to secure this equilibrium and to assist in removing possible causes of disturbance.

This policy was not new; it was the only policy open to a nation of traders possessing vast colonial territories and defending them by sea-power without a large military land force. Palmerston's method of improvisation was also the only method open to him. After the Napoleonic war Castlereagh had hoped much from regular meetings of the Great Powers; within a short time it was clear that the Continental monarchies wanted to use these meetings as occasions for interference in the affairs of small States, that is to say, to use them for the suppression of constitutional movements of which English opinion approved. After Castlereagh's death in 1822 Canning kept clear of the 'European Areopagus', and left England free to act as English interests might determine. One of these interests was in maintaining the independence of the rebel American colonies of Spain. Canning therefore took the lead in the negotiations which were followed by President Monroe's message of December 1823 to Congress that no European interference would be tolerated in the American continents. This message would have been little more than a gesture if English sea-power had not been

[1] Prince Albert of Saxe-Coburg–Gotha was a man of second-rate ability and superficial education to whom England owes a great deal. He was more serious-minded than most English politicians of the early years of the Queen's reign and his influence on the Queen helped to regain for the monarchy the respect which it had lost under George IV and had not recovered under William IV.

strong enough to cut off attempts at interference in the Americas. A few years later the fact of sea-power made it possible – and necessary – for England to secure the independence of Belgium[1] and once again to prevent the control of the estuary of the Scheldt from falling into the hands of a Great Power.

Sea-power was, however, of less use in dealing with a more distant threat to the European balance of power and to British interests in the Near and Middle East. In the eighteenth century the Eastern Question had been the problem of Poland. After 1774, when Russia had obtained large and dangerously vague rights of interference in favour of the Christian subjects of the Sultan, Russian control over the declining Ottoman Empire became a possibility. The development of British power in India and the increased importance of Levantine and Eastern markets made English opinion extremely sensitive to every advance of Russian power at Turkish expense. Moreover the overland route[2] to India lay through territory under Turkish sovereignty. Thus the maintenance of the Ottoman Empire became a leading feature of British foreign policy, but there was more than an incongruity in defending the rule of the Sultan over unwilling Christian subjects in Europe. The Greek rebellion which broke out in 1821 had been an embarrassment both to Russia and to England. Alexander of Russia disliked supporting rebels against a legitimate authority. England disliked supporting a tyrant against justifiable rebellion.

The Greek question was settled, or half-settled, by a compromise. The main problem still had to be faced and the only Continental war in which England was engaged between 1815 and 1914 broke out over the question of Turkish sovereignty. Years afterwards Gladstone described this war as 'just but unnecessary'. The judgment is reasonably fair. Russia, if left unchallenged, would have gained control over Turkey, yet the challenge need not have taken the form of war. In 1831–3, and again in 1839–40, when the

[1] At the Congress of Vienna the former Austrian Netherlands were joined with the kingdom of the United Netherlands. The reason for this union was a desire to strengthen the Belgians against a possible revival of French aggression. In 1830 the Belgians denounced the union and set up an independent state – the kingdom of Belgium.

[2] There were two 'overland' routes; one of them through Syria to the Mesopotamian rivers, and the other across the isthmus of Suez. The route from Suez down the Red Sea was much less important until steamships could go long distances without replenishing their supplies of coal and water.

Sultan came near to losing his empire to a rebellious vassal, Mehemet Ali, Pasha of Egypt, a war between the European Powers was avoided by diplomatic action. The crisis of 1852–4 might have been settled peacefully if the British Government had been clearer as well as firmer in their policy and if the Russians had been more moderate in their demands. England had not provoked this crisis; it had arisen out of Napoleon III's assertion of ancient French rights over the Holy Places of Palestine. Russia put forward much larger counter-claims which would have opened the way to complete domination of Turkish domestic and foreign policy.

On this issue the war was fought. The fighting was inconclusive because the war ended before either side had brought more than a small part of its resources into play. The Crimean campaign justified the high reputation of the rank and file of the British army, but added nothing to the reputation of its commanders and revealed on the administrative side an astonishing incompetence and backwardness. It is probable that this incompetence was no greater than in the initial stages of earlier wars; for the first time the facts were known quickly and fully owing to the presence of war correspondents in the battle area. The increase in size and circulation of newspapers gave the reports of these correspondents a wider publicity and the general rise in administrative standards made the shortcomings of the military organization more intolerable.

Palmerston had not been responsible for the conduct of the negotiations which failed to prevent the Crimean War. By popular consent he became Prime Minister when public anger at the military confusion forced the resignation of Aberdeen.[1] Except for a short time between February 1858 and June 1859 Palmerston remained Prime Minister until his death in 1865. His support of Italian nationalism was popular in England and allowed the success of Garibaldi; the British fleet could easily have stopped Garibaldi's Redshirts from crossing to the mainland from Sicily. The two minor wars – they were hardly more than punitive expeditions – against China in 1840–2 and 1858–60, appear as examples of Palmerston's high-handedness. He defended his policy

[1] Aberdeen hated war too much to take the firm line which alone might have kept the peace. He was the only English Prime Minister – except the duke of Wellington – in the nineteenth century who had seen war at first hand; his hatred of it went back to the sight of the battlefield of Leipzig in 1813.

in terms of exaggerated patriotism, but, taking all the circumstances into account, it is doubtful whether war could have been avoided except by the impracticable alternatives of the cessation of trade with China, or surrender to fantastic Chinese claims.

Palmerston was more careful in his attitude towards North and South in the American Civil War. At the outbreak of this war, when both sides still accepted slavery, English opinion was divided. After Lincoln's edict of emancipation in January 1863 practically the whole of England favoured the North. There were no outstanding questions of dispute with the United States. Since the war of 1812–14 Anglo-American relations had been settled on a basis of cold and reluctant common sense. If the reluctance was mainly on the American side, the reason was partly that most of the matters concerned were boundary disputes which touched American opinion more sharply than they could touch opinion in England. During the Civil War dangerous ill-feeling was caused in America and England over the question of maritime rights. The Northern Government angered British opinion by arresting envoys from the southern states on a British ship. The British Government was accused, with considerable reason, by the North of culpable negligence in allowing privateers to leave British ports. These gusts of anger mattered less because Palmerston and his Cabinet were agreed that 'the only thing for us to do seems to be to lie on our oars, and to give no pretext to the Washingtonians to quarrel with us'.

The maintenance of the unity of the United States was the most important issue in world politics during Palmerston's tenure of office as Prime Minister. The disputed succession to the Duchies of Schleswig and Holstein – a question of minor significance in itself – appears in retrospect as a turning-point in European history since it resulted in the first, and, indirectly, the second and third of the wars which established Germany as the greatest military Power in Europe and Prussia as the controlling force in Germany. Palmerston, who had fought his first general parliamentary election in the year of the Prussian defeat of Jena, was unlikely to regard Prussia as a greater danger to world peace than France. Nevertheless, if he had had his way, he would have prevented the detachment of the Duchies from Denmark and the annexation of the naval port of Kiel by Prussia. Public opinion, however, in England was unwilling to go to war and Palmerston himself knew that England could fight a Continental war only with France as an ally. At the same time he was afraid of a French alliance because he thought that Napoleon III might use it to gain territory in the Rhineland.

Palmerston died before the second and third stages in the aggrandizement of Prussia-Germany. When the Franco-Prussian war began in 1870, English sympathies inclined more to Prussia than France. The victory of Prussia came as a surprise and the harshness of the peace terms imposed on France was generally condemned. No political leader in England seems to have realized that these terms would have the effect of making a Franco-German combination against England impossible for many years to come.

CHAPTER XVII

Mr Gladstone and Ireland: Imperialism: The South African War

AT THE END of 1867 Gladstone became leader of the liberal party; two months later Disraeli succeeded Derby as Prime Minister of a conservative government. For the first time in the nineteenth century the leaders of the two great parties were men born after 1800. For the first time also for many years each party had a leader of outstanding political ability. Gladstone was more inclined by temperament to discipline and administrative order. He was, except on rare occasions, less incisive in phrase but always more magnificent in oratory than Disraeli. Moreover he was a very strong man, while Disraeli, who was only five years older, lost after 1875 a great deal of his vigour. Disraeli had a more difficult road to high office than Gladstone, since he had to overcome much prejudice, some of it due to his flamboyance. Although Gladstone made too much use of righteousness as a political argument in doubtful cases and Disraeli assumed too easily that vague general ideas could take the place of principles, each of the two men had a certain nobility of mind. Gladstone impressed contemporaries more deeply, but, for better or worse, there were more elements in Disraeli's policy which could be described as prophetic.

The balance of ability between parties and the inexperience of the new electors enfranchised under the Reform Act of 1867 were among the reasons for the 'swing of the pendulum' which produced a large majority for the liberals in 1868, for the conservatives in 1874, and for the liberals again in 1880. From this time the Irish question brought another period of instability; Gladstone's policy of home rule divided his party much as Peel's policy of free trade had divided the conservatives.

The Irish question in the first half of the nineteenth century had been one of an increasing population pressing upon a limited amount of land. It is doubtful whether improved methods of cultivation and more humane conditions of tenure could have solved the problem. The population of Ireland rose from over six million in 1815 to eight and a half million in 1840. The standard of life of the peasantry was very low; most Irish peasant families lived mainly on potatoes. Hence the failure of the potato crop in 1845 and 1846 brought terrible famine. Responsibility for inadequate measures of relief cannot be laid with fairness entirely upon the English Government, but in the last resort Irish opinion could not place it anywhere else, since the English parliament had refused to carry out a revolution in Irish land tenure or to permit the Irish to undertake this revolution for themselves. After the famine the economic position began slowly to improve. About two million Irish emigrated – mainly to America – between 1847 and 1861. They left Ireland with bitter hatred of English rule and transmitted this hate to a younger generation which knew nothing of the change for the better in English policy. In 1858 a society, known as the Fenian[1] brotherhood, was founded in the United States. The Fenians gained recruits from disbanded Irish soldiers after the American Civil War. They planned revolution in Ireland, but had little active support from the Irish peasants. A few outrages in England did the Fenians and their cause more harm than good.

The failure of Fenianism led Gladstone to the conclusion that if the main grievances of the Irish were remedied, Ireland might be reconciled. If the Act of 1869, disestablishing the Irish Church and the Land Act of 1870 had been passed a generation earlier, they might have had the consequences for which Gladstone hoped. Even so remedial measures passed by an English parliament would probably not have weighed much against the long history of Anglo-Irish antagonism. In 1829 the agitation directed by Daniel O'Connell had secured catholic emancipation; O'Connell himself regarded emancipation as a step towards the repeal of the union and the re-establishment of an Irish parliament in Dublin. Before his death O'Connell was regarded by a younger generation as too moderate; the nationalist movement throughout Europe affected Young Ireland as it affected Young Italy. English reforms in Ireland were always too late, but the trouble was not merely a matter of timing.

The English parliament after 1870 did far more to save Irish than

[1] The name is taken from the Fianna, or armed force, of Irish legend.

English agriculture. Yet once again the *damnosa hereditas* of centuries blinded Irish and English alike to any cool examination of the facts. In the year of the Land Act a 'Home Government Association of Ireland' was founded in Dublin. In 1874 fifty-nine 'home rulers' were returned to the house of commons. Four years later Charles Stewart Parnell[1] became leader of this Irish party. Parnell's methods of organized obstruction of business in the house of commons and of organized resistance in Ireland compelled the English Government to concentrate upon Irish affairs. In the last resort these tactics were mistaken. Parnell forgot that there might be an English as well as an Irish patriotism; he also made the mistake of assuming that the English view of the rule of law was mere humbug. Irish agrarian crime shocked English opinion, and the violence of Parnell's hatred of England was more of an embarrassment than a help in persuading an English electorate that the grant of home rule would not endanger the security of Great Britain.

Hence, when Gladstone became convinced, after another Land Act in 1881, that home rule was the only solution of the Irish question, he could not carry the whole of his party with him. The home rule bill of 1886 was defeated by 30 votes; the majority against it included 93 liberals and among them was Joseph Chamberlain. The liberals were then defeated at a general election. Before they returned to office Parnell was dead. A second home rule bill in 1893 was defeated in the house of lords; Gladstone's colleagues forced him to accept the defeat. On a long view it might be said that the cause of home rule had been won, since a majority in the house of commons had voted for it and the time would come when the lords would be unable to resist popular feeling.

The sequel to this defeat was Gladstone's retirement in 1894.[2] Lord Rosebery took his place as Prime Minister but was unable to keep a majority in parliament for more than fifteen months. The

---

[1] Parnell's father was an Anglo-Irish landlord; his mother was American. A year before Parnell's death his political career was wrecked by the discovery that he was living with the wife of a Captain O'Shea. Neither Irish catholics nor English nonconformists would allow conduct of this kind in the private life of a political leader. These events, however, did not decide the fate of the home rule bill.

[2] Gladstone's retirement could not have been long delayed; he was 84, and although his superb constitution never failed him, his sight and hearing were beginning to be a trouble.

conservatives and liberal unionists[1] then formed a government and held power under Lord Salisbury and later under Balfour. The liberals were returned in the elections of 1906 but already the labour party had begun to encroach upon liberalism in many industrial areas. At the other end of the scale most of the English whigs had left the liberal party on the home rule issue; their defection made it more necessary for the liberals to depend upon Welsh, Irish, and Scottish votes. Only in 1906 was there a liberal majority in the English constituencies. At this election the conservatives would have lost fewer seats if they had adopted a programme of social reform.[2] During the last quarter of the nineteenth century and to some extent earlier the conservative party had for a time taken the lead in domestic legislation of a social kind. They were less dependent upon the manufacturing interest and less convinced of the merits of *laisser-faire;* the landowning class, with its traditions of local government, retained something of the old paternal sense of administrative responsibility. Disraeli was not less sincere in his concern over the 'condition of England' because he realized that there were votes to be gained by a party interested in matters of public health.

The Public Health and Housing Acts of 1875 were conservative measures; Joseph Chamberlain, as radical mayor of Birmingham, worked more easily with the conservative ministers in London than with his own liberal colleagues when he was a member of Gladstone's 1880 administration. Between 1885 and 1895 the liberals were so much occupied with the Irish question that they had little time for a broad programme of domestic social reform. Salisbury and Balfour therefore had a chance of reverting to the policy of Disraeli. Their failure to do so revealed a flaw in temper and imagination. Under Salisbury's leadership conservatism tended merely to 'conserve'. Salisbury's cool, unheroic wisdom suited the direction of foreign policy but was too much detached from the details of

---

[1] The 'liberal unionists' who had left Gladstone continued to vote with the conservatives. The term 'unionist' came into use to designate both sections of this combination. The term was applied officially down to 1914, but the conservatives were much the larger of the two sections, and, especially after the original 'seceders' from the liberal party had died or retired, the general appellation 'conservative' reasserted itself.

[2] The most important social measure of the Balfour administration – the Education Act of 1902 – was, from a party point of view, a liability, since it failed to satisfy the nonconformists.

ordinary life. Balfour was more to be blamed from the point of view of tactics. He was a younger man, who might have felt the generous indignation of his time at social evils which thirty or forty years earlier had still seemed part of the nature of things.

The unionist government, however, was not overthrown on the issue of domestic reform but on two questions: the introduction of Chinese labour into the South African gold mines and the abandonment of free trade. Each of these questions arose out of the imperialism of the later nineteenth century. The significance of British colonial expansion was not understood for a long time after 1815. The revolt of the South American colonies of Spain and Portugal seemed to confirm the view that colonies 'dropped off the tree when they were ripe'. British interests were more in markets, such as those of South America, than in costly territorial acquisitions. The West Indies were tarnished with slave labour. Cape Colony was a naval base and port of call, Australia a penal settlement.[1] New Zealand was not formally annexed until 1840. Canada was of importance for lumber, furs, and fish, but there was little public concern about the development of the country. The English people indeed showed little imagination about their overseas possessions. Neither Byron nor Shelley in their writings about liberty ever mentioned the freedom of Englishmen overseas. The colonies counted for little in English politics. The whigs cared more for colonial patronage than for colonial development. Peel made no reference to the Empire in his Tamworth manifesto. Disraeli's imperialism was concerned with India and the Near East, and not with Africa or the great English-speaking colonies.

The colonists themselves were poor, scattered, and uninterested in theory. Their politics developed out of practical needs and their desire for 'responsible' government meant a government which understood the problems of lumbermen or traders, or of small

---

[1] The name Australia was not used officially until 1817. In 1875 an edition of the *Encyclopedia Britannica* began an article on Australia with the words: 'Australia or New Holland'. Bentham had proposed a settlement in South Australia to be named Felicitania. British authority over the whole continent was not formally asserted until 1829 when the French showed some intention of establishing a settlement there. The annexation of New Zealand was accepted reluctantly by the British Government, partly to put an end to the anarchy introduced by traders – British and others – and partly to forestall a French expedition which arrived in 1840 only to find that the country had been annexed to the British Crown.

farmers in danger of being overwhelmed by native risings. In other words 'responsible' government meant control of local affairs by local men; there was no wish for separation from Great Britain. This local control was impossible as long as the colonial authorities – directed from London – disposed of independent revenues from Crown lands. The demand for local self-government therefore became a demand for responsible government as Englishmen knew it; that is to say, control of finance and of the executive. English opinion at home was unlikely to refuse these demands. They were granted first to Canada, and Canada was the first colony to adopt federation (1867).

The change of attitude towards the larger colonies came through the slow but steady increase in their population and economic importance. Canada could not export wheat on a grand scale until cheap transport had opened the lands west of the Great Lakes, but Australian wool had become a considerable export before the discovery of gold in 1851. In the first half of the century England had scarcely felt the competition of other countries in her staple manufactures. After 1870 her foreign customers began to produce these staples for themselves and to put up tariffs against British goods. British trade increased, but the export of machinery, ships and coal played a larger part in it. The machines and ships were used in competition with those of the exporting country; the coal might have been consumed at home. Even textile manufacturers had to look for expanding markets in Asia rather than in Europe or America. Hence more interest was taken in the colonies. They were no longer 'millstones round the neck' of the mother-country.

With the cheapening of transport by rail and by sea the hinterland of Africa (as well as of Canada) became a profitable area of expansion. The history of British advance in Africa is a curious example of continuity with an earlier tradition and of contrast with the development of British rule in India. The expansion of British power in India had been due mainly to political and military reasons. After the Indian Mutiny of 1857[1] the East India Company was formally abolished; it had long been no more than the

---

[1] The Mutiny, though dangerous for a short period, was not a political rebellion of India. The political consequences were out of proportion to the event itself, since they included memories – on each side – which widened the distance between Indians and Europeans.

channel of official control. For the rest of the century the history of India is mainly – from the English point of view – a record of public work carried out by a benevolent if unimaginative bureaucracy.

The Colonial Office in London worked on principles different from those of the India Office. Private enterprise, in the old form of Chartered Companies, opened Africa to trade; the Royal Niger Company (1886), the British East Africa Company (1888), and the British South Africa Company acted as pioneers and even found difficulty in preventing the government from giving away to others the fruits of their work. The older generation of statesmen and civil servants was indeed not much touched by the so-called imperialist movement of the last decade of the century. This movement, which is still analysed too superficially in economic terms, was not English alone; it was more blatant and lasting in Germany and more naïve in the United States, but its most remarkable literary memorial is in English literature. Kipling's prose and verse show imperialism at its best – as a substitution in an age of religious decline, of the concept of duty for dogmatic belief – and at its worst as a crude glorification of material power supported, in theory, by an equally crude mis-statement of the Darwinian hypothesis of natural selection.

There is something of a paradox[2] in the fact that colonial questions were raised to major issues in English politics by a former radical, Joseph Chamberlain. In 1887 an informal conference of colonial[3] Prime Ministers was held in London during the first Jubilee of Queen Victoria. A second conference took place in 1894, and a third at the time of the Queen's Diamond Jubilee. At this third conference Chamberlain was Colonial Secretary. For ten years he had regarded the colonies as 'undeveloped estates'. He now had his chance. He wanted colonial federation, but the colonies were more concerned with their own self-government. Even on the economic side their interests did not altogether harmonize with those of Great Britain. The colonies wanted imperial preference because they could dispose of their main products in a protected British market; the advantages were less for Great Britain owing to

---

[1] Rhodes is a good example of the power of this substitute.

[2] Not wholly a paradox. In the earlier years of the century the radicals – Lord Durham, Gibbon Wakefield, and others – had been more interested than politicians of other parties in colonial matters.

[3] The term 'colonial' was used until 1911, although the logic of facts had already differentiated the self-governing Dominions from the Crown Colonies.

the smallness of the colonial markets. The colonial representatives repeated their views at the conference of 1902. At the same time they refused to consider any scheme for closer political union or to make a larger contribution to imperial defence. They could argue that the Boer War had shown their willingness to make sacrifices and to support Great Britain in time of need.

Colonial support in this war had indeed convinced Chamberlain that satisfaction ought to be given to these demands for imperial preference and that without such economic strengthening the Empire might fall apart. Chamberlain announced his views in the early summer of 1903. He recommended not only imperial preference but fiscal retaliation against foreign tariffs. He thus broke the unity of the conservative cabinet and gave the liberals a good 'slogan' – the defence of free trade – for the next election.

The liberals hardly needed this gift because the conservatives made the mistake of sanctioning the employment of Chinese labour on the Rand. No question was more likely to arouse English opinion. The importation of indentured Chinese coolies and their maintenance in closed compounds came dangerously near to a reversion to slavery. The offence was greater because the coolies were working for the mining interests whose activities had already caused much searching of heart among the English people. For many years relations with the Dutch republics of South Africa had been difficult. The Dutch farmers who had made the 'Great Trek' between 1835 and 1837 across the Orange River into new country had been freed from their allegiance to the British Crown. In 1877 the Transvaal was annexed as the simplest means of protection against attack from the Kaffirs and especially from the Zulus whom the Boers had in fact done much to provoke. The destruction of the military monarchy of the Zulus left the Boers without any reason for accepting annexation. The British Government did not offer them responsible government. Hence the Boers broke into rebellion. Although they defeated a small British force at Majuba Hill, they could have been crushed without great difficulty if Gladstone had been willing to fight for annexation. He refused to do so, and the Boers regained their independence.

Paul Kruger, the leader of the revolt, became the first president of the restored republic. He represented the narrowest type of Boer hostility to English rule, but his stubborn opposition would have mattered little outside his own sphere if gold had not been discovered on the Witwatersrand in 1886. At once this barren ridge became the centre of activities of a crowd of adventurers, not all of them British subjects. Kruger allowed them to work the mines and tapped their profits by levying enormous duties on the machinery which they imported for mining. Out of the disputes between the Boer Government and these Uitlanders, or foreigners, and through the intermediate stage of the Jameson Raid,[1] arose the South African, or as it was generally called at the time, the Boer War. It may still be argued whether this war was, in Gladstone's words about the Crimean War, 'just but unnecessary', or whether it was even just. A more skilful diplomacy might perhaps have avoided it. On the other hand Kruger's refusal of civic rights to the foreigners whom he admitted – and taxed – made trouble inevitable. Once rebellion had begun, British intervention would have followed. Otherwise colonial opinion generally would have assumed that no protection could be expected from the home country.

Nevertheless the case was not a good one. The gold-mining companies of the Rand had nothing of the glamour of Elizabethan plunderers of Spain. Neither Rhodes nor Jameson inspired much moral respect. The suppression of two small republics by a Power which had always claimed to support the liberties of small states was humiliating to English pride. The war lasted two and a half years.[2] During this time there was considerable division of opinion in England and even among those who accepted the necessity of war not much sympathy for the Uitlanders as such. In any case the reason for fighting had not been to allow the mining companies to introduce Chinese coolies into South Africa.[3]

---

[1] At the end of December 1895 Dr Jameson, administrator of the British South Africa Company, and a friend and confidant of Rhodes, led an absurd raid into the Transvaal with the intention of supporting an outbreak at Johannesburg. The small body of raiders was easily captured by the Boers. The Raid, incidentally, produced a telegram of congratulation from Emperor William II to Kruger on his success in putting down the raiders without appealing for the help of 'friendly Powers'.

[2] If the war had been fought little more than a decade later, in the age of mechanized transport and armoured cars, it might have lasted only a few months, since the tactics used with such skill and determination by the Boers would have been ineffective against a fast-moving and well-protected force.

[3] The introduction of coolies was recommended by Milner and accepted by Balfour. Milner was by temperament an administrator rather than a politician. Balfour's failure to realize the reaction of his countrymen is less easily explained.

CHAPTER XVIII

The Early Twentieth Century and the First German War

THE CONVERGENCE OF the issues of protection and Chinese labour brought about a severe unionist defeat. The liberals obtained 377 seats, the new labour party 53, and the conservatives (with the liberal unionists) 157. Even without the 83 Irish nationalists the liberal party had a secure majority. Their Prime Minister, Sir Henry Campbell-Bannerman, was a shrewd, well-to-do Scot, not very imaginative but capable of far-sighted political action such as the grant of self-government to the Transvaal in 1907.[1] His cabinet included Asquith, Grey, Lloyd George, Morley, Haldane, and Bryce. No administration since Peel's government of 1841 had assembled such brilliance. This fact is not without significance. Although the term 'Victorian age' has led to misunderstanding of the phases of English social, economic, and political development, the accession of Queen Victoria five years after the passing of the first reform bill can be taken as a convenient date for the beginning of a new age. The accession of Edward VII in 1901 is an equally convenient date. The queen and her son reflected rather than led the times in which they lived; 'Victorianism' was a reaction against the looseness of morals – the *dégringolade* of an aristocratic culture – in the Regency period; 'Edwardianism' was in turn a reaction against the stricter social tone which an earlier generation had accepted as a necessary corrective.[2] Neither term applies very well

---

[1] He resigned owing to ill-health in 1908 and was succeeded by Asquith.

[2] It must not be forgotten that many Victorian writers, for example Carlyle, J. S. Mill, Ruskin, Matthew Arnold, and most of the great novelists were severely critical of their age. The Pre-Raphaelite movement, in its own sphere, was also a part of the reaction against contemporary standards. Furthermore the attempt of the Victorians, at their best, to establish society on a Christian basis was troubled by doubts about the truths of revealed religion. These, doubts – as Tennyson's *In Memoriam* shows – were raised by the evidence of geology before

to economic development unless Queen Victoria is associated with railway-building and King Edward, a little less incongruously, with the coming of the motor-car.[1] There was, however, one factor common to the earlier years of Queen Victoria (though not to her majestic old age) and to the short reign of Edward VII. A new generation after 1900 – perhaps owing to the mere fact of the beginning of a new century – felt the urgency of social reform just as Peel's generation had felt the need of an overhaul of the main administrative system of the country. The liberal party, which was prepared to carry out such reforms, thus worked on a rising tide of opinion and attracted, as Peel also had attracted, those politicians who wanted reform without revolutionary change.

The conservative party, therefore, were defeated in 1906, on something deeper than immediate political issues and the liberal victory, from a party point of view, was almost too great. The labour party were prepared to go further than the liberals, just as the liberals themselves had gone beyond the limits thought safe by Peel. Until the outbreak of the first German war the significance of the voting in 1906 was obscured not only because the liberals failed to interpret it rightly but also because the conservative opposition in the house of lords was blind to the movement of opinion. The folly of the conservative peers turned against themselves. In 1909 Lloyd George, as Chancellor of the Exchequer, had to find an additional £15,000,000 in taxation. Part of this sum was for old age pensions – the first instalment of social reform; another part of the increase was due to the naval building programme, which the conservatives had supported and indeed would have made still larger. Lloyd George added twopence to the income tax,[2] increased the death duties, established a super-tax, and proposed the taxation of unearned increment from land. It could be said that this tax was unfair in that it singled out one form of unearned increment for special taxation. Nevertheless in rejecting the budget which contained the proposal the house of lords was acting against all recent precedent and, therefore, breaking an unwritten but established convention of the constitution.[3]

Darwin's study of the evolution of species shook the foundations of Christian belief.

[1] The sewing-machine and the bicycle – two inventions of immense social importance – were Victorian.   [2] The rise was from 1s. to 1s. 2d.

[3] Since 1671 the house of lords had been denied the right of amending money

The action of the lords gave Lloyd George full scope for his own type of oratory in denouncing peers, landowners, and the whole of the conservative party as drones trying to evade taxation. At the general election which followed the rejection of the budget the conservatives were again defeated, but the liberal majority was reduced; there were now 275 liberals, 273 unionists, 40 labour members, and 82 Irish nationalists in the house of commons. The liberal party had never given up Home Rule; the house of lords had always opposed it. The liberals could therefore count on the Irish vote in any measure against the lords. The attack was delayed for a time owing to the death of Edward VII. The new king, George V, was better suited to the difficult position in which he was placed for the next few years. George V had a more sensible upbringing than his father. He had travelled widely and had served for fifteen years in the navy.[1] He was not a clever man, but he judged people more soundly than Edward VII and listened to sounder advisers. He proposed a conference between parties on the question of the lords. After the breakdown of this conference another general election took place (December 1910). The election brought little change in the representation of parties: 272 liberals, 272 unionists, 42 labour members, 84 Irish nationalists.

A third general election was out of the question. Either the lords would accept measures restraining their own powers or the liberals, according to precedent, would ask the king to create sufficient peers to give them a majority in the upper house. Although the liberals did not want to take the latter course, a number of 'die-hard' peers nearly forced them into it. Finally the lords gave way, and in August 1911 the Parliament Act laid down that money bills should become law without the consent of the lords and that other bills passed in three successive sessions and rejected each time by the lords should become law if two years had passed between the second reading in the first session and the third reading in the final session of the commons.[2]

bills. After 1860 all such bills were included in a single 'budget'. Therefore the house had to reject the 'budget' as a whole in order to reject any tax contained in it.

[1] George V was the younger son of Edward VII. His elder brother died in 1892.

[2] The act, which also reduced the legal duration of a parliament from seven to five years, passed the lords by 131 to 114 votes; the two archbishops, 11 out of 13 bishops, and 29 conservative peers voted for it.

The action of the house of lords between 1909 and 1911 was in a sedate form a strike against the constitution. As such it may be reckoned one of the reversions towards violence which stand out in the years immediately before 1914 because they took place against a background of increasing respect for law and order. The militant supporters of the women's suffrage agitation had begun this disregard of legality about the year 1906; it is possible that their tactics did more harm than good to their cause. At the time of the parliament act this social unrest spread to the working class, partly owing to the attention given to the programme of revolutionary syndicalism[1] in France. The French movement faded out after the government had broken a railway strike in October 1910 by the mobilization of railway servants. In Great Britain a wave of strikes lasted for over two years. Some – not all – of these strikes were about real grievances; the most serious of them, a dispute in the spring of 1912 over the establishment of minimum wage rates in the coal-mining industry, could have been settled without a strike if the men's leaders had been less headlong in their tactics.

The abolition of the veto of the lords had other consequences. It enabled the government to pass a National Insurance scheme against the opposition of the conservatives and to satisfy Welsh non-conformists by disestablishing and disendowing the anglican Church in Wales. There seemed also an opportunity of satisfying the Irish nationalists by the grant of Home Rule. The Home Rule bill was not merely a return for the services rendered by the Irish vote. In many respects the chances of a lasting settlement of the Irish question were better than at any time since the union. John Redmond, the leader of the parliamentary nationalist party, was a moderate man without Parnell's pathological hatreds. Ireland was more peaceful; the land question had been settled at the expense of the British taxpayer.[2] The liberal plan was on a federal basis, which might have been extended to other parts of the United Kingdom. The conservatives were not altogether opposed to a plan of this

[1] Syndicalism derives its meaning from the French term for a trade union. The syndicalist movement was a development of socialist theory away from parliamentary methods towards joint action through the trade unions and culminating in a general revolutionary strike.

[2] The Irish Land Purchase Act of 1903 went far beyond earlier legislation on the subject in establishing, on easy terms for the purchaser, a landowning peasantry in Ireland.

kind. The favourable moment was lost because an agreement could not be reached on the question of Ulster. It is possible that currents of feeling in Ireland were too strong to allow a compromise in this matter. There might have been a chance of persuading the nationalists to allow Ulster the right to decide when, if ever, the protestant north-east of Ireland should be included in the scheme; the Ulster protestants might have been persuaded to accept the safeguards which Redmond and his party were prepared to allow them. Asquith, however, delayed a decision until each side had taken up an extreme position. He refused to face the fact that English opinion would not allow the expulsion of loyal subjects wishing to remain in the United Kingdom. On the other side the unionists also refused to face the consequences of supporting in Ulster armed resistance to law. The drift from legality became more dangerous when the unionist leader, Bonar Law, acquiesced in something like a 'strike' of army officers, that is to say, a threat of resignation if they were ordered to take part in the coercion of Ulster.

Thus in the spring of 1914 the risk of civil war was most serious. There were two 'private armies' in Ireland; the Ulster volunteers and a rival body – not under Redmond's control – in Dublin and the south. The government could not drop the Home Rule bill; Redmond could not agree to the exclusion of Ulster. Ulster, with the support of one of the English parties, continued to refuse inclusion. In June 1914 Bonar Law and Carson, the Ulster leader, offered to withdraw opposition if an area in the north-east, slightly smaller than the present area of Northern Ireland, were excluded (with the right to come in by plebiscite at any time). Redmond would not and indeed could not accept these terms. This was the situation at the time of the outbreak of war. Redmond then made a gesture which might have been the means of reconciliation. He offered Irish nationalist support in the defence of France and Belgium. This offer, which was an act of courage, was not treated with much imagination by the Cabinet or the War Office. Nevertheless it is doubtful whether any friendly British gesture would have had a lasting effect. The nationalist movement in Ireland was passing out of the hands of Redmond and the parliamentary party, as years earlier it had passed out of the hands of O'Connell. An irreconcilable minority, inflamed with the fierce and deep-set passions of twentieth-century nationalism, was likely to gain the support –

active or passive – of catholic Ireland, and to get what it wanted, if
only because the English voters were more than weary of incessant
Irish demands. In fact the Home Rule bill was passed, but its
operation was suspended until after the war in order to allow a
settlement of the Ulster question. No one supposed that the war
would last until 1918.

The origins of the war of 1914 extend in time far beyond the
formation of the liberal government of 1906, and cover events over
which British policy had no control. The war had no single cause,
but, at the risk of over-simplification, it is possible to say that it
would not have occurred if Germany had not used her national
power in such a way as to threaten not only Great Britain but all
countries not directly within the German system of alliances. This
threat took two main forms: a challenge to British sea-power and a
south-eastern movement which would have cut across Russian out-
lets to the Mediterranean and the Persian Gulf and endangered
British interests in India. It is doubtful whether, even in official
German policy, these two main challenges were made as part of a
concerted plan for world domination. Such a plan had its advocates
in high military and political circles in Germany and appealed to a
large section of German public opinion which was envious and
crudely resentful of the established position of Great Britain. Under
the clever but unstable William II imperial Germany abandoned
the 'limited aims' to which Bismarck had adhered. William's
acceptance of Admiral Tirpitz's plan for a large German battle fleet
was due to a mixture of jealousy and admiration of British naval
power. German colonial expansion was more a matter of prestige
than of economic necessity. This confusion of thought can be seen
in the German attitude towards Great Britain at the turn of the
century. At the outbreak of the South African War, Great Britain
was isolated and indeed friendless in Europe. For many years past
the unsatisfactory condition of Anglo-French and Anglo-Russian
relations had inclined British policy towards an understanding with
Germany. English naval strength was calculated in terms necessary
to meet the French and Russian navies. Colonial disputes with
France were more serious, or at all events were concerned with
larger issues than colonial disputes with Germany. In the Far East
and in Turkey, Russia and not Germany had long been regarded as a

danger. Thus in spite of the clumsy and truculent methods of German diplomacy an Anglo-German alliance was not out of the question. Joseph Chamberlain made no less than three attempts at an agreement. He failed because the Germans believed that owing to Russian pressure on England they could secure such an agreement at any time and at their own price, and that meanwhile they need not run the risk of war with Russia in English interests. Tirpitz and the German Admiralty based their plan for a high-seas fleet rather than a navy suited only to defensive 'cruiser warfare' on the view that England could never risk, in relation to France and Russia, the losses which she would incur in destroying a weaker German fleet. The German fleet could thus be used as an instrument of blackmail.

German diplomacy maintained too long this conviction that France and Russia could never come to terms with Great Britain on the basis of a common fear of German aggression. In the Far East the Germans drove Great Britain into an alliance with Japan by refusing to join in opposing Russian encroachments on Chinese territory. The fact that the first important step in leaving the policy of 'isolation' was taken in the Far East is evidence that British policy was not based upon a plan to 'encircle' Germany. Without careful diplomatic handling the Russo-Japanese War (1904–5) might have involved Great Britain in war with Russia and France. The consequences of the Russian defeat in this war were serious for France since she could no longer rely on strong Russian military support against Germany. Meanwhile a French *rapprochement* with England had already taken form, and indeed was a logical consequence of the most recent Anglo-French colonial dispute. In the autumn and winter of 1898–9 the two countries had been on the verge of war over the control of the upper waters of the Nile. France had given way because she could not afford to go to war with England without weakening herself in relation to Germany.[1] If the French could not oppose England they might as well make the best possible bargain with her.

[1] The political reason for the Anglo-French *entente* was so obvious that there is no need to regard it as a clever move by Edward VII. Edward VII had little to do with the formulation of policy, although his good manners and affability (which he displayed as much on a visit to Berlin as in Paris) helped to gain popular support in France for the policy wanted by the British and French Governments.

The Anglo-French agreement of 1904 was a colonial agreement; an attempt to smooth out existing differences and possible sources of conflict. The agreement was made by a conservative government. The liberals accepted it, and later applied the same method to the improvement of Anglo-Russian relations. Neither Lansdowne nor his successor Grey appears to have realized the full significance of this new direction of policy. They were influenced by Lord Cromer whose first consideration was the settlement of the long-standing rivalry of Great Britain and France in Egypt. They felt uneasy over the general attitude of Germany. They could not but see that they had nullified the basis upon which the new German battle fleet was being constructed; the German fleet would lose blackmail value if Great Britain no longer regarded herself as threatened by the navy of France. The French understood more clearly than the English negotiators of the agreement that they were changing the balance of power in Europe to the disadvantage of Germany. The Germans (as the French expected) also saw the fact but failed to give it the right interpretation. They might have taken it as a warning that their own policy was leaving other Powers with the alternatives either of submitting to German dictation or of defending themselves against it. Germany might have accepted the Anglo-French *entente* and have negotiated a similar agreement with Great Britain. On the other hand, if the Germans tried to destroy the Anglo-French *entente*, the inference was that they were aiming not at European co-operation, but at European domination.

It is still uncertain whether the Germans acted out of folly or for more sinister reasons in their decision to break the *entente*. For their purpose they used the Moroccan question. Under the terms of the Anglo-French agreement France had recognized the British position in Egypt in return for a free hand in the disintegrating sultanate of Morocco. If Germany objected to French control of Morocco and France did not obtain English backing, French public opinion might think that the agreement with Great Britain was a bad bargain.

The German attempt failed; Great Britain and France would have been blind indeed if they had not seen that the German anxiety to break the *entente* gave them a stronger motive for maintaining it. There was, however, still a chance for the German Government to avoid bringing about their own isolation in Europe. Instead of meeting the liberal desire for a reduction of armaments they pushed their naval policy a stage further and decided upon a direct challenge to Great Britain in capital ships. Their calculations were again foolish but not altogether wild. In 1905 the conservative government, on the recommendation of Admiral Sir John Fisher, began to build capital ships of a new type; the first of these *Dreadnoughts* was launched in February 1906. The *Dreadnoughts* were faster as well as more heavily gunned than any other capital ship. If Fisher's programme had been carried out Great Britain would have had an overwhelming lead in these *Dreadnoughts* before Germany had constructed one of them. Moreover the ships set Germany a serious problem because the Kiel Canal was not wide enough to take them.

In their desire to reduce expenditure on armaments and in the hope of reaching a naval agreement with Germany the liberal government did not carry out the Fisher programme. Thus the Germans had a chance of overtaking the British lead. They seized the chance and in 1908–9 came near to success. They had laid down in the previous year four *Dreadnoughts* to two laid down by Great Britain. They proposed to lay down another four in 1909. By devices such as the assembly of material in advance of laying down the ships they might complete this programme before the time anticipated by the British Admiralty and thus reach not merely equality but for a short period even superiority in new capital ships. The British Government discovered what the Germans were doing and decided at once to lay down four *Dreadnoughts* with four more if they were needed. Parliament insisted that all the eight ships should be laid down.

The Germans had again shown their hand, and lost. Although they had now no chance of overtaking the British lead, they had increased the distrust felt about their intentions. Even before this miscalculation the signature of the Anglo-Russian Convention of 1907 had disproved the German assumption that Great Britain and Russia could never settle their differences. The Anglo-Russian Convention, like the Anglo-French agreement, was a settlement of outstanding questions. It was welcomed by Morley as Secretary of State for India for reasons similar to those which had led Cromer to advocate the agreement with France. It is, however, unlikely that Russia would have signed the Convention if the second area of German advance – along the line of the Baghdad railway to the Persian Gulf – had not threatened Russian interests.

The Anglo-Russian Convention made a conflict of interests between Russia and Germany more probable. Russia had been checked in the Far East by Japan. She now agreed to limit her expansionist aims in the Middle East. She was therefore likely to take a more active interest in questions affecting Constantinople and the Balkans. This likelihood was greater after the 'Young Turk' party had expelled the Sultan Abdul Hamid. The Turkish revolution affected both Austria-Hungary and Russia. For different reasons neither wanted a strong Turkey. Austria-Hungary wished to keep Bosnia and Herzegovina of which she was the occupying Power. Russia wished to obtain the opening of the Straits. The two Powers appear to have made a bargain to act together, but the Austrians anticipated that there would be opposition to the Russian demands and therefore decided to be sure of their prize at once. In October 1908 they announced the annexation of the two provinces. Their action caused great anger in Serbia since the Serbs had hopes of uniting the southern Slavs of these provinces in a larger Serbian kingdom. Russia supported Serbian opposition. France was bound to support Russia. Germany was bound to support Austria-Hungary – her one remaining ally,[1] and indeed announced the fact in provocative language.

Russia gave way because at this time she was not prepared to go to war. The Russians were unlikely to give way a second time. In these circumstances, instead of reverting to a policy of caution, Germany again asserted herself about Morocco. Her claim for compensation elsewhere as the price of recognizing French control was not unreasonable, but the claim was put forward by the typically German method of sending a warship to the Moroccan port of Agadir. This move was especially alarming to Great Britain since there was already some agitation in Germany in favour of obtaining a port on the Atlantic. Once more the Germans themselves strengthened the Anglo-French *entente*.

In spite of the difficulty of dealing with Germany, the liberal government in Great Britain continued to try for an agreement on the limitation of naval building. Although the negotiations came to nothing, the war of 1914 did not break out on the question of Anglo-German rivalry or indeed on any question directly affecting British

[1] Italy – the third partner in the Triple Alliance – was already known to be unreliable.

or German interests. In the autumn of 1912 Serbia, Bulgaria, Greece, and Montenegro declared war on Turkey. Within eight months they were quarrelling over the spoils of victory. The quarrel ended with the defeat of Bulgaria and considerable territorial gains for Roumania (who had kept out of the first war), Serbia, and Greece. The increase of Serbian power was especially dangerous to Austria-Hungary because there was already serious risk of the disruption of the Habsburg Empire at the death of the Emperor Francis Joseph. For this reason Russia supported Serbian claims and pretensions.

Francis Joseph was eighty-three years old. A considerable party in Austria-Hungary thought it necessary to fight Serbia at once in order to save the Empire. They could not venture on war – war with Serbia meant war with Russia – unless they were sure of German support. During the winter of 1913–14 it seems clear that Germany also decided that war to save Austria-Hungary was inevitable, and that the early autumn of 1914 would be the most favourable time.[1] Once this decision had been taken any pretext would have served. The assassination of the Archduke Francis Ferdinand, heir to Francis Joseph, on 28 June 1914, was the best occasion which could have been found. The Archduke was murdered by Austrian subjects of Serbian irredentist sympathies; they had plotted the murder on Serbian territory. On 23 July, after getting a promise of full German support, the government of Francis Joseph sent the Serbian Government an ultimatum in terms which would have meant surrender of Serbian independence.[2] To the surprise of her enemies Serbia accepted all but two of the conditions.[3] Austria-Hungary, however, broke off relations with her and began to mobilize. On 27 July Germany refused an invitation from Grey for a conference in London.

On 28 July Austria attacked Serbia. This attack – as the Germanic Powers knew – would cause Russian mobilization. Once

[1] The widening of the Kiel Canal would then have been completed. In 1913 Germany raised a capital levy of a thousand million marks for non-recurrent military expenditure. A measure of this kind could not be repeated indefinitely. In the early part of 1914 the German Government increased the gold stocks of the country by collecting commercial debts at high rates of discount.

[2] Grey said of this ultimatum: 'I have never before seen one State address to another independent State a document of so formidable a character.'

[3] The Serbian Government was willing to submit these outstanding points to the decision of The Hague court.

G

this slow process had begun, German mobilization was bound to follow, since the German war plan provided for an immediate attack on France before Russia could make an important diversion in the east. Germany would secure a quick decision in the west and then turn eastwards with her full strength. She hoped to defeat Russia before the winter. Hence a naval blockade by Great Britain had little significance for her.

The attitude of Great Britain was thus not a deciding factor from the German point of view. This attitude was still uncertain. Grey could not promise support to France because the Cabinet would not agree to give it. Even on the morning of August 2, more than a day after the despatch of a German ultimatum to Russia, a minority of ministers had argued against telling the French ambassador that the British fleet would be used to prevent an attempt by the Germans to land on the French coast.[1] Only on the evening of August 2 (when the Germans had entered Luxemburg and delivered an ultimatum to Belgium) was the decision taken to declare war on Germany if the Germans violated Belgian neutrality.

This decision was both inevitable and right. If the most favourable interpretation be put upon the German motives for allowing and indeed encouraging Austria-Hungary to begin the war of 1914, there is no doubt that a victorious Germany would have seized the chance of world domination. The German war plan against France and Russia nearly succeeded. The German armies in Russia were ultimately successful; the terms then imposed upon the Russians show what would have happened to Great Britain if she had left Europe to its fate. In the first as in the second German war something vaster and more important than the destiny of England was at stake. The deepest responsibility of Germany goes beyond the ineptitude of the statesmanship and diplomacy which brought her to the position of risking the existence of the Reich on the question whether Austria-Hungary should continue to rule over unwilling subjects. This responsibility was summed up by British and French opinion in the term 'Prussian militarism'. 'Militarism' was not limited to Prussia, or indeed to Germany, but in no other country was its characteristic feature – the glorification of force – deployed with such arrogance and accepted by such large sections of the population. In the last years of the nineteenth century the

[1] The Germans had no intention of making a landing of this kind.

Socialist Bebel commented that the German people was 'still drunk with victory'. Most foreigners who knew Germany before 1914 made similar judgments. German aggression against Belgium, in spite of the treaty obligations of the German people, was typical of the consequences of the German philosophy. The triumph of German arms would have fastened upon Europe for an indefinite time this philosophy of the supremacy of force over law, and would have brought with it a reversal of the patient achievement of more than thirty generations of Europeans.

The first German war lasted four years. Looking back over the course of the fighting the Germans seem to have lost the war before the end of 1914, with their failure to capture the Channel ports. The Allied counter-attack which saved Paris and drove back the German armies from the Marne to the Aisne maintained the situation in the west and allowed time for Great Britain and ultimately the United States to develop their immense resources.

If the chances of a complete German victory diminished after the early winter of 1914–15, the Allies were unable to defeat the Germans until the late autumn of 1918. In the trench warfare of these four years the advantage remained on the side of the defence; machine-guns, barbed wire, artillery barrages, and, later, fortified strong posts destroyed the momentum of every attack after a few miles had been won at fearful cost. In contrast to the second German war the inventiveness of the Allies was curiously small in relation to their resources. The tank was not used until the autumn of 1916 and even then the British commanders did not understand the value of their new weapon. The conditions of the South African War had brought cavalry commanders to prominence in the British army. In 1914 and throughout the war the high command and staff were too much in the control of officers drawn from the least intellectual branch of the army. This fact goes some way, though not very far, to explain why no British commander had enterprise enough to call upon the skill and immense productive power of his countrymen to find some method of breaking a line which stretched from the North Sea to the Alps.[1]

There was, however, a similar failure on the part of the French

[1] Grey records that, after the formation of this line, Kitchener said to him more than once: 'I don't know what is to be done. This isn't war.'

High Command. Even the Germans, who had given more attention than any other people to the study of war, failed to produce any remarkable invention. The German use of poison gas[1] was the employment not of a new invention but of a weapon prohibited by the intention if not by the letter of The Hague Convention of which Germany was a signatory. Even this act of treachery was not carried out with much intelligence. The gas was used on too small a scale to produce a decisive result before means of protection were improvised against it.

The consequence of this intellectual failure on the part of the soldiers was a loss of life on an unprecedented scale. The flower of a generation was lost in the waste lands between the opposed trench-systems. In the absence of a decisive break through the German lines in the west the alternative might have been an attack far behind these lines. A diversion of this kind would have been in the tradition of English use of sea-power, but the western Allies were handicapped by the German alliance with Turkey and by Turkish fears of Russia. The attempt in 1915 to open the Dardanelles might have shortened the war and have saved Russia from military disaster and political collapse. The expedition nearly succeeded; it was wrecked by a division of opinion at home and, as a result, by delays, bad tactics, and incapable corps commanders. Although after this failure the Allies seized a bridgehead at Salonika[2] an advance into Austria-Hungary was impossible until the Central Powers had been greatly weakened.[3]

Hence each side continued to waste divisions in attacks on the western front. The Germans failed to take Verdun early in 1916; later in the year a great English offensive on the Somme also failed to make more than local gains. In May 1916 the German High Seas Fleet fought its one battle in the war. This action off Jutland brought heavy losses to each side; the German fleet narrowly escaped complete destruction and henceforward did not venture upon more than two sallies taking them any distance into the North Sea. Instead the Germans –again breaking the laws of war – turned to an intensified submarine campaign. For a time their attacks were

[1] As early as the Crimean War the British Cabinet had rejected a proposal for the use of asphyxiating smoke-clouds at the siege of Sebastopol.

[2] The port of Salonika was too small to supply a large force.

[3] Lloyd George, who succeeded Asquith as Prime Minister in December 1916, favoured an 'eastern' strategy, but never produced a feasible plan.

a very grave danger; they were countered – after too long delay – by the use of the convoy system and by improved methods in the detection of submarines. The German illegalities at sea brought the United States into the war and thus, from the German point of view, destroyed any hope of a stalemate. On the other hand the military collapse of Russia, followed by the Bolshevik revolution in November[1] 1917, gave Germany a temporary advantage in man-power on the western front. The advantage was greater owing to the collapse of a French offensive in April 1917 with serious results on the morale of the French army.[2] During the interval before American troops were ready to take the field, the position was held by a continuous British attack to the east of Ypres over the sodden and difficult terrain around Passchendaele. Here in particular a terrible price was paid for the failure to devise means of breaching fortified lines other than by methods which were only local in effect and increased the difficulties of attack.

In the late autumn of 1917 the Allied position also worsened owing to the collapse of the Italian front;[3] complete disaster was prevented by a late rally of the Italian armies and by the dispatch of Allied troops who could not easily be spared from the western front. The British victories in Palestine at the end of the year, although of far-reaching importance, could have little immediate effect upon the long-drawn battle in the west. On this western front the Germans made a last effort in March 1918 before the arrival of the Americans in force. The attack gained more ground than anything of its kind since 1914. The weather favoured the attackers and the position was more difficult than it need have been because differences between Lloyd George and Haig, the British commander-in-chief, had the effect of keeping in England large numbers of troops who might have been in France.

The Germans were, however, unable to provide the necessary weight to continue their attack until they had won a decisive victory. The Allies did not retreat in panic. They knew that they had only to hold out until the balance of strength turned in their favour. At this late hour also the Allies found a great commander. Full powers,

[1] October in the 'Old Style' Russian calendar.
[2] The date and place of this offensive became known to the Germans who were therefore able to make their dispositions to meet it.
[3] Italy entered the war on the Allied side in May 1915.

or very nearly full powers, were given to the French General Foch. Foch's coolness and intellectual grasp enabled him to wait until the Germans were exhausted and then to attack at the right time and place. From the first counter-attack in August the Allied armies began to advance. Furthermore, the effect of sea-power was at last decisive both in the enforcement of a blockade on Germany and her Allies and in the transport of huge American armies. Austria-Hungary, more severely tested and less united at home than Germany, Turkey and Bulgaria, with less heart in the war, collapsed. The Habsburg Empire broke up. Finally the German High Command lost its nerve and surrendered on 11 November 1918, before a single Allied army had even reached German territory.[1] The first German war was over.

[1] This fact was turned to political advantage almost at once by the German army commanders. They brought forward the 'stab in the back' legend according to which the German armies were never broken but were compelled to surrender owing to political revolution at home.

CHAPTER XIX

Great Britain between the Two Wars: Domestic Politics and Economic Problems

THE COST OF the war in lives to Great Britain was 764,000, or 88 out of every 1,000 males between the ages of 20 and 45.[1] These figures, though tragically large, do not of themselves suggest a 'lost generation', but the dead included a much higher proportion of the outstanding young men between twenty and thirty years old who, if they had lived, would have come to control the political life of the country for the next quarter of a century. The survivors of this *élite* had not sufficient collective influence to break through to the positions of power to which the older men clung for too long. 'The men who came back from the war counted for less, perhaps, in the political life of their country than any generation during the last two or three centuries.'[2] In the words of an ancient historian about the loss in battle of the youth of Athens, 'the spring had gone out of the year'.

The immediate reaction of soldiers and civilians alike was to get back to 'normal' pre-war conditions. The slogan 'business as usual', which had been employed with some steadying effect to meet the immediate shock of the outbreak of war, might have been taken as the wish of most Englishmen after the signature of the armistice. Nevertheless the war had modified their attitude towards social and political change. In many respects the effects of these bitter years were disintegrating and disruptive. The suddenness of the catastrophe (few people in Great Britain during the summer of 1914 expected a European war) was the more numbing because the experience of warfare between large armies had been unknown to the British people for over half a century. As the months of fighting

---

[1] The comparable figures for the Dominions were: Australia, 60 out of every 1,000, New Zealand, 73, Canada, 30, and for other belligerents, France, 182, Germany, 155, and the United States, 3.

[2] Baldwin was one of the few political leaders who realized these facts.

stretched out almost endlessly, and the zones of battle extended to the air, the nervous strain was intensified. The loosening of old beliefs and restraints was rapid, especially among the young, owing to the removal of many thousands of men and women from their homes, as well as through over-excitement and danger.[1] The fall in the value of money, the rise in taxation, the profits of some and the losses of others brought about a shift in wealth and a transfer of purchasing power to new classes. There was some ostentatious spending by 'war-profiteers', but their number was exaggerated. In the long run, and as far as the transfer of purchasing power raised the standard of life of the lowest-paid workers, the change was to the good.

It would be misleading, however, to draw attention only to the phenomena of war-strain or to changes in income-levels. The war had other domestic consequences and taught unexpected political lessons. In particular, the British people had practical experience of state-planning and of interference with long-established interests and liberties hitherto regarded as inviolable. Food rationing, though less rigorous than in the second German war, was as novel as air-raids. The introduction of conscription, the far-reaching powers of public authority under the Defence of the Realm Acts, the control of industry and transport, the direction of labour, the excess profits tax, and a hundred lesser examples of governmental activity tended towards a new conception of political society and of social and economic adjustment. If measures of a most drastic kind were feasible to ensure victory in war, could they not be employed, without risk to the British way of life, to bring about desirable social change in time of peace?

In other words, the *communitas* of Englishmen, to use a medieval term, possessed greater positive control over their destinies than anyone had imagined. These hopes were fostered, not only by the actual course of events, but also by encouragement from politicians, notably Lloyd George, that the war would be followed by a 'better world'. To some extent such forecasts were made rashly – war is not a good prelude to social reform – and as a stimulus to effort and

[1] At certain periods of the war the expectation of life of young infantry officers drafted to the front was about six weeks. At home enemy air attacks caused dislocation and anxiety (sometimes bordering on panic) out of proportion to the damage they inflicted.

endurance; after the Bolshevist revolution there was a deliberate attempt to outbid Russian propaganda. Nevertheless, although, for the moment, the average man had had enough of state interference directed to one particular end, the promises of a brighter future were not forgotten, at least by those to whom they were made.

Even without a general improvement the tasks of recovery from the material losses of the war were difficult for a people nervously and physically overstrained. The direct material damage done by the war – the destruction of shipping, the running-down of machinery, the postponement of necessary repairs as well as of new construction of buildings – was probably equal to what would have been the normal increase in wealth between 1914 and 1918. Most of this loss, except in house-building, was made good by the end of 1920, but the disturbance of trade and the huge increase of debt incurred for economically unproductive expenditure remained. The National Debt rose from £650,000,000 in 1914 to £7,830,000,000 in 1920. About 10 per cent of British capital investments abroad had been sold during the war; another 4·5 per cent in Russia and elsewhere could be regarded as lost. Markets for British exports also had been lost, especially to the United States and Japan, and the machinery of selling had ceased to operate. Many changes disadvantageous to British industry could have been and in some cases were foreseen in pre-war years. The trouble after the war was that the rate of change accelerated rapidly, and that a host of problems which might have been dealt with singly came up for solution all at once. British coal exports were affected by the increasing use of oil and hydro-electric power; these losses in the export trade were cumulative, since for example, the change from coal to oil in ships meant that less coal was needed for bunkering. There had been severe competition in the iron and steel industries. British firms had shared in the increasing world demand, but their share had been at a declining rate. The development of textile industries in India and Japan would also have taken place in the decade after 1914 even if there had been no war. The skill required for these industries was relatively low and the large exports of textile machinery from Great Britain had foreshadowed increasing competition from the purchasing countries. From the point of view of domestic unemployment the situation was made worse by the war, since the war-time demand and immediate post-war boom had attracted workers into the staple industries which were bound to decline.

The prospects for British industry, however, were not altogether dismal. There had been considerable realization before the war that British industrialists were too complacent, and that they neglected technical advance. These defects were being remedied, but some time was bound to elapse before the effects of modernization were felt. On the other hand new industries were being developed. Indeed, if this had not been the case, it would have been impossible to provide unemployment relief – the so-called 'dole' – in the declining industries and to increase expenditure on social services.[1] If certain lines of manufacture were being lost to foreigners, other industries – begun abroad – soon established themselves in Great Britain. The manufacture of motor-cars had developed in France[2] earlier than in Great Britain, but before 1914 British firms led the way in the making of motor buses, and in the 1920s and 1930s took the lead in the production of cheap cars on the American pattern. An English economic historian[3] has pointed out the transformation of a manufacturing area such as Birmingham which in 1884 was the centre of a 'multitude of hardware trades based on iron or brass' and which had become by 1914 'a light engineering centre based mainly on steel, much of it imported into the district' and which possessed important new industries such as the manufacture of chocolate and cocoa and rubber tyres.

Changes of this kind were happening all the time; they were less noticed because they came piecemeal and not as the result of an advertised state planning. There were other signs of initiative in

[1] There was a good deal of criticism of an apparent increase in luxury expenditure after the war. This supposed increase was a little misleading to contemporaries. Much spending was transferred from great country houses to the towns, and specially to parts of London, where it was more visible. In fact the number of very rich people fell between 1914 and 1925 very considerably. At the other end of the scale, whereas about 1912 in Great Britain some twelve out of every hundred families in five representative cities were found to be living on or below the poverty line, the number in 1923–4 had fallen to four families. This is not to say that a more rapid transfer of purchasing power was not urgently desirable. Some 13 per cent of income receivers still took 40 per cent of the national income accruing to individuals. See also above, p. 152.

[2] As is shown by the number of French words in the industry, e.g. chassis, garage, chauffeur.

[3] W. H. B. Court, *A Concise Economic History of Britain from 1750 to recent times.*

meeting more intensive competition; for example, the amalgamation of smaller undertakings into large combinations. Altogether these changes, which have been much accelerated since 1945, may be summed up in figures; in 1907 newer manufactures formed one-fifteenth of the output of British industry, in 1924 they were about an eighth and in 1935 about a fifth. Nevertheless the rate of new growth was not sufficient to compensate for the falling-away of the old 'staples'. The new light engineering and other trades tended also to establish themselves away from the older industrial centres with the result that these older centres – soon to be described as the 'depressed areas' – suffered from chronic unemployment. Their difficulties were increased in 1925 when Great Britain returned to the gold standard and the £ sterling was restored to its pre-war parity with the United States dollar. It is now generally agreed that this valuation was too high and that it added to the prices of British exports, and therefore contributed to further unemployment.[1]

The coal industry, especially in the older mining districts of south Wales and north-east England, was almost continuously 'depressed'. The industry was insufficiently mechanized in comparison with its continental competitors;[2] labour relations, which had been bad before the war, became worse after the failure of the miners to get the nationalization of the mines after 1919. The so-called 'general strike' of 1926 arose out of a dispute over wages in the coal industry. Neither the owners' nor the miners' representatives were without blame for the breakdown in negotiations which led the Trades Union Congress to give their support to a general strike. The strike began on 4 May. There were some local acts of violence, but as a whole the strike was peaceful. Except for a few extremists, the T.U.C., which described the stoppage not as a 'general strike', but as a 'national strike' of a sympathetic kind, did not want a political strike and were very far indeed from intending to lead a revolutionary movement. Baldwin, as Prime Minister, was more sympathetic than some of his own colleagues (including Churchill) with the men's side in the coal dispute. On 12 May, after the miners' leaders had refused terms which the other large unions thought a

[1] The fact that 'real' wages were higher in Great Britain than in any other European country added to the difficulties of competition in exports.

[2] As late as 1936 British output per shift was not much more than 14 per cent above the figure for 1914, whereas in the decade 1927–36 the increase in the Ruhr mines was over 80 per cent and in the Polish coalfields over 50 per cent.

suitable basis for settlement the T.U.C. called off the general strike; the miners continued a futile strike in their own industry for another three months and then slowly went back to work.[1]

In 1926 Stanley Baldwin was Prime Minister for the second time. Baldwin had sat in the House of Commons since 1908; he did not hold Cabinet office until 1921.[2] He had taken the initiative in 1922 at a Conservative meeting in proposing the withdrawal of the party from the coalition under Lloyd George. Baldwin did not expect his action to have any result other than his own retirement, but in the four years since the armistice Lloyd George had lost the outstanding position which his energy and courage had given him during the war. Asquith must take a considerable share of responsibility for the split in the Liberal party which had followed his own enforced resignation in 1916. Public opinion in general was convinced, rightly or wrongly, of Asquith's failure as a war leader. If he had been readier to give up office, the breach between him and Lloyd George might not have been irreparable. As things were, his following in the Liberal party was small, but it included most of the Liberal Ministers of pre-war years. Lloyd George had therefore been compelled to rely for his parliamentary majority upon Conservative votes. It is doubtful whether he could have kept these votes permanently. The Conservatives, though they had supported him as Prime Minister, had never really trusted him; they had reason for thinking that, if it suited him, he would throw them over for a radical programme which might reunite the Liberal party. Lloyd George's treatment of nearly all post-war questions deepened the dislike and anxiety of the Conservative rank and file. The Prime Minister's actions seemed to be a series of ingenious expedients not based upon any consistent principles. He became increasingly autocratic in his methods; the Conservatives regarded his personal direction of affairs as lowering the character of British politics.

[1] The Government, which had anticipated the possibility of a general strike, had organized emergency services, on the whole, with considerable success. The T.U.C. had no comparable plans of their own for conducting a strike which they had not wanted; they had also taken insufficient account of the number of middle-class volunteers capable of working emergency transport services and of the growing importance of road transport. The withdrawal of labour from the railways could no longer endanger the food supplies of the great cities.

[2] Baldwin was Financial Secretary to the Treasury in 1917; his first office of Cabinet rank was the Presidency of the Board of Trade in 1921.

Apart from the question of unemployment, once the post-war 'replacement' boom was over, Lloyd George's most serious problem in domestic politics was Ireland. Here he inherited the bitter pre-war controversy which had been intensified by the rise of a party – known as Sinn Fein ('ourselves alone') – in Ireland demanding complete separation and not merely 'home rule'. In 1916, with an indifference, explicable on historical grounds, to the patriotism and interests of any community except their own, the Irish extremists had launched a rebellion in Dublin at a critical time for the fate of Great Britain and France and, for that matter, of a small catholic country like Belgium. The rebellion was soon suppressed, and did not have much popular support, but the formal court-martial and execution of sixteen of the rebels caught while attempting to kill British soldiers caused intense Irish resentment. Efforts by the British Government and the moderates in Ireland to bring about a compromise settlement during the war broke down on the old difficulty of allowing self-determination to Ulster. The leadership of Irish nationalism now fell almost completely into the hands of Sinn Fein – still only an active minority – but with strong financial support from Irish Americans (many of whom, again for under-standable historical reasons, were violently anti-English). This group believed that force alone could extract from Great Britain real independence for Ireland, though they were still unwilling to extend to Ulster the right of choice which they claimed for them-selves. They set up a secret administration of their own, an assembly and courts of law; they applied terrorist methods of murder and assassination against the police who were responsible for public order in the Irish countryside. Their forecasts were correct in one important consideration; the Irish people accepted them and their methods as they had always accepted successful violence.

The British Government could either surrender to terrorism or try to put down the terrorists by superior force – a process which would have meant little less than a military occupation of all Ireland outside Ulster. The British people were unlikely to acquiesce in any military reconquest. They had just ended a war in which the peace settlement had been based on the right of small nations to determine for themselves their political allegiance. If catholic Ireland refused to accept less than independence, British opinion would not want to keep her within the United Kingdom. The British electorate no longer had a bad conscience about Irish land questions. Further-more, after the destruction of German naval power, there seemed no risk that an independent and unfriendly Ireland might be used as a base for operations against Great Britain. Great Britain, however, was bound to keep her pledge to the people of Ulster whose deter-mination to stay out of a national Irish parliament and administra-tion was only strengthened by the terrorist happenings outside and often by terrorist raids into the Ulster province.

The position was made more acute because Lloyd George allowed the recruiting of an undisciplined 'auxiliary' police force – known from the colours of their uniform as 'Black and Tans' – to deal with the Irish rebel guerrillas. This recourse on the British side to the barbarous methods of Sinn Fein shocked British opinion, and public sentiment compelled Lloyd George to try for some agree-ment. It is uncertain whether the Irish extremists could have held out much longer if British military – not 'Black and Tan' – pres-sure had increased. On the other hand, the melancholy history of Irish rebellion had shewn that military suppression had never been followed by lasting pacification. After difficult negotiations (De Valera,[1] the Sinn Fein political leader, was an elusive and pedantic negotiator), a settlement, described only with technical inaccuracy as a 'treaty', was signed on 6 December 1921, in which Great Britain recognized the status of Ireland as a self-governing Domin-ion – a 'Free State' within the British Commonwealth of Nations. Ulster was given, and exercised, the right to contract out of the Irish Free State and to retain her existing status.

The treaty was welcomed by the majority of the Irish people; it was accepted with difficulty by the Irish leaders. A minority, in-cluding De Valera, repudiated the terms and, with their supporters, took to arms against the Provisional Government formally estab-lished under the treaty. The civil war which now followed between the Irish factions was of the same terrorist character as the previous fighting against the British forces. It ended, inevitably, with the

[1] Edward (he later changed his baptismal name to Eamon) De Valera was the son of a Spanish father and an Irish mother. He was born in the United States, but brought up in Ireland. He came into prominence during the Dublin rebel-lion. He was among those sentenced to death after the rebellion; the sentence was commuted on the ground of his American citizenship. He was imprisoned, re-leased on amnesty, and later rearrested. He escaped from prison, and went to the United States where he collected large sums for the Sinn Fein cause. On his

defeat of the rebel minority and the establishment of the Free State on the terms laid down in the treaty.[1]

The Irish settlement did not cancel the discredit brought on Lloyd George by the 'Black and Tans'. Lloyd George had also to meet the disappointment of those who had hoped for a 'new world' after the war. In spite, however, of its failure – for which it cannot altogether be blamed – to find work for the unemployed the government was less unpopular in the country than among the politicians, and especially the Conservatives. Lloyd George's name and his war-time services still counted for much with the electorate; his skill in manœuvre might have kept the coalition in being for a longer time if he had not made a serious blunder in foreign affairs. The Allied plans for the partition of the defeated and broken Ottoman Empire had been upset, at least in Asia Minor, by a successful military revolt led by Mustapha Kemal.[2] Kemal set up at Ankara a rival government to that of the Sultan at Constantinople and began to attack the Allied forces in Asia Minor. Lloyd George encouraged the Greeks, who looked for Smyrna, parts of eastern Thrace, and even Constantinople as their reward, to attack the Turks. After some initial success, the Greeks were completely defeated by Kemal, who had obtained large quantities of munitions from Russia, and also, though the French and British were supposed to be enforcing a common policy, had the secret connivance of France. Kemal re-occupied Smyrna in early September 1922, and then moved towards the neutral zone extending from the Black Sea to the Asiatic side of the Dardanelles which the Allies were occupying under the terms of the treaty of Sèvres with the Sultan. Kemal's army thus reached

return his colleagues accepted him as the head of the rebel political organization. De Valera objected to any formal inclusion of Ireland within the British Commonwealth; he was willing to accept an 'external association' by means of a treaty with the Commonwealth.

[1] Michael Collins, who led the Free States forces, was killed in an ambush in August 1922, possibly owing to treachery within his own party. Collins had been born in 1890. He came to London at the age of 16 and worked as a clerk in the Post Office.

[2] Mustapha Kemal (who later took the title of Ataturk, or Chief Turk) was the son of a Turkish father and an Albanian mother. He was born at Salonika in 1880. He entered the Turkish army, and during the war of 1914–18 was Turkish commander at Gallipoli.

the neighbourhood of a small British force holding Chanak on the Asiatic coast of the Dardanelles.

The Cabinet decided on 15 September 1922, to warn Kemal, who was hoping to take Constantinople, that an attempt to pass through the neutral zone would mean war. The Cabinet at the same time authorized telegrams to the Dominions explaining the crisis and inviting them to send troops. On 16 September – in order to inform the British public – the Cabinet issued a statement to the press. This statement reached the Dominion Prime Ministers before the telegrams were deciphered. The Dominion Governments, already sensitive on the question of consultation in foreign policy, felt that they were being asked to commit their peoples to war on a matter of British interest about which no consultation had taken place. New Zealand alone gave an unqualified promise of support. Fortunately for the British Government, General Harington, who was in command of the British force in the neutral zone, was able to arrange with Kemal that the Turkish forces would not enter the zone. The crisis was over, but Lloyd George's 'personal' methods of conducting foreign policy – though he shewed his usual courage and decision in resisting Kemal when France, Great Britain's ally, was in fact supporting the other side – had resulted in abandoning the Greeks to defeat, bringing Great Britain close to war, and causing an unnecessary crisis of confidence with the Dominions.

After the Chanak affair the Conservative party decided that they must leave the Coalition. In the general election which followed Lloyd George's resignation and the appointment of Bonar Law as Prime Minister the Conservatives secured 347 seats, the 'Lloyd George Liberals' only 57, and the 'Asquithian Liberals' 60 seats. The Labour Party increased its representation from 59 seats (in 1918) to 142. The disparity between the total number of Conservative and Liberal votes – about $5\frac{1}{2}$ millions to just over 4 millions – was less than the disparity between the number of Conservative and Liberal seats, but on the British electoral system, which no party in power was likely to be willing to exchange for one of proportional representation, the Liberals were almost certain to remain, as they have remained for another forty years, under-represented in the House of Commons.

Bonar Law, the Conservative Prime Minister, was an uninspiring and somewhat enigmatic figure; modest and unambitious, though he rarely refused to be pushed forward by his friends; honest, though it is still difficult to explain his part in the fall of Asquith in 1916; clear-headed in debate, remarkably good at figures, without ideas of his own or much interest in the ideas of others; personally not ungenerous, but in his approach to problems lowering the intellectual interest of politics. Bonar Law's health was not good; he resigned in May 1923, and died six months later.

The choice of Stanley Baldwin – another rich business man – as Bonar Law's successor shewed the change in the Conservative party. The old aristocratic influence was no longer dominant; Bonar Law and Baldwin never assumed, like Salisbury and Balfour, and, for that matter, the great whigs, that their class had a right to govern England. Baldwin, in particular, was deeply concerned with the improvement of industrial relations. Unfortunately he had few other qualifications for the office of Prime Minister except an astute and subtle skill in handling parliament. He was not an idle man, but he disliked trouble and evaded rather than solved difficult problems. After an error of judgment, at the end of his first period of office, in thinking that the British electorate was ready to accept a protective tariff, Baldwin was unwilling to take political risks. Baldwin's defeat in the general election of 1923 brought about a curious position. The Conservatives, with 258 seats, were still the largest party; Labour had increased its representation to 191 seats, and the two wings of the Liberal party had between them 158 seats. There was thus a free trade majority against the Conservative policy of protection; the Liberal and Labour parties had little else in common. In these circumstances Ramsay MacDonald, the leader of the Labour party, was invited to form a minority government. MacDonald has been more spitefully treated from within his own party than any other politician of the left. He had obvious faults. He was vain, imprecise, and often 'woolly-minded'; he disliked criticism and was jealous of his colleagues, but he understood more clearly than most of the Labour party that they could not hope to carry through their programme unless they won the sympathy of moderate opinion. From this point of view MacDonald's vagueness was not altogether a disadvantage. The Labour party had accepted 'socialism' in 1918, but 'socialism' and 'socialization' were somewhat loose general terms. One section of the party held to what the

Webbs[1] regarded as orthodoxy, a form of collectivism under which the essential means of production and essential services were nationalized, and controlled by a central bureaucracy; a smaller section of the party, influenced by pre-war syndicalism and Guild socialism, and much excited by the Russian Revolution, wanted a greater measure of workers' control. This latter demand, which in a last analysis, was a protest against the depersonalized harshness of the existing industrial order, had been especially strong among the miners, for whom nationalization was, openly, only a stage in a frankly revolutionary change of ownership.

Five years after the armistice the Labour party had increased its vote, but its programme had lost some of its glamour. The British people, and, in particular, the soldiers who came back from the war, had not wanted a society transformed by revolution. They were content to get back to the society they had known, with certain definite social and economic improvements – more pay and amenities, shorter hours of work, less unemployment, better housing; they had no liking for the all-pervading bureaucratic direction which they had endured during the war years. Although the demand for a greater share in management was too deep-seated to disappear, the practical difficulties of any form of workers' control were becoming obvious; there was less incentive to take over industries at a time when the enterprises to be 'taken over' were working at a loss. The example of Russia became less attractive as more British labour representatives saw Soviet dictatorship at first hand, and as the Soviet Government continued to abuse British Labour leaders and their policy.[2]

A member of the Labour Government has described the constant preoccupation of his colleagues 'to keep the party fairly quiet

[1] Beatrice Potter (1858–1943), daughter of a well-to-do business man, married Sidney Webb (1859–1947), a civil servant, in 1892. Mrs Webb was an attractive woman of great ability, though too confident about her own rightness; Sidney Webb was also an able man whose method of bringing about the permeation of society by collectivism (see above, p. 154) was one of universal 'wire-pulling'. Sidney Webb was mainly responsible for the Labour manifesto 'Labour and the New Social Order' issued by the Labour party in 1918.

[2] The Webbs described Soviet Russia in 1920 as 'the servile State in being'. Mrs Philip Snowden, whose husband was Chancellor of the Exchequer in the Labour Government of 1923, was shocked on a visit to Moscow by Lenin's cynical comment that the way to get rid of property-owning peasants was to invite the non-property-owning peasants to murder them.

and the permanent officials satisfied'. On the whole MacDonald succeeded in convincing moderate opinion in the country that a Labour government did not threaten social and economic order. MacDonald's Government fell, however, partly because he could not control the small but vociferous left wing group, partly because he gave way to this left wing in accepting commercial and general treaties with Russia on conditions more favourable to the Soviet Union than to Great Britain, and finally owing to his own *maladresse* in dealing with a letter which, if genuine (and the genuineness was doubtful), shewed Russian propagandist interference in British affairs.

Baldwin was back as Prime Minister in November 1924. In the spring of 1926 he had to deal with the general strike, but his five years of office were, on the whole, the quietest domestic period between the two wars. These years were marked by a formal recognition of the change which had come about in the relations between Great Britain and the self-governing Dominions. Lloyd George's sudden appeal to the Dominions over the Chanak crisis had brought into the foreground the fears of the Dominion Governments that they might become involved, without previous consultation, in a war on behalf of a purely British interest which did not concern them. The Dominions had made a remarkable contribution to the victory over Germany,[1] and had shewn their great collective power as self-governing communities under the British Crown. The realization of their own status in the world made them even less likely to agree to any form of closer union with Great Britain. They were concerned with securing for themselves a greater part in decisions on foreign policy within the existing constitutional relationship, but they did not want a greater share in control to carry with it greater responsibility or commitments. In other words they were concerned primarily with their right to 'contract out' of any policy which seemed to them outside their sphere of interests, and, after the destruction of German naval power, they were less occupied with European politics. Canadians were inclined to take the common American view of the incurable turbulence of the European states.

The Dominions had already obtained individual representation at the Peace Conference. Their representatives had signed the

[1] See p. 191.

treaty of Versailles on behalf of their Governments, and their Parliaments had accepted the treaty before it was ratified by the Crown on behalf of the British Empire. The Dominions had also secured separate membership of the League of Nations. They were in fact more qualified for recognition as sovereign independent States than most of the newly created States of the peace settlement. They had reached their present position by peaceful stages. Their parliamentary institutions, their courts of law, their systems of local government, their traditions of a free press and personal liberties were long established. They had no feelings of inferiority, no plans of aggression. Sooner or later further constitutional changes would give them in form the complete independence which they already possessed in fact. For a time there had seemed no need to hurry on these final changes, and, if the Chanak crisis had not occurred, this last stage might have been delayed, though not for very long.

In 1923 an Imperial Conference, described carefully as a 'conference of representatives of the several Governments of the Empire', considered the problem. They laid it down as desirable that treaties should not be concluded by any one member of the Empire without consulting the other members; a recommendation which could be taken to assume the right of the Dominions to conclude treaties without even the nominal approval of the terms by the British Government. The Labour Administration in 1924 did not consult the Dominions before giving diplomatic recognition to the U.S.S.R. In 1925 the Conservative Government did not invite Dominion representatives to the Locarno Conference[1] because they knew that the Dominions did not wish to be represented. No one of the Dominions adhered to the Locarno treaty; the obligations affected only Great Britain.

The Imperial Conference of 1926 recognized the actual situation in its description of Great Britain and the Dominions as 'autonomous Communities within the British Empire, equal in status, in no way subordinate one to another in any aspect of their domestic or external affairs, though united by a common allegiance to the Crown, and freely associated as members of the British Commonwealth of Nations'. The next step was a recognition in legal form of the consequences of this definition. This step was not completed until the passing of the Statute of Westminster in 1931.

[1] See below, pp. 213–14.

The Statute, which was agreed between the British and Dominion Parliaments, gave complete legislative freedom to the Dominions even if their laws should conflict with British legislation.[1]

The Statute of Westminster might be regarded as the final defeat of Joseph Chamberlain's hopes of a closely knit British Empire bound by economic ties. Nevertheless Chamberlain and all the theorists with schemes of federation had failed to understand the considerations of world power which had kept and might still keep together the great English-speaking Dominions. Twelve years after the Dominion Prime Ministers at the Conference of 1902 had rejected Chamberlain's proposals for closer union the Dominions – to the surprise of the enemies of England – had voluntarily made very great sacrifices in a common cause with the Mother-Country. Eight years after the Statute of Westminster the Dominions, when they were legally without any obligation to do so, once again came to the assistance of Great Britain. In each case these independent nations, which had rightly been careful to assert their full autonomy and power of choice, realized (as, on the other hand, the smaller States of Europe in 1939–40 failed to realize until too late) that only by concerted action could they maintain their liberties.[2]

The domestic activities of Baldwin's Government from 1924 to 1929 were not insignificant. They included pensions for widows (with allowances for children), the reorganization of local government, the creation of a Central Electricity Board for the distribution of electric power on a national basis, and the establishment of the

[1] The term 'Dominion status' which came into common use after 1919 (see below, p. 228), was never properly defined. The term 'British Commonwealth of Nations' was older. Rosebery had used it as early as 1884. Fabian Socialists also employed it because it had no imperialist associations. On the other hand, it too was a vague term, and unlikely to appeal to Indians or the Afrikaner population of South Africa.

[2] De Valera (see above, p. 198) who won an electoral victory in 1932, and whose single-track mind was as determined as ever to secure an independent Irish republic, took immediate advantage of the Statute of Westminster. He abolished the oath of allegiance to the King as Head of the Commonwealth; five years later he announced a new constitution giving to the Irish Free State the name of Eire and declaring the country a sovereign, independent democratic State under a President. The British Government refused to allow any alteration in the status of Ulster but otherwise accepted the changes; British public opinion was indifferent to them. In the second world war Eire remained neutral, and, in spite of American pressure, withheld from the Allies the use of Eire ports for naval purposes. In 1949 De Valera announced the complete secession of Eire from the Commonwealth.

B.B.C. as a public corporation. Nevertheless the Conservatives did not solve the problem of unemployment – the figure was still over a million – and had no programme likely to attract the electorate. At the general election of 1929 Baldwin's leading theme for the voters was 'safety first'. Asquith had accepted a peerage in 1925, and had left active political life. Lloyd George was trying to get a Liberal revival; he produced a comprehensive programme of social and economic legislation, but he had not won back the confidence of the country, while the Labour party outbid his programme and seemed more likely to be able to put it into effect.

The electors returned 287 Labour members, 261 Conservatives, and only 59 Liberals.[1] Labour once more took office as a minority government with MacDonald again as Prime Minister. The Labour plans were unexpectedly deranged before the end of the year by the grave financial crisis beginning with the collapse of the Stock Exchange boom in the United States, and, as a consequence, the withdrawal of short-term American foreign loans. The fall in commodity prices, which reduced the purchasing power of countries producing raw materials, affected British exports and brought about a disastrous rise in unemployment. The Labour Government was divided over possible remedies, temporary as well as long-term. Lord Beaverbrook, a Canadian business man who had acquired a considerable control of the cheaper British press, used his newspapers to advocate what he called 'Empire Free Trade' – complete freedom of trade within the Empire sheltered by a tariff from the rest of the world. The plan had no chance of success because the Dominions did not want free entry for British exports which competed with their own manufactures.[2]

While Government and Opposition were disputing with each other, and among themselves, on measures to meet the situation, the crisis suddenly became worse. In June 1931, the unemployment figures rose to nearly 2¾ millions. In the following month there was

[1] The Conservatives had passed an act lowering from 30 to 21 the age qualification for women voters. This measure, and the removal by the property qualification hitherto imposed on women voters, increased the electorate by over 7 millions.

[2] Beaverbrook and his fellow newspaper proprietor Lord Rothermere (brother of the late Lord Northcliffe) continued their attacks on the Conservative leaders. Baldwin finally turned on them, and in a speech of March 1931, accused them of distorting facts in their newspapers in order to get power for themselves, 'power without responsibility, the prerogative of the harlot throughout the ages'.

a collapse of confidence in Germany. The mood spread to Great Britain where at the end of July a special Committee on National Expenditure (appointed five months earlier) recommended severe cuts in Government expenditure, including unemployment benefit. The effect abroad of the Committee's report was to increase doubts about the stability of the £ sterling. These doubts grew when the Cabinet was obviously disagreeing about the economy measures. Finally Ministers were openly divided on the amount of the reduction to be made in unemployment pay. MacDonald then asked for the resignation of his colleagues. They expected that he too would give up office, but next day – 24 August – he told them to their surprise that after consultation with the King and the Conservative and Liberal party leaders, he had agreed to the formation of a National Coalition government, with himself as Prime Minister, to tide over the economic crisis.

The National Coalition had the support of the Conservatives and most of the Liberals. Only two important Labour Ministers in the Commons – J. H. Thomas and Snowden – joined it. The Government satisfied high financial opinion abroad that it really intended to cut down expenditure, but three weeks later protests (magnified by press accounts into a 'naval mutiny') by sailors of a detachment of the fleet at Invergordon (Scotland) over cuts in their pay shook foreign confidence again and on 21 September forced the Government to abandon the gold standard. Devaluation brought none of the expected disasters. The fall in the dollar value of the £ gave a temporary advantage to the export trades; wages did not fall and unemployment benefit continued to be paid.

The National Government now decided upon a general election. Their wish to shew the world that they had strong support in the country was not unreasonable. Moreover the Conservatives believed that only a protective tariff could supply a permanent cure for the economic sickness of Great Britain. Such a remedy could hardly be tried without a popular mandate. The election was held early in October 1931. The National Government obtained the immense majority of 497 seats over their opponents.

The events which led to the resignation of the Labour Cabinet, the formation of the National Government and the general election of 1931, have been the subject of angry controversy. Labour supporters have described the crisis as 'unreal', 'a bankers' ramp'; they have suggested that MacDonald acted out of personal ambition, and that he planned to get rid of his Labour supporters and become Prime Minister of a coalition government. Conservative writers have accused the Labour Cabinet of giving way to the pressure of the Trades Union Congress and the extreme left wing of the party. There is an element of truth in all these exaggerated charges. Foreign holders of sterling and foreign bankers who could provide credit were uneasy at the failure of the Labour Cabinet to take firm hold of the situation, at the negative attitude of the T.U.C. and at the vociferous anti-capitalist speeches of the extreme left wing. MacDonald may have thought of himself as a possible man of destiny, but there is no reason to suppose that he had been intriguing throughout the critical period to get for himself the leadership of a coalition (of which there had already been considerable talk). It is clear that at the time he regarded such a coalition merely as a temporary expedient to deal with the financial difficulties. The Conservatives certainly used the election to obtain a mandate for protection; they had every right to try to do so – only the extreme free traders still looked upon the advocacy of protection as immoral and sinister. In such confusion – political and personal – it is not easy to draw conclusions; the electors by their votes shewed that, rightly or wrongly, they distrusted the capacity of the Labour party to meet a financial crisis and that they did not want the socialist remedies outlined in the party election manifesto.

The record of the National Government is so much over-shadowed by its disastrous failures in foreign policy that its domestic policy is often overlooked. This domestic policy was dominated by the energy and efficiency of Neville Chamberlain. MacDonald was already in failing health; he gave up the Prime Ministership in June 1935. Baldwin, his inevitable successor, had not grown more enterprising or assertive with the years, though he supported Chamberlain's measures. Neville Chamberlain's real interests were in social reform. He had refused the Chancellorship of the Exchequer in 1924 in order to return to the Ministry of Health which he had held for a short time in Baldwin's first Cabinet. He had been responsible for important reforms in rating and local government, and had initiated housing plans which within five years brought about the building of nearly a million houses. He went back to the Ministry of Health in the National Government until Snowden's resignation from the Chancellorship of the Exchequer over the introduction of protection. Chamberlain then became Chancellor and in this capacity introduced a general tariff, and later by a successful conversion measure secured a very considerable reduction in the National Debt charges.

Chamberlain was clearly marked out – in a Cabinet not notable for the high ability of its members – as Baldwin's successor. Baldwin retired in May 1937, six months after his firm but tactful handling of the personal crisis leading to the abdication of King Edward VIII. Chamberlain was excellent in the conduct of business, and in private life a civilized man, interested in music and gardens. On the other hand he lacked many of the qualities essential in a Prime Minister. He was obstinate, cold and even rasping in manner, and a poor judge of men, whether they were colleagues or opponents. The economic position of the country improved under the National Government, and the Ministers can take some credit for this improvement which was due to the cumulative effect of a number of practical measures rather than to any grandiose plan. Unemployment, however, remained high; the figures fell from the highest level of about 3 millions at the end of 1933 to about $1\frac{1}{2}$ million in the summer of 1937. British exports never recovered fully, but the country secured a slightly larger share of a much diminished world trade. The amount spent on housing had something of the effect of a large public works programme in providing employment. The agreements concluded with the Dominions at the Ottawa Conference of 1932, though not as beneficial to British trade as the Government had hoped – the Dominions were as reluctant as ever to risk competition with their own industries – gave certain advantages to British exporters in return for increased preferences to Dominion primary products. Trade agreements, mainly on a quota basis, were made with most European countries. British agriculture, assisted by marketing boards and, in certain cases, by subsidies, increased its productivity by about a sixth without raising domestic prices. Protective duties and reorganization schemes benefited the heavy industries. Steel-making plant increased and shipbuilding recovered from its worst years, when nearly two-thirds of the workers in the industry were unemployed, but the figure in 1937 was still about 25 per cent. In coal-mining the most important step – important because it made easier later on the nationalization of the mines

– was the nationalization of mining royalties with compensation to the owners. One notable feature of these years was the extension of the principle of the large public corporation to new fields. Thus the British Overseas Airways Corporation was set up in 1939 to cover civil air services and, earlier, all London transport undertakings were brought together under the control of the London Passenger Transport Board.

The generation which has grown up in Great Britain since 1939 is apt to look back on the inter-war years as a period of almost unbroken domestic gloom. It is true that chronic unemployment, especially in the 'depressed' areas, was a grave social evil with demoralizing effects. Nevertheless in 1939 an unemployed man with a family received more every week in purchasing power from unemployment relief than an unskilled workman in full work had earned before 1914. The average height and weight of children had improved remarkably over a quarter of a century. The expectation of life was longer than at any earlier time; housing was better – slum clearance schemes, though very far from complete, had rehoused over a million people within a decade. Food was more varied, and on the whole the diet of the poor was better chosen and less monotonous. In 1939 there had been for a hundred years an increasingly greater awareness of social injustice, and an increasing amount of public spending to remedy it. Before 1914 the working class paid more in taxes than they received in social services; between the wars the balance was reversed. Great Britain could not yet be described as a 'welfare state', but between 1919 and 1939 her people were moving towards this kind of community more rapidly than in periods which were looked back to as golden ages of peace and prosperity.

CHAPTER XX

British Foreign Policy from 1919 to 1939

THE PEACE SETTLEMENT of 1919, and, in particular, the treaty of Versailles with Germany disappointed all those – including the majority of the British people – who had not realized the extreme difficulty of getting agreement between allies upon the terms to be imposed upon an enemy after a long and fiercely contested war. The dominating influence at the time of the German defeat was President Wilson who insisted upon taking as the basis of the settlement certain ill-defined and often contradictory principles laid down in his own speeches. In the sudden catastrophe of total defeat – after total victory had seemed so near – the Germans would have accepted almost any conditions; they did in fact pledge themselves to accept the Allied interpretation of Wilson's XIV Points without making any detailed enquiry about their application, though this pledge did not prevent them later from complaining bitterly of the terms which were imposed upon them.[1]

The terms of the treaty of Versailles were in general much better than the Germans, who could not resign themselves to the loss of military hegemony in Europe, were ever willing to admit. The political and territorial clauses followed, as far as was practicable, Wilson's principle of national self-determination. The unity of the German Reich was maintained, whereas the Habsburg and Ottoman Empires were broken into fragments and the Russian Empire lost immense territory on its western and southern frontiers, including the economically and strategically important Baltic provinces, Finland, and Russian Poland. The loss to the German Reich of Alsace-Lorraine and part of Slesvig after military defeat was as inevitable as their earlier annexation after military victory. The

---

[1] The critical German attitude towards the treaty was reinforced in 1919 by the brilliantly written but unfair attack in J. M. Keynes' *The Economic Consequences of the Peace.* Keynes, who could speak with authority only on the financial terms, delivered a violent polemic not only against the treaty as a whole but against the good faith and intelligence of the Allied leaders.

restoration of an independent Polish state was an act of historical justice explicitly announced in the XIV Points. The loss of German colonial territories was also foreshadowed by Wilson and expected by the German Government.

The reparation clauses were most severely criticized. Lloyd George, after making some rash statements before the opening of the Conference, would have been more moderate in his demands than many of his own financial experts, but, apart from the popular clamour on the Allied side that Germany should make good the material losses which she had inflicted upon the countries attacked by her, the problem of fixing the actual amount to be paid was insuperable at the conference. No one knew how much Germany could pay when she had recovered (as she was expected to recover) her economic prosperity. The figure was at first greatly overestimated, and then underestimated; finally, in a time of panic at the world economic depression, reparation payments disappeared altogether.[1]

The treaty of Versailles included the Covenant of the League of Nations; the admission of Germany to the League was contemplated after she had given satisfactory evidence of her intention to fulfil her obligations. The establishment of a world-wide organization for keeping the peace might have been the starting-point of a new era in history; it was wrecked, primarily, by the refusal of American opinion – badly handled by President Wilson – to accept it, and by the unwillingness of Soviet Russia to alter, until it was too late, her absolute hostility to the western parliamentary democracies. Even so, the League (with its machinery for peaceful change) and the new states set up by the peace treaties might have provided the basis of a lasting peace if the Germans had not been so completely unable to realize that, in the opinion of their enemies, they were primarily responsible for provoking the war and for the savagery with which it had been fought, and also that the fear of another outburst of German aggression – a war of revenge – was a real and dominant factor in the attitude of France. In these circumstances, with the Germans doing their utmost, one might say, conscientiously to evade as much as possible of their obligations under the treaty, the short-sighted American withdrawal into political isola-

---

[1] The small amount of reparation actually paid by Germany came mainly from American loans.

tion from Europe would have been less disastrous if Great Britain
and France had worked together. Unfortunately the two Powers
were almost continuously in disagreement. There was an uneasy
rivalry between them for power and influence in the Near and
Middle East. They differed very considerably about the treatment
of Germany. The French, afraid of German superiority in man-
power and productive capacity, thought in terms of their own
security; they knew that they would hardly find it possible to repeat
the immense effort which they had made between 1914 and 1918.
After the American rejection of the treaty of Versailles, the offer of
a joint Anglo-American guarantee to France lapsed, and the military strength of Great Britain faded away with the demobilization
of her armies. The French, having abandoned their attempt to
secure the Rhine frontier (which their military advisers had regarded as necessary for their safety,) now tried to insure themselves
by alliances with the new or enlarged states of central and south-east
Europe which had an equal interest with France in maintaining the
treaty settlement. The French Government had paid less of its
war expenses out of taxation than the British Government and had
the task of restoring the devastated territories; it was therefore
determined to recover the largest possible sums from Germany,
whatever the effect might be on the German economy. Great
Britain, on the other hand, was suffering from unemployment and
the dislocation of world trade; she wanted the economic recovery of
Germany and did not really fear new German aggression when the
country had recovered its economic prosperity. Finally, the leading
personalities in England and France did not get on well together.
Neither country made sufficient allowance for the special difficulties
of the other, and the long-standing historical distrust, which cooperation in war had not altogether broken down, revived in the
post-war years.

There was a temporary improvement in the international situation with the Locarno agreements of 1925. British and French
statesmen were for once in harmony. The French had learned
something from the failure of the occupation of the Ruhr to solve
the problem of getting reparation from Germany; the British had
realized the need to meet the deep-seated French demand for
security; the German leader Stresemann, while maintaining all the
German hopes of recovering their position in Europe, had realized

the futility of stubborn attempts to evade the terms of Versailles. British opinion was unduly optimistic about the possibility of settling Franco-German differences and fears by an Anglo-Italian guarantee of the western frontier of Germany and the eastern frontier of France. Too little attention was paid in Great Britain to the opposition to Stresemann's policy in Germany and to the danger of admitting that, apparently, the clauses of the peace treaties dealing with the frontiers of France and Germany were more sacrosanct than other parts of the settlement. Even so, the Locarno agreements, the conciliatory speeches with which they were accompanied, the welcome of Germany into the League of Nations, and, still more, the fact that the undertakings now entered into by Germany were made out of free will, and could not be described in terms of a *Diktat*, gave new ground for hope. It was not for nothing that the term 'appeasement' (or in its French form 'apaisement') was used by every politician at the Locarno Conference – including Mussolini! – to describe the improvement in the relations between France and Germany, and, therefore, the possibility of a lasting European pacification.

Unfortunately it became clear before the political collapse following the world economic depression that the so-called 'spirit of Locarno' had vanished. Franco-German hostility had not been 'appeased'. A more favourable treatment of the reparation problem had not satisfied Germany. On the contrary, it seemed all too likely that as soon as she was strong enough to do so, Germany would repudiate all that remained of her financial obligations. Germany, however, could not do much in the way of repudiation with safety until she were rearmed. By a pledge unique in history the victorious Powers had pledged themselves, as a counterpart to the disarmament of Germany, to reduce their own armaments to the lowest level compatible with their national safety. For Great Britain and France this limit would be determined by their view of German intentions. A Germany still clamouring against the peace settlement, and at the same time demanding equality with the other Great Powers in armaments, was bound to alarm French opinion; the French would refuse to give up the one sure gain of the war – their military superiority in face of a practically disarmed Germany. The Germans would then claim that their former enemies were themselves not fulfilling their treaty obligations.

Successive British Governments, to their ultimate undoing, refused to support the French view. MacDonald, both as head of Labour Governments, and as Prime Minister in the National Government during the Disarmament Conference, thought that the only way to safety for France as well as for Great Britain was to rely on the 'collective security' provided by the League Covenant; the French refusal to disarm to the German level or to allow German rearmament thus seemed an obstacle to 'appeasement', and more than dangerous because, unless the Germans were satisfied, they were likely to repudiate the military clauses of the treaty of Versailles. British opinion would certainly be unwilling, and French opinion, when it came to acting alone, would hardly be willing to go to war with Germany to prevent her rearmament. MacDonald, before his resignation, had begun to be alarmed at the evidence of illegal German rearmament, as well he might be after Hitler had become Chancellor of the Reich, and, having failed to get Anglo-French consent to immediate German equality in armaments, had taken Germany out of the League of Nations. By this time the breakdown of the League was becoming increasingly clear to the governments of the Great Powers, though the British electorate was still much influenced by the well-organized 'pressure group' tactics of the supporters of 'collective security'.

The test of the League had come, not in Europe, where the framers of the Covenant had expected it, but in the Far East. Here Japan had secured for herself a great military advantage in the treaties reached at Washington in 1922. In return for a mere promise to settle disputes by negotiation Japan obtained British and American consent to the prohibition of new fortifications at Hong Kong or other British or American possessions in the Pacific from which she (Japan) might feel threatened. Japan had thus safeguarded her own sea communications with Korea and Manchuria, while Great Britain had no adequately fortified base until the construction of Singapore. Great Britain had also given up the Anglo-Japanese alliance to satisfy the wishes of the Dominions and the United States, and could no longer protect her Far Eastern interests without American support. The Japanese occupation of Manchuria began in 1931; their attack on the Chinese at Shanghai in 1932 was followed later in the year by the establishment of the puppet state of Manchukuo, and, in 1933, by the invasion of Jehol – a northern province of China – and the withdrawal of Japan from the League of Nations after the League had pronounced against Japanese action. Meanwhile the naval agreements made at Washington in 1922 and London in 1930, under the guise of a general reduction in naval armaments, had lowered British naval superiority over Japan.

In December 1933, two months after he had announced the withdrawal of Germany from the League, Hitler, contrary to the terms of the treaty of Versailles, re-established conscription in Germany. With Germany and Japan out of the League the attitude of Italy was more important. Mussolini, however, had no interest in the maintenance of a collective world order, and when the League Powers tried ineffectively to prevent him from making aggressive war upon Abyssinia, he brought Italy out of the League, and joined the other law-breaking powers. The failure of the powers to use the League as an instrument for enforcing peace was now obvious. It could be argued that the attempt to involve every state in the pursuit of aggressors was a mistake, since it merely prevented the localization of wars; every war would become a general war. On the other hand it could also be argued that the extravagant and 'absolute' nationalism of the dictator states was bound to lead to general war, and that the democracies were in danger of destruction one by one if they did not combine to stop aggression, and, above all, if they lost their superiority in armaments.

The years between Mussolini's Abyssinian adventure in 1935 and Hitler's attack on Poland in 1939 were thus years of missed opportunities and fatal mistakes of policy, especially for Great Britain who might have used her strength to maintain the rule of law without paying the terrible price ultimately exacted from her. In retrospect it is difficult to account for the short-sighted folly of British statesmen and of British opinion. One may observe – though this is no excuse – that the United States and, for different reasons, the Soviet Union were equally blind to the threat to civilization from the fascist dictators. There is no need to assume a deterioration of the British character; the second world war shewed that the British people were as capable as at any time in their history of courage, endurance, and hard effort. One factor indeed in British public opinion was not discreditable; the British nation need not be ashamed of its reluctance to believe that in other countries the national leaders would intend, and prepare their countrymen for a renewal of general war. There is less excuse for the failure to realize the significance of new factors such as air-power on British security or even to understand that the changed economic position of Great Britain had weakened her political power in the world. British elections were fought mainly on domestic issues; the electorate had little understanding of the trend of world affairs, and was given too little enlightenment by its leaders. Each of the political parties misread the international situation. A dominant section of the Conservatives thought that by conciliation and concession they could bring Italy and Germany back to a policy of peaceful co-operation (they were less hopeful about Japan) or at least that they could persuade Mussolini that Italian interests would suffer from the continental hegemony of National Socialist Germany. On the other hand left-wing opinion refused too long to see that the League of Nations was only as strong as the military force of its supporting states, and that increasingly after 1935 a temporary coalition of the law-breakers might be more powerful than an Anglo-French combination. The Labour party inside and outside Parliament had blamed the British Government, or French obstinacy, for the breakdown of the Disarmament Conference, and, so far from recognizing that they could hope to negotiate only from a position of military strength, they refused to support the rearmament of their own country unless they could be sure that the arms would be used to support what they called a 'League policy'.

The confusion of thought can be seen in the so-called 'Peace Ballot' of 1935, a private referendum organized by a self-appointed body closely connected with the supposedly non-party League of Nations Union. This ballot shewed about ten million voters in favour of the use of economic and non-military sanctions against an aggressor, but under seven million favoured and over two and a half million opposed military sanctions. The outbreak of civil war in Spain added to the intellectual confusion. The young volunteers from Great Britain who went to fight on the side of the Spanish Government in this civil war may have assumed too easily that they were fighting for liberty as the term was understood in their own country; General Franco, however, was clearly not a champion of democracy in any form and a victory won by him with German and

Italian assistance was likely to be a serious threat to Anglo-French security.[1] The most dangerous consequence of the preoccupation of left-wing opinion with the Spanish affair was that it diverted the attention of a large section of British public opinion from the grave problem created by the much faster increase in German than in Anglo-French rearmament. As late as 1938 Germany spent five times as much as Great Britain on armaments.

Thus, with their minds turned away from realities, and without wise and informed leadership, the British nation allowed the military initiative to pass to the side of unreason and aggression. The Locarno policy of European appeasement degenerated into a policy of appeasement in the sense of satisfying the appetite of a beast of prey by allowing it to seize its victims. What one might call parliamentary chance worked against the adoption of a wiser British policy. Baldwin had not been altogether blind to the danger, but after a heavy Conservative defeat at a London by-election in 1933, he thought that a Conservative appeal to the country on the issue of rearmament would bring a Labour victory which would make matters worse, since a Labour Government would do less than the Conservatives were doing to meet the German threat. Winston Churchill, who, almost alone on the Conservative side, realized the enormous risk which Great Britain was taking, had been at odds with his party on other questions and was at this time regarded as an unstable and even eccentric political figure. The choice of Neville Chamberlain as Baldwin's successor was doubly unfortunate because Chamberlain was fantastically hopeful that he could persuade the dictators, or at least one of them, to accept a general European settlement. At the same time Chamberlain knew little about Europe and the fateful effects of National Socialism upon the German people. In his self-confident and obstinate way he also thought that his professional advisers at the Foreign Office were mistaken; he neglected their advice in favour of far less competent

---

[1] The view of the British Government that Spanish opinion would be more favourable after the civil war to those states which had not interfered in it turned out to be correct. The refusal of General Franco to enter the second world war on the German side was a disappointment to Hitler and an immense advantage to the western Allies. It must be remembered, however, that Great Britain and the United States were in a position to cut off the seaborne supplies upon which Spain depended, especially in her exhausted condition after the civil war, and which Germany could not provide.

judges. His Foreign Secretaries were of little help in correcting his errors. Eden had failed in 1936 to see that resistance to Hitler's repudiation of Locarno and remilitarization of the Rhineland offered the last chance – and even so not an easy chance – of getting rid of him and the Nazi regime without a long and catastrophic war. The British Government therefore, instead of stiffening French resistance, strongly advocated concession, and the opportunity faded out in a cloud of words. Eden, at all events, resigned over Chamberlain's futile efforts to conciliate Mussolini; Lord Halifax, who became Eden's successor, agreed uncritically and weakly with the Prime Minister's policy.

The Munich agreement of 1938, in which Great Britain and France accepted nearly all Hitler's outrageous demands on Czechoslovakia, humiliated the Western Powers without giving them much of a respite. It is indeed still a matter of controversy whether Great Britain and France would have been better placed if they had gone to war in 1938. The military arguments are fairly even, though perhaps the gain of time in which Great Britain was able to build up a force of fighter aircraft just sufficient for her defence in 1940 and to develop the radar system of warning (which immensely increased the defensive power of a numerically smaller air force) may be held decisive. Political considerations were certainly on the side of delay. The western Powers could not have saved Czechoslovakia from being overrun in 1938. Opinion in the Dominions and in the United States was much less agreed in 1938 in thinking that Hitler could be stopped only by force. There is no reason to suppose that the Russians would have been more willing in 1938 than they were in 1939 to risk a war with Germany; they would have been unable to provide direct help to Czechoslovakia and their army was still disorganized by Stalin's 'purges'.

The total repudiation of the Munich agreement by Hitler in the spring of 1939, the destruction of Czech independence, and the obvious German threats to Poland and other countries at last convinced Chamberlain and his Cabinet that German lawlessness could be checked only by armed resistance. Great Britain and France now tried to get a coalition of Powers strong enough to meet the danger. Success depended on bringing into a defensive alliance either the United States or the Soviet Union; the smaller European Powers did not dare to offend Hitler. Italy, though in no position to go to war, had committed herself too deeply to draw away from Germany. The United States was still in a mood of unrealistic isolation; President Roosevelt obtained from Congress only with difficulty in November 1939 the removal of the neutrality legislation which forbade the export of war material to belligerents, and would have prevented the Allies from obtaining the munitions and weapons essential to make up their deficiency in relation to Germany. Russia, still affected by Stalin's political and military purges, had no wish to defend bourgeois democracy against fascism; Russian interests would be better served by a long war fought to exhaustion between Germany and the western Powers. If Germany offered the Russians an agreement by which they could avoid war and also regain lost territory which might strengthen them against a later attack, the Soviet oligarchs would certainly accept the offer. The remarkable fact is that, Great Britain and France, ignoring Stalin's plain warning of March 1939 that Russia would not allow herself to be dragged into war on behalf of other Powers, still thought it possible to get Russian cooperation on terms which the defenders of international law could accept. Even if their diplomacy had been more skilful – the guarantee to Poland was given without consultation with the U.S.S.R., and without considering whether the Poles would be willing to admit Russian troops to Polish territory to repel a German attack – the western Powers could not have denied their own political principles by conniving at Russian claims to interfere with the independence and indeed to take virtual possession of the Baltic States. On the other hand it is hardly necessary to point out that the Russians paid heavily for their duplicity in dealing with the Allies. Instead of the Anglo-French armies fighting an exhausting war of attrition with the Germans, to the ultimate advantage of the U.S.S.R., the rapid collapse of France in 1940, and Hitler's rash decision to attack Russia before he had defeated Great Britain, involved the Russians for a long time in meeting the main strength of the German forces on land; in other words, the Russians brought upon themselves the very situation which they hoped to avoid by their agreement with Hitler.

CHAPTER XXI

The Second German War and After

FOR GREAT BRITAIN the war of 1939–45 was a longer and in some respects a more terrible experience than the war of 1914–18. The loss of life was smaller, the material destruction greater; casualties and hardships among the civilian population were more numerous; food rationing, which had ended (except for sugar) within a year of the armistice of 1918, lasted after the second war until 1950. The months between June and December 1940 were more anxious than any comparable period in the first war, and the disasters of the first half of 1942 hardly less depressing than the short weeks of the German offensive of 1918. The country had not been in such danger as in the summer of 1940 since the Spanish Armada of 1588 sailed up the Channel to protect the landing of a Spanish army of invasion. For the first seven months of the war the British Government had believed, or had acted as though they believed, that time was on their side. They knew that until they had built up their forces they could not take the offensive except at sea against Germany. They expected a long war, and thought that their greater economic strength would take them a long way towards ultimate victory.

The Allied failure to expel the Germans from Norway in April 1940 was a sharp warning that Germany held the initiative and intended to use it ruthlessly and without regard to neutral rights. Chamberlain's administration did not long survive the Norwegian disaster. Chamberlain resigned on 10 May – the day of the opening of the German offensive in the west – after he had failed to get support for a coalition under his leadership. Winston Churchill took office in a National Coalition which lasted until after the German surrender. The first six weeks of this new government were filled with disaster; the only relief was the successful evacuation of the British Expeditionary Force (with the loss of most of its equipment) from France. After the military defeat and political capitulation of

France the invasion of an almost defenceless Great Britain seemed to her friends as well as to her enemies almost certain. The invasion did not take place because the German air force was unable to win control over the areas in which the landing would have been made. The British return, however, first to an assurance of survival and then to confidence in complete victory was necessarily slow. Not until the entry of the United States into the war in December 1941, was Churchill (and all England with him) able to say that at last there was no doubt of victory.

There was no single cause of victory. One may list certain factors: (i) the leadership given by Churchill, and the national response to this leadership; (ii) an efficient coordination, after May 1940, of the whole of British resources in the prosecution of the war; (iii) the cooperation of the Dominions and the United States (before as well as after the latter became belligerents); (iv) the endurance and ultimate victories of the Russian armies and people; (v) the political and military errors of Hitler, and, in a last analysis, the baseness of his character.

(i) It is impossible to overestimate the contribution of Churchill to victory both in his firm direction of policy and in his appeal to national feeling. There had been no leader – not even the first Elizabeth or William Pitt Earl of Chatham – since Alfred the Great[1] over a thousand years earlier who had shewn such mastery in counsel and action, no one who had appealed in such direct and unforgettable words to the common man. One might mention two critical matters in 1940 in which Churchill's influence was decisive. On 26 May 1940, the day before the beginning of the Dunkirk evacuation, and before it could be known how much of the British army would be saved, M. Reynaud, the French Prime Minister, came to London to propose, on behalf of the French Government, a joint Anglo-French approach to Mussolini in the hope that he (Mussolini) might not want too great a German predominance in Europe, and might therefore suggest to Hitler an offer of moderate terms to the Allies. Halifax, who was still Foreign Secretary, was not altogether opposed to such an approach. Churchill saw at once not only that Hitler would reject it even if Mussolini could be persuaded to sponsor it, but also that the fact of making it would have disastrous effects upon British morale. Chamberlain and Attlee sup-

[1] See above, pp. 17–18.

ported Churchill, and the Cabinet agreed to reject the French proposal.[1] The second decision in these early days which had momentous consequences was Churchill's refusal to waste the last reserves of British fighter strength in the air by throwing them into the battle of France which was already lost. The first of these two decisions confirmed the British resolution not to surrender; the second kept in being the necessary resources to defeat the German air attack which was to have been the prelude to invasion.

The response of the British people to Churchill's leadership was immediate and profound. One might note, in particular, the absence of any general panic during the German air attacks upon the civil population,[2] and the formation of a Home Guard to assist in meeting an invasion.[3]

(ii) The coordination of British strategy and the use of all the nation's resources for the requirements of total war surpassed anything in the war of 1914–18. The great error of this first war was the failure of the high military command – a failure which Asquith did little to correct and Lloyd George was not altogether successful in correcting – to make use of the great engineering and other technical resources of the country to solve the military problem of breaking the deadlock in trench warfare. All was changed in the second war, and the change was due not so much to the initiative of the military authorities as to Churchill's open-minded recourse to scientific and technical advice. There were, of course, differences of opinion over strategic policy and serious mistakes were made, but Churchill's hold on his Cabinet and Parliament and the military chiefs of staff prevented anything like the unfortunate dissensions between Lloyd George and Haig and Robertson in the first war.

(iii) As in the earlier war the cooperation of the Dominions was of immense military value, especially in 1940, both at home and in

[1] The French, contrary to M. Reynaud's own judgment, insisted on making an approach which was ignominiously rejected by Mussolini.

[2] The first severe German air attacks on London were directed against the poorer quarters in the east end of the city. If the population of those areas had not, as a whole, set an example of steadfastness, the German aim of demoralizing the British people by 'terror' attacks might have succeeded.

[3] This volunteer body was formed in the first instance largely by veterans of the first war who came together almost spontaneously. Obviously they could not have been a match for the German army, but their local knowledge and previous war experience would have enabled them to take important delaying and harassing action.

the Middle East. The part played by the United States was decisive. Without American help Great Britain – and Russia – would have lost the war. American cooperation of a practical kind began long before the United States became a belligerent. President Roosevelt's provision of aid under the 'Lend-Lease' plan enabled American supplies to be continued after British dollar resources had been exhausted. The 'Atlantic Charter' was drawn up while the United States was still, technically, neutral. Anglo-American staff conversations, which laid the foundations of future cooperation, also began before the Japanese attack upon Pearl Harbour. The Combined Anglo-American Chiefs of Staff Committee in Washington worked extremely well; the decision to concentrate on the defeat of Germany before attacking Japan in full strength was of the highest importance though it was never fully accepted by the United States naval command. There were significant Anglo-American differences about the date of a cross-Channel invasion, of which the Americans at first underrated the difficulties. Fortunately Churchill's discussions with Roosevelt persuaded the Americans to make the North African landings rather than attempt prematurely the opening of a second front in Europe for which the Russians (having previously left western Europe to its fate) were clamouring many months before there was any chance of success.

(iv) Notwithstanding their unreasonable and impractical demands on their Allies, and their lack of political collaboration after full victory was in sight, the Russian contribution to the defeat of Hitler was very great. Without the Russian victories in the east, and the continuous drain on German man-power, the Anglo-American invasion of northern France in 1944 would hardly have been possible.[1]

(v) Finally it is important to notice the enormity of Hitler's mistakes. On the military side the invasion of Russia and the incitement of Japan to attack the United States were acts of self-destruction. Politically, Hitler's inability to shew generosity, imagination or pity was ultimately his undoing. If in 1940 and after, the 'New Order' promised by the Germans for Europe had been made genuinely attractive, and not merely a thinly disguised state of serfdom for non-Germans, Great Britain might have been isolated in

[1] In the summer of 1941 most – not all – British military opinion expected the collapse of the Russians within a few months.

European opinion as a disturber of the good order and peace of the Continent. The savagery of the German armies – not only the special Nazi formations – in Russia at Hitler's orders wrecked any possibility, if one had existed, of a separate Russo-German peace. The full horror of the German concentration camps was not known generally until after the war was over, but there was evidence enough to make every European country, including Germany's former associates, welcome the Anglo-American armies as liberators.[1]

The final stages of the war against Germany were prolonged by the frantic determination of Hitler to fight to the last whatever the cost to the German people. The Allied demand for unconditional surrender (which had been enforced in theory though not in practice against the Italians and the Balkan satellites of Germany) did not prolong the war and was not the reason why Hitler did not ask for terms. The Allies in any case could not have come to terms with the Nazi leaders or have countenanced the survival of any part of their regime or allowed them to keep any of their conquests. On the other hand the internal opposition to the regime was not sufficiently strong or well-organized to be able to overthrow it until it had been broken by total defeat.[2]

After the German surrender the war against Japan was ended early in September 1945 after the American use of the newly devised atomic bomb. The Americans had expected that the defeat of Japan would take another year and exact a heavy cost in lives. Historians will continue to discuss whether in fact Japan could have held out much longer, and therefore whether the use of the bomb

---

[1] Hitler's almost childish belief in the decisive value of his 'new weapons' was in the end a sign of despair, though, if British bombing raids on the German experimental station at Peenemunde had not delayed the production of the German pilotless bombs and rockets, the Anglo-American invading armies might not have been able to concentrate in sufficient strength in English harbours along the south coast.

[2] Approaches to the British Government were made from time to time by Germans for assistance in plans to get rid of Hitler and his *entourage*. The British Government was in difficulty about these approaches. They could not be sure whether they were genuine (some were known to be initiated by the German secret service). They also did not know whether the Germans concerned were likely to be able to carry out their promises to remove Hitler. Nearly all the German opponents of the Nazi regime laid down as a necessary condition of securing popular support that Germany should keep most of Hitler's territorial gains before 1940.

was necessary from a military point of view to secure her immediate surrender.

Woodrow Wilson had brought his country into the first world war with a general idea of the kind of peace which the United States would wish to enforce, if necessary, against the wishes of their European Allies.[1] For many months in the second war Great Britain was fighting for survival and could form no clear idea what the international situation would be after Germany had been defeated. Even if, as the British Government and people hoped, their victory were complete, the position of Great Britain would be much weaker than in 1918, and the tasks of recovery more difficult, but British opinion envisaged a world order dominated at least for a time by the United States, the U.S.S.R., and the British Commonwealth. The U.S.S.R., however, shewed itself coldly aloof, and indeed hostile before the war was over. American opinion suspected British 'imperialism' and inclined to regard it as more dangerous than the imperialism of the U.S.S.R.[2] Thus the Americans would not support Churchill's policy of taking a firm line with the Russians while the British and United States armies were at full strength. The Russian intention to enforce communist regimes in such areas of central and south-east Europe as they were able to control was clear even before the Potsdam Conference of July 1945, but Great Britain could do little to stop them without American support. In any case public opinion in Great Britain and America had been encouraged to regard Russia as a partner in the cause of democracy, and would not have understood or accepted threats of force to ensure that the Soviet Government honoured its engagements.

Fortunately for herself and for the free nations of Europe the United States did not return to a policy of isolation and did not take long to realize that there was little or no chance of Russian cooperation. Within five years of the end of the war with Germany the

[1] Technically the Americans were not allies in the first war. Wilson insisted on the term 'Associated Power' for the United States.

[2] 'Imperialism' to most Americans (including President Roosevelt) meant the acquisition of overseas territory. Territorial expansion in the sense of pushing forward land frontiers by conquest or other means seemed far less blameworthy, and, as far as the past history of the United States was concerned, might be explained in terms of 'manifest destiny'. Russian expansion in central Asia was little known in the United States.

organization and frontiers of the 'free world' had taken roughly their present shape. The 'Marshall plan' for European recovery in 1947–8 had saved the European economic situation; the Soviet refusal to allow the states under their control to participate in this plan had shewn the sharp division – in Churchill's phrase, the 'iron curtain' – between communist and non-communist Europe. The success of the Chinese communists in 1949, after bitter civil war, extended the 'iron curtain' to Asia. The United Nations, in spite of the lessons which might have been drawn from the failures of the League, was unable to give a united leadership, since Russia used her veto on the Security Council against any measure likely to strengthen the non-communist world. In these circumstances Great Britain had little freedom of action in foreign policy. She took the lead in supporting the regional organization of security in the North Atlantic Treaty Organization; her interests were strongly favourable to an ending of the 'cold war' between the communist and non-communist worlds, but there was little that she could do, except in matters of detail and emphasis, to influence American policy, and nothing to change the attitude of the U.S.S.R. or China.

On the other hand the transformation of the British colonial empire during the two decades since the second war has itself had a profound effect upon the international balance of power. The break-up of the colonial empires of the European Powers would have come even without the war, and the tempo of change might not have been very much slower. For Great Britain the most significant surrender of power was her withdrawal from India.[1] There had been some concessions to the small but active body of nationalist

[1] India, with Burma, is twenty times the size of Great Britain, and in 1921 had a population of nearly 320,000,000, most of whom were villagers. India had 12 major languages and about 220 vernaculars. British rule in India was not much more remote from the ordinary villager than that of the earlier Hindu or Moslem dynasties. The British governing minority was almost incredibly small – some 3,500 senior officials who were always overworked. The provinces of Bengal and Madras were bigger than Italy. India was a 'welfare state' before Great Britain in the sense that the aim of British rule was the well-being of the population, but, however just and efficient, this rule was foreign, and disliked by a self-conscious Indian minority because it was so inflexible and all-pervading, and yet so aloof. Under British control the two rival religions, Hinduism and Islam, existed side by side with only occasional outbursts of violence since neither controlled power, and the British authorities were neutral. The Indians could not 'share' India with the British; the latter were too strong and too competent,

opinion in India before the war of 1914, but the movement had been transformed by the extraordinary personality of Gandhi and his ascendancy over the Indian masses. Gandhi[1] was regarded as a holy man, in a country where religious ideas and customs have always had more influence than secular law. He preached his doctrines of 'passive resistance' and 'non-cooperation' to millions of excited and ignorant men. When 'passive resistance' turned to violence, he absolved himself from responsibility by saying that the transformation was contrary to his intention.

The British Government was unable to deal with this peculiar eastern type of holiness. The Government of India Act of 1935, passed after long discussion, created an all-India federation, and established practical self-government in the provinces. These concessions were not enough; anyhow the war came before they had a fair trial. During the war the British Government offered India full Dominion status[2] under a constitution drawn up by Indians. This offer also was rejected by Indian party leaders. Meanwhile, with the prospect of independence, the Moslems had become alarmed at the probable consequences to them of government by a permanent Hindu majority. After the war the British Government could get no agreement between Hindus and Moslems. Finally Attlee announced in 1947 that Great Britain would leave India not later than June 1948. Since there was no agreed single Indian authority to whom power could be handed over, the partition of the country into two states of India (Hindu) and Pakistan (Moslem) was inevitable.[3]

Withdrawal from India has been followed by withdrawal from

---

and, whatever the consequences, there was no half-way solution between submission and independence.

[1] Mohandas Karamchand Gandhi was born in 1868. He came to England in 1888 to study, and after practising at the Indian bar for two years went to South Africa where he stayed for twenty years organizing the Indian community. Gandhi knew no history beyond school level; he despised science, and cared nothing for economic and administrative questions.

[2] See above, p. 205.

[3] The process of partition after the British withdrawal was accompanied or followed by disastrous attacks upon the respective Hindu and Moslem population, mainly, though not entirely in the border areas. Both India and Pakistan remained in the Commonwealth, but elected in 1949 to become republics. A meeting of Dominion Prime Ministers agreed that this change should not mean their exclusion from the Commonwealth.

Africa. The former British colonial empire is therefore now an association of states, in a Commonwealth of which the majority of the members are no longer of European origin. It is impossible to forecast whether such an association can survive the harsh and excited nationalism of the new African states and what hope of lasting success there is for the attempt of Great Britain to leave these states on their independence, as she has left India and Pakistan, with the working machinery of modern democratic communities. The experiment implies a faith in liberal institutions and in the ultimate value of the historic civilization of Europe which in their present mood the people of former colonial territories are apt to dismiss superficially as a mere instrument of exploitation. If the experiment succeeds, the world will not have been the poorer for the period of British imperial rule.

The Labour Government which took the momentous step of withdrawing from India had been elected within three months of the capitulation of Germany. Labour had refused to continue the war-time coalition, and the parties went separately to the polls. To their surprise the Conservatives were defeated. Labour was returned with 393 seats to the Conservative 213. The defeat was a heavy blow to Churchill, but it did not affect his popularity or the immense esteem in which he was held by the British people. The electors who voted against him were passing judgment upon the foreign and domestic policy of the pre-war National Government. There was also a wish to get away from the hardships of the war. Churchill had offered 'blood, sweat, and tears', and the nation had responded to his appeal. The time for heroic action now seemed over; the electors expected something different, and chose a different set of men to give them the fruits of victory.

Clement Attlee, the new Prime Minister, was, as one of his colleagues said of him, a man 'easily underestimated', and with 'a capacity for making everything seem sensible and unimportant'. He was not an orator, and never attempted an emotional appeal, but he knew his own mind, and was neither browbeaten by the Opposition nor stampeded by the extremists of his own party. He introduced a programme of social change which was not less sweeping because it was presented in a moderate way. The economic position of the country did not look favourable to heavy social expenditure.

The sudden ending of 'Lend-Lease' by the United States left Great Britain in a situation from which with the utmost rigour she could hardly expect to extricate herself at least for several years. During this period she was bound to rely on American help. One of the earliest papers submitted (14 August 1945) to the new Cabinet stated that, without substantial new aid from the United States, Great Britain would be 'virtually bankrupt, and the economic basis for the hopes of the public non-existent'. American aid was given, at first after somewhat bitter wrangling over the terms, and later with more generosity.[1] Under the shelter of American dollar credits, therefore, the Labour party was able to introduce its social legislation.

This legislation put into effect a good part of the socialist programme of nationalizing the means of production which the party had adopted after the first war. The coal industry and the supply of electricity and gas, road transport and the railways were nationalized; a National Health Service and an enlarged National Insurance scheme were set up on the basis of the 'Report on Social Insurance and Allied Services' drawn up by Sir William Beveridge during the war and accepted by the Conservatives; the Bank of England was brought under public ownership. These measures were not unpopular at the time, but in the next general election (1950) the Labour majority over the Conservatives and their supporters fell to 18, and, in 1951, after the resignation of the Labour Government, the Conservatives were returned with a majority of 26.

There were a number of reasons for the Labour loss of popular support. The Labour party had carried out the main items of the programme which it had put forward in 1945. The results of nationalization were disappointing. They did not even include the elimination of wasteful competition, for example, between rail and road transport, or gas and electricity. Labour relations in the national industries did not shew any change for the better; there was no greater amount of workers' control. The electors were tired of the restrictions which, somewhat unfairly, they attributed to socialist planning and not to the financial troubles of the country due to the

[1] The American loan did not solve the problem for Great Britain, since the British Government was required to restore the convertibility of sterling in 1947. Other European countries were also in difficulty, and the situation was saved only when General Marshall, the U.S. Secretary of State, proposed a plan for European recovery with American help.

war. Some of the Government's plans, for example a grandiose scheme for growing nuts in Africa, were ill-conceived and wasteful. In spite of restrictionary measures, the Government seemed unable to prevent continual rises in the cost of living or to solve the problem of the balance of payments. Marshall Aid was of immense help, but the £ had to be devalued in 1949, and there was another financial crisis in 1951. Furthermore the leading figures in the Government were elderly and tired; some of them – including Attlee – had been in office almost continuously since the coalition Government of 1940. Ernest Bevin, the most attractive Labour politician of his generation, died in the spring of 1951. There was also evidence of a deep division over policy between the moderate and extreme wings of the party. Aneurin Bevan, the leader of the left-wing dissidents, was a brilliant, if harsh debater, without much administrative ability; he resigned from the Cabinet in April 1951, nominally over a minor dispute about National Health expenditure, but actually over the whole policy of the Government.

The decade between 1951 and 1961 was one of unexpected Labour eclipse, but in retrospect the mutual recriminations of party politicians since the war may seem disproportionate to the amount of common ground between the parties. Both parties disliked spending large sums on armaments which (especially after the atom bomb was succeeded by devices of even more terrible power) could hardly be employed without bringing about the destruction of Europe; only a minority of the Labour party and of the electorate thought that unilateral disarmament on the part of Great Britain might be a solution of the problem. In domestic policy each of the two parties was committed to increasingly expensive schemes of social improvement; the National Health Service more than doubled in cost between 1948–9 and 1952–3. Both parties also accepted – the Conservatives to a less degree than the Labour party – the redistribution of wealth by taxation. The cumulative effect of these measures was the emergence of a new category of highly paid workers; one can hardly use the term 'new social class' to describe them, but they were typical of the new 'welfare state' and in many urban constituencies held the electoral balance between the parties. These new electors were indeed in one respect no different from their parents and grandparents. They held left centre opinions in politics – with the centre itself moving slowly leftward. The rejection of one party or the other was nearly always by a narrow majority and implied that its policy had inclined too much to the right or left.

The movement to the right in and after 1951 was accentuated by the disarray into which the Labour party had fallen. Aneurin Bevan continued to divide the party; the doctrinal feuds also tended to become personal. Attlee was 72 in 1955. He had a slight stroke in the summer of that year, and retired from the party leadership in December. Bevan had already left the Opposition 'Shadow Cabinet' and was unlikely to be chosen as Attlee's successor. The choice was between Morrison and Gaitskell. Herbert Morrison – born in 1888 – was the older man; he had had wide ministerial experience and had made a good name for himself as chairman of the London County Council. On the other hand he had been a failure as Foreign Secretary after Ernest Bevin. Only a minority of forty – thirty less than the supporters of Aneurin Bevan – voted for him, whereas Gaitskell had 157 votes.[1] Hugh Gaitskell was under 50; he had been Chancellor of the Exchequer, and a strong supporter of the moderate official Labour policy against the Bevanites. Bevan died in 1960, and Gaitskell two years later. Before his death he had done much to reconcile the two wings of the party. After his death Harold Wilson, a Bevanite, was chosen as Leader.

Meanwhile the Conservative leadership had also changed. Churchill retired in 1955 and was succeeded by Eden. During the war Eden had been a good Foreign Secretary and Churchill's closest collaborator. He had been specially valuable in getting Churchill to accept 'second thoughts' on some of his imaginative but not very practical projects and had done much to restore the Foreign Office to the position which it had lost under Chamberlain and Halifax. It is therefore the more surprising that Eden should have made what most of his fellow-countrymen regarded as a mistake in launching with the French (after great provocation) an attack to coerce President Nasser of Egypt into keeping his international obligations. The attack was made in the face of certain Russian opposition and without being sure either of American support or even of the ability of the forces immediately available to achieve quickly their military objectives. Eden's health was not

[1] The Leader of the Labour party (who would normally become Prime Minister when his party succeeded to office) was chosen by the votes of Labour members of the Commons.

good, and, apart from the Suez fiasco, he could not have continued long as Prime Minister. He resigned in January 1957. The succession lay between R. A. Butler and Harold Macmillan, both of whom accepted the changes which were transforming the Conservative party. In 1963, after early success and later failure and discord, Macmillan also resigned owing to ill-health. His successor, Sir A. Douglas Home,[1] who was chosen in a way unlikely to unite the leading personalities of the Conservative party, lost a general election by a narrow majority in the late autumn of 1964.

With the retirement of Churchill in 1955 the historian should bring his commentary to an end, since he cannot make an accurate assessment of the last ten years – they form part of an epoch which is not yet closed. The problems of this decade have not been solved; at home, the difficulty of a policy of industrial expansion without running into trouble over the balance of payments; the difficulty of combining full employment with stability of prices and of meeting without inflation the immense and increasing social expenditure of the modern 'welfare' state upon which the working class has become accustomed to rely as of right, and without counting the cost; the grievous burden of modern armaments, and the failure to obtain in present conditions any plan for their reduction acceptable both to the communist and non-communist states, the confused voices in the United Nations, and the burden of British military commitments overseas.

Historians rarely make good prophets, and an Englishman, thinking of the probable future of his country, must be content to look back rather than to deliver oracles. He may remember that over a hundred years ago, the Duke of Wellington, who took the gloomiest view of the future of England at the very time when she was entering on the greatest decades of her power, once said, during the Chartist troubles, that the English were a quiet people. There have been periods when this judgment could be questioned, but English history, including the history of English revolutions, has been much less violent than that of her great European neighbours. The English, by nature conservative, have adapted themselves and their

[1] At the time of his appointment as Prime Minister Sir A. Douglas Home was the Earl of Home. He at once gave up his title; Parliament had passed in the previous summer a measure enabling peers who wished to sit in the House of Commons to renounce their peerage.

institutions to change and have also shewn a very remarkable firmness in the face of great danger. They have given up an Empire over 500,000,000 people without any sense of humiliation or defeat, since ultimately they could not confine to themselves their belief in the merits of political liberty and self-government. The next stage – a closer integration of Great Britain with the states of continental Europe – may be less easy for a nation which still thinks of itself as an Island Power, with its own particular ways, and is still fearful of the consequences of any important surrender of national sovereignty. Nevertheless this transition will be made, and made, so an Englishman may hope, without loss of the distinctive English characteristics which, for all their shortcomings, have been in the past of some service to the world.

Index

Aberdeen, 4th Earl of, 163
Aboukir Bay, battle of, 145
Africa, 86, 170–2; see also South Africa
Agincourt, battle of, 49
Aidan, St, 10
Albert, Prince, 161
Alfred, King, 16–19, 65
American Civil War, 164
Anglo-French *entente*, 181–4
Anglo-Russian convention, 183–4
Anjou, 26, 46–7
Anne, Queen, 117–18, 121, 125, 127
Anselm, St, 30
Aquitaine, 46
Architecture, medieval, 43–5, 66
Armada, the Spanish, 87–8
Asquith, H. H., 175, 179, 188, 196, 206
Astrology, medieval, 64
Athelstan, King, 19
Attlee, C. R., 229, 231–2
Augustine of Canterbury, St, 9
Australia, 170, 191

Bacon, Francis, 71, 91
Badonicus, Mons, battle of, 8
Baldwin, S., 191, 195–6, 201, 203, 205–6, 208–9, 218
Balfour, A. J., 169–70, 174
Bank of England, 114
Bannockburn, battle of, 37
Bede, 18, 55
Belgium, 162, 186–7
Bentham, Jeremy, 149, 170
Bessemer steel, 160
Bevan, A., 231–2
Bevin, E., 231–2
Birmingham, 115–16, 169, 194

Black death, 58–9, 77
Blake, William, 135
Blatchford, Robert, 154
Boadicea, 3
Boleyn, Anne, 76, 83
Bosworth, battle of, 54
Boyle, Robert, 112
Boyne, battle of the, 121
Bracton, 35
Bristol, 124, 131
Burke, Edmund, 126, 129
Byron, Lord, 170

Cabinet, development of the, 126, 129–30
Caesar, Julius, 1–2, 9
Calendar, reform of the, 135
Campbell-Bannerman, Sir H., 175
Camperdown, battle of, 145
Canada, 138–40, 142, 191
Canning, George, 161
Canterbury, 9, 10, 16
Canute, 15, 19, 20
Cape la Hogue, battle of, 121
Cape St Vincent, battle of, 145
Caractacus, 3
Carson, Sir E., 179
Carta, Magna, 33, 40
Cassivellaunus, 2
Castlereagh, Viscount, 161
Catherine of Aragon, 71–3, 76, 79
Caxton, 66
Ceorls, 12–13
Chamberlain, Joseph, 168–9, 172–173
Chamberlain, Neville, 208–9, 218–219, 221
Charles I, 89, 93–9, 100–5, 107, 110, 115–16, 119

Charles II, 107, 109–10, 115–18, 126
Chartism, 153, 155
Chaucer, 38
Chester, 4
Chinese labour, 173–4
Churchill, Winston S., 195, 218, 221–4, 229, 232
Clarendon, 115, 117
Clive, Robert, 138–9
Coal, 133–4, 147–8
Cobden, R., 158
Coffee, 138
Colonial conferences, 172–3
Connecticut, 111
Conquest, Norman, see Harold II: William I
Coram, Thomas, 135
Corn Laws, repeal of, 158
Cranmer, Archbishop, 76, 78–9, 84
Crecy, battle of, 48
Cromwell, Oliver, 103–15
Cromwell, Richard, 109–10
Cromwell, Thomas, 77–8, 107–8

Danish invasions, 15–19
Darby, Abraham, 133
Darien, 124
De Valera, E., 198, 205
Disraeli, Benjamin, Earl of Beaconsfield, 152, 158, 166, 169–70
'Domesday' survey, 14, 24
Douglas Home, Sir A., 233
Drake, Sir Francis, 86–9
Dudley, John, Duke of Northumberland, 79
Dunbar, battle of, 107
Dunstan, St, 27

East India Company, 112, 124, 138, 142, 171
Eden, R. A., 219, 232
Edgar, 19
Edmund Ironside, 19
Edward I, 36–41, 43
Edward II, 41–5
Edward III, 46–8, 50–3, 69

Edward IV, 53–4, 67
Edward V, 53
Edward VI, 78–80, 100
Edward VII, 175–7, 181
Edward VIII, 209
Edward the Confessor, King, 20, 23
Edward the Elder, King, 19
Elizabeth, Princess, 96, 122
Elizabeth I, Queen, 79–85, 87–90, 94–5, 100
Enclosures, 89, 98, 132
English language, 65–6
Essex, 2nd Earl of, 89
Ethelred II, King, 19, 20, 23
Exchequer, the, 28, 31, 34
Exhibition, Great, 160

Fabian Society, 154
Factory Acts, 150, 152
Falkirk, battle of, 37
'Feudalism', 14, 23–4
Fisher, Sir J., 183
Forests, royal, 33, 56, 97–8
Franchise reform, 112, 153–4, 156, 166
Friars, 59, 107

Gandhi, M. K., 228
Gavaston, Piers, 41
George I, 125–7, 130
George II, 126–7, 130, 138
George III, 129–30, 139–40, 142
George IV, 130, 161
George V, 177
Gibraltar, 110, 123
Gilbert, Humphrey, 86
Gilds, craft, 67
Gilds, merchant, 32, 67
Gladstone, W. E., 158–9, 162, 166–8, 173
Gloucester, 3, 45, 104
Goldsmith, Oliver, 135
Grafton, Duke of, 141
Gray, Thomas, 135
Greek rebellion, 162
Greenwich observatory, 133
Gregory I, Pope, 9–10, 18

Grenville, G., 141
Grey, Sir E., 175, 182, 185–7

Hadrian's wall, 3
Harold II, 15, 20–22
Harvey, William, 91
Hastings, battle of, 1, 21
Hawkins, Sir John, 86, 88
Hengist, 7
Henry I, 25–6, 28, 30, 32
Henry II, 27–31, 33, 36, 38, 46
Henry III, 34–5, 37, 43
Henry IV, 52
Henry V, 48–9, 52, 70
Henry VI, 53
Henry VII, 53–4, 70–2, 85, 93
Henry VIII, 70–3, 75–8, 81, 84
Hitler, A., 216, 218–20, 222, 224–
    225
Hogarth, William, 135
Home Rule Bills, 168, 177–80
Hooker, Richard, 83, 91
Howard, John, 135
Hugh of Lincoln, St, 27
Humphrey, Duke of Gloucester,
    62–3

Independency, 105–7
India, 137–9, 162, 171, 227–8
Investiture, lay, 30
Ireland, 10, 16, 36–7, 75, 89, 99–
    101, 107, 112, 121, 145, 158,
    166–9, 177–80

James I, 89–90, 93–6, 110
James II, 116–22
Jameson, Dr, 174
Japan, 181, 215–17, 224–5
Joan of Arc, St, 49
John, King, 33, 39
John of Gaunt, 50–4, 60
Johnson, Dr, 67, 136
Jutland, battle of, 188

Kent, 7, 9, 12
Kipling, R., 172
Kruger, P., 173–4

Labour representation, 155
'Laisser-faire', 149
Lansdowne, Marquess of, 182
Laud, Archbishop, 84, 94, 97–9,
    103, 116
Law, A. Bonar, 179, 200–1
League of Nations, 204, 212, 214–
    217, 227
Liverpool, 124, 131, 140, 150
Lloyd George, D., 175–7, 188–9,
    192, 196–200, 206, 212
Lollardy, 61, 77
London, 4, 9, 17, 21, 31, 53, 104,
    113, 117, 119, 131, 133, 135,
    149–50, 152, 172, 210, 223
Louis XIV, 116–23, 144

MacDonald, J. R., 155, 201, 203,
    206–8, 215
Macmillan, M. H., 233
Marlborough, Duke of, 122
Marlowe, C., 91
Marshall, Gen. G. C., 227
Mary I, 71, 79–80, 84, 100
Mary II, 117–21, 127
Mary Stuart, 81–2, 93
Maryland, 110
Massachusetts, 110–11, 142
Matilda, Empress, 26, 73
Melbourne, Viscount, 157
Mercantilism, 111
Mercia, 15–17, 19–21
Milton, 103, 112, 155
Monck, General, 109
Monmouth, Duke of, 118
Monroe, President, 161–2
Montfort, Simon de, 34–5, 39
More, Sir Thomas, 77
Morocco, 182, 184
Morris, William, 154
Morrison, H. S., 232
Mussolini, B., 214, 216–17, 219,
    222–3

Napoleon I, 144–6
Napoleon III, 163, 165
Naseby, battle of, 104

Nationalism, rise of, 69–70
Nelson, 145–6
Newcastle, Duke of, 137, 139
Newmarket, 118
'New Model', The, 104–5
Newton, Sir Isaac, 133
New Zealand, 170, 191
North, Lord, 129, 140
Northumbria, 10, 15, 17

Oates, Titus, 118
O'Connell, Daniel, 167, 179
Offa, King, 15–16
Oglethorpe, William, 135
Oswald, King, 10
Ottawa Conference, 209
Oxenham, John, 86–7

Palmerston, Viscount, 160–1, 163–165
Parliament Act, 177
Parliament, Development of (to 1640), 38–42, 50–1, 83–4, 93–5, 97–8
Parliament, the long, 99, 101–7
Parnell, C. S., 168
Parties, parliamentary, 118, 126–9
Patay, battle of, 49
Peace Ballot, 217
Peel, Sir Robert, 130, 157–9, 166, 170, 176
Pensions, Old Age, 152
Philip II of Spain, 80, 85–8, 109, 144
Pilgrim Fathers, The, 110
Pitt, William, Earl of Chatham, 128, 131, 137, 139–41
Pitt, William, the younger, 128, 130, 143–4
Plassey, battle of, 139
Plautius, Aulus, 2
Poitiers, battle of, 48
Pope, Alexander, 135, 155
Population, (15th century), 70, (18th century), 131–2, (19th century), 151
Postage, penny, 149

Prime Minister, office of, 127–8
Puritanism, 94, 108, 113–14

Railways, 148–9
Raleigh, Sir Walter, 85–6
Redmond, John, 178–9
Reformation, English, 73–82
Remonstrance, the Grand, 101
Revolution, American, 140–3
Rhodes, Cecil, 172, 174
Richard I, 32, 38
Richard II, 52
Richard III, 53–4, 93
Rights, Declaration of, 120–1
Rockingham, Marquis of, 141
Roosevelt, F. D., 224, 226
Rosebery, Earl of, 168, 205
Royal Society, 113
Russell, Lord John, 160

Salisbury, Marquis of, 169
Schleswig-Holstein, dispute, 164–5
Schools, charity, 134
    elementary, 152, 159–60
    girls, 159
    grammar, 64, 91, 159
    medieval, 64–5
    public, 112
    technical, 160
Scotland, 3, 16, 37–8, 46–7, 71, 81, 93–4, 98–9, 104–7, 109, 112, 124–5, 151, 192
Settlement, Act of, 122, 124–5
Seymour, Edward, Duke of Somerset, 78–9
Shaftesbury, Earl of, 118
Shakespeare, 83, 90–1
Ship-money, 98
Sluys, battle of, 48
Smith, Adam, 143
Snowden, P., 207–8
South Africa, 170, 173–5
'South Sea Bubble', 134
Spenser, Edmund, 90
Stamp Act, 141–2
Steam engine, 134, 147
Stephen, King, 26–7

Sugar, 66, 111
Swift, Jonathan, 123, 135

Table manners, 66
Tea, 138, 142
Teeth brushes, 112
Tennyson, Lord, 175
Test Act, 117
Theatres, 91, 113
Theodore of Tarsus, 10–11
Thomas of Canterbury, Saint
    (Thomas Becket), 30
Thomas of Lancaster, 42
Tiptoft, John, Earl of Worcester, 62
Tobacco, 90
Towns, medieval, 22, 31–2, 67
    Roman, 3–6
Townshend, C., 141
Trade Unions, 152–5, (T.U.C.)
    153, 155, 195–6, 208
Trafalgar, battle of, 146
Treaties, Aix-la-Chapelle, 138
    Amiens, 143, 145
    Dover (secret), 117
    Locarno, 213–14, 219
    Ryswick, 121
    Utrecht, 123
    Versailles, 211–14, 216
    Washington (1922), 215–16
Trial by ordeal, 29
Turkey, 162–3, 184, 199–201
Turnpikes, 148

U.S.S.R., 202–3, 212, 216, 219–20,
    222, 224, 226–7, 232
United Nations, 227, 233
Universities, 60, 62–5, 91, 112,
    134, 136, 159

Victoria, 130, 160–1, 172, 175–6
Vienna, Congress of, 162
Villeins, 14, 24, 56–9
Virginia, 85–6, 110–11

Wales, 2, 16, 36–7, 151, 169, 195
Walpole, Horace, 141
Walpole, Sir Robert, 127–8, 137

Wars, American Independence,
    140–3
    Anglo-American (1812–14),
        143
    Anglo-Dutch, 98, 111–12, 117
    China, 163–4
    Crimean, 163, 174, 188
    1st German (1914–18), 185–92
    2nd German (1939–45), 221–6
    Hundred Years, 46–9
    Revolutionary and Napoleonic,
        143–6
    of the Roses, 53–4, 68–9
    Seven Years, 137, 139–40
    South African, 173–4
    Spanish Succession, 122–3
Waterloo, battle of, 146
Webb, S. & B., 202
Wedgwood, Josiah, 133
Wellington, Duke of, 146, 163, 233
Wentworth, Thomas, Earl of Straf-
    ford, 97–9, 101
Wesley, John, 134, 136
Wessex, 8, 11–12, 15–20, 65
West Indies, 88, 110–11, 124,
    144–5
Westminster, Statute of, 204–5
Whitby, Synod of, 10
Wiclif, John, 60–1
William I, 1, 14, 20–5, 28
William II, 25, 27
William III, 117, 119–121, 124,
    127
William IV, 130, 161
William II, German Emperor, 174,
    180
Wilson, J. H., 232
Wilson, Woodrow, 211–12, 226
Winstanley, Gerrard, 106
Wolsey, Cardinal, 72–3, 75, 77
Women's suffrage, 178
Wool trade, 47–8, 59
Worcester, battle of, 107
Wordsworth, William, 144
Wren, Sir Christopher, 112

York, 3, 4, 21, 31, 42, 152